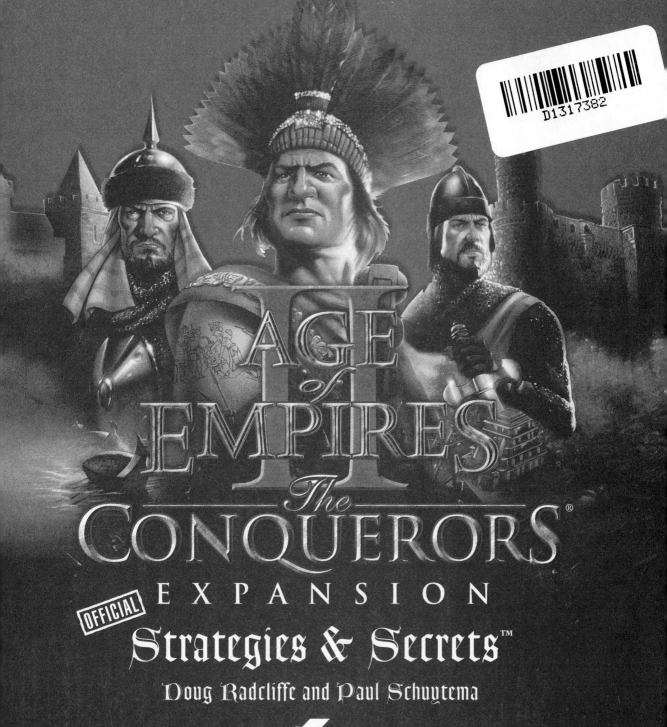

Age of Empires II

The Conquerors

EXPANSION

OFFICIAL

Strategies & Secrets™

Doug Radcliffe and Paul Schuytema

SYBEX

San Francisco · Paris · Düsseldorf · Soest · London

Associate Publisher: Dan Brodnitz

Contracts and Licensing Manager: Kristine O'Callaghan

Acquisitions and Developmental Editor: Willem Knibbe

Editor: Brett Todd

Associate Production Editor: Kelly Winquist

Proofreader: Rich Ganis

Book Design: Van Winkle Design Group

Book Production: Van Winkle Design Group

Cover Design: Alan Davenport & Associates

Library of Congress Card Number: 00-105392
ISBN: 0-7821-2859-9
Manufactured in the United States of America

10 9 8 7 6 5 4 3 2 1

To Rob Wright and Todd Rosenbaum...

reuniting with my greatest friends has been long overdue.

—Doug Radcliffe

Acknowledgments

First, a huge thanks to the talented team over at Sybex. Your continued support ignites my excitement for current and future projects. Special thanks to Dan Brodnitz for his enthusiasm and kind words. A welcome and thanks to the "new kid on the block," Willem Knibbe, who provided much-needed insight during the project's initial days. Thanks to Brett Todd for a gentle copyediting touch, Michael Rymaszewski for his in-depth tech edit, Diana Van Winkle for her mad layout skills, and Kelly Winquist and the rest of the Sybex production staff for shepherding the project along.

Many thanks also go out to Karen Sparks, Greg Street, and Bruce Shelley at Ensemble Studios for their wonderful contributions. James McDaniel at Microsoft also provided invaluable assistance. I'm also grateful to Tim Seitz (Out4Blood) for his expert additions to the guide. Finally, a big thanks to Paul Schuytema, my coauthor once again, who continues to excel despite the demands of his "day job."

—Doug Radcliffe

Contents

Introduction

Microsoft and Ensemble Studios' *Age of Empires II: The Age of Kings* is one of the most successful real-time strategy games of all time. Expertly blending resource management, technology research, and combat, Ensemble Studios' masterpiece places you in command of over a dozen civilizations, each with unique attributes, technology trees, and units.

With *Age of Empires II: The Conquerors Expansion,* the official expansion pack to *Age of Empires II: The Age of Kings,* Microsoft and Ensemble Studios have introduced five new civilizations in the Aztecs, Huns, Koreans, Mayans, and Spanish; tweaked game balance by implementing important changes to several of the original 13 civilizations and units; added unique technologies to all civilizations; and introduced several new global units, including the petard, halberdier, and hussar.

Conquering *The Conquerors* requires expert analysis of the game—provided only by this official *Strategies & Secrets* guide, written with the full support of the Ensemble Studios and Microsoft design teams. Inside you'll find advanced resource-gathering and combat techniques, build orders straight from multiplayer experts, exhaustive analysis of all 18 civilizations, and a detailed look at how the new units, technologies, and changes affect single-player and multiplayer gameplay.

How to Use This Book

Since you're playing *The Age of Kings: The Conquerors* expansion pack, we assume you have sharpened your skills somewhat on the original game. Chapters 1 and 2 look at necessary and advanced strategies for the two fundamental aspects of the game: resource gathering and combat tactics. Changes in *The Conquerors* refine both elements, so it's important to begin your journey here. The tactics detailed can be applied to single-player and multiplayer situations.

In Chapter 1: Building a Strong Economy, you'll learn essential techniques for generating an efficient economy. You'll discover how to organize and maximize early-, middle-, and late-game economies to advance through the ages more quickly and ensure a large economy for endgame battles. *The Conquerors'* changes addressed here include reseeding farms and smart villagers, both of which make managing an economy much easier.

Chapter 2: Building a Strong Army shifts the focus to combat, covering both offensive and defensive strategies. This chapter details tactics needed to produce an effective military and keep your opponent off balance.

Note We'll be posting updates on our web site to cover the evolving multi-player strategies and tactics, especially those relating to the new game modes and five new civilizations. Visit the *Age of Empires: The Conquerors Expansion* area of www.sybexgames.com for these new strategies.

The four chapters that follow detail *The Conquerors'* single-player campaigns, played at Moderate level. Complete walkthroughs will help you accomplish every optional and required objective in the mission. These chapters also include insightful strategies, as well as historical and game design notes, from Ensemble Studios' Greg Street and Karen Sparks, two of the game's designers. Note that for the purposes of the walkthroughs, "north" refers to the top corner of the map (twelve o'clock), "east" is the right corner (three o'clock), "south" means the bottom corner (six o'clock), and "west" is the left corner (nine o'clock).

There are thousands of ways to complete each mission. The walkthroughs here present a proven, but by all means not only, solution. In general, you should strive to max out your population with military units before attacking. Some generalizations are made in the walkthrough since each player will have his or her own personal unit preferences. For example, we consider a "moderate-sized" army to be 30–35 units. When necessary, specific unit suggestions are provided in the walkthrough to maximize battle success.

The rest of the book concentrates on multiplayer strategies. Chapter 7: Civilization Strengths and Weaknesses offers an in-depth look at *The Conquerors'* five new civilizations, as well as the original 13 from *The Age of Kings*. It's here that you'll find hard-hitting strategies for each civilization from expert player Tim Seitz (Out4Blood). Tim's contribution includes resource and task assignments for each new villager you produce. Mastering his strategies will lower your Feudal and Castle Age times and improve your ability to put quick, offensive pressure on your opponent.

Cheat Codes

The following table includes cheat codes applicable to both *The Age of Kings* and *The Conquerors* expansion pack. Using cheat codes will significantly unbalance gameplay, so activate them only as a last resort.

Introduction

To use these cheats, hit Enter during gameplay to access the chat prompt. Type in the desired code and hit Enter again to receive your reward. Cheat codes are disabled by default in multiplayer but can be activated by the host during the pre-game.

Cheat Code	Result
CHEESE STEAK JIMMY'S	Adds 1,000 food to your reserve
LUMBERJACK	Adds 1,000 wood to your reserve
ROBIN HOOD	Adds 1,000 gold to your reserve
ROCK ON	Adds 1,000 stone to your reserve
MARCO	Uncovers map to explored status
POLO	Removes shadow to reveal all units and buildings
AEGIS	Instantly build units and gather resources
I R WINNER	Fulfills victory conditions in current mission
BLACK DEATH	Destroys all enemies on map
RESIGN	Instantly lose current mission
WIMPYWIMPYWIMPY	Eliminate yourself from map
TORPEDO#	Kill opponent #
NATURAL WONDERS	Control nature
I LOVE THE MONKEY HEAD	Gives VDML
HOW DO YOU TURN THIS ON	Gives a cobra car
TO SMITHEREENS	Gives a saboteur

Building a Strong Economy

The Age of Empires *series fits into the classic "grow, then conquer" design scheme. It is your job to take a civilization and nurture it to a position of strength so that you can conquer your enemy.*

No matter how deftly you might try an alternate approach, The Conquerors is designed to favor the aggressor. As a player, you must eventually go on the offensive to secure a victory. You can't dig yourself into a purely defensive position (unless you grow to the point where you are defending a wonder).

Yet an aggressive campaign against your enemies is a very expensive proposition. You'll need a rock-solid economy to marshal a potent fighting force to defend your home territory, create reinforcements, and provide your troops with the most deadly technologies available. In short, the "grow" side of the "grow, then conquer" approach must be handled with care and skill, for it is the foundation upon which you will build your mighty empire.

This chapter explores the key concepts behind building a strong, vital economy in The Conquerors. In the sections that follow, you'll learn about balance, management, resource gathering, and getting out of the gates fast.

Golden Rules

While managing a strong civilization is a daunting task, several "rules of approach" can help you avoid costly errors. All of the rules outlined below can be summed up in one statement: Keep it simple and keep it efficient.

Maximize Your Efforts

> **Tip** Use the Single Player: Standard Game screen to set up a game with all players controlled by the computer. You can learn a lot by watching how the AI begins to grow its civilization. While computer-controlled players aren't terribly imaginative, they know the game inside out and don't waste a single action. Get to know the flow and pace of the computer players, because your goal is to beat them at the early economic game to gain an early advantage.

The game world is a complicated, busy place, and any inadequacies in the civilization you create will be magnified as play progresses. Your foremost goal in the early stages of the game is to create a robust and efficient economy.

Setting up a thriving economic foundation takes a lot of work, but you can make your job far easier by using the most efficient means of resource gathering possible. Also, get familiar with your civilization's technologies, particularly those that enhance its economic output.

The foremost rule of efficiency in *The Conquerors* is simply this: Don't make your villagers walk. Villagers are slow and often bump into each other as they travel from resources to their drop-off points. Try to construct these drop-off points as close to resources as possible.

> **Note** Remember that your villagers are smarter in *The Conquerors*, and will begin gathering a resource immediately after building a resource drop-off point.

The second rule is this: Don't let your villagers loiter…not even for a second. An idle villager is a wasted asset. Automatically assign newly created villagers to a task by selecting the town center, then right-clicking the resource you want them to harvest. Also use the Idle Villagers button on regular occasions to seek out slackers and put them to work immediately.

Don't Force Yourself to Micromanage

As the leader of a civilization in *The Conquerors*, you don't want your economic foundation to drain your time when you should be focusing on tactical issues. An ideal economic machine works well on autopilot, until you step in and make a course correction (which you'll certainly need to do from time to time).

Organize your villagers in "packs" for tasks like resource gathering and large building construction. Commit a group of villagers to a specific job, such as berry gathering or lumber work, and treat them like a single entity, group-selecting them and moving them to new areas and tasks. A pack of four or five villagers is ideal (see Figure 1.1). If you place working villagers in clumps like this, it's easy to do a quick drag and select and send a whole group from the forest to the stone mine, if you need a quick influx of stone for some new walls.

Figure 1.1:
Using villagers in packs to act as a single unit can greatly speed up tasks. Here, four villagers are quickly building a group of four houses.

Tip Having an "on call" pack of five villagers makes great sense. While your other villagers are gathering resources, you can command this pack to churn through all of your building and repair tasks in rapid time.

With practice, you'll get the hang of the ebb and flow of resources in the game and when your villagers should be concentrating more on one resource than another. In the early stages, food and wood are the most vital commodities, while gold and stone grow in importance later. By using the pack approach, you can move your villagers from one priority to another in just a few seconds.

Once you get an idea of the lay of the land around your town center, plan for the resource-gathering endeavors that your growing civilization may need. First, locate the best places for lumber camps, stone mines, and gold mines. If you're on the coast, search out shore fishing and open sea fishing opportunities, since shore fishing and fishing boats are some of the lowest maintenance food-gathering approaches in the game.

Make the Economy Serve Your Goals

A strong economy won't do you much good if it doesn't allow you to execute tactical plans for a given scenario. While the balance of a scenario in *The Conquerors* will shift as you move through the ages, use up resources, and alter your tactical plans, you should always be striving toward a clearly defined strategic goal.

Before you press the start button on any scenario, visualize your end goal and allow this to help you decide on tactical positions as the game progresses. In many scenarios, this may be as straightforward as defeating all other foes, or it may focus on defending a wonder or another similar goal. It is this "master strategic goal" that your economy should serve at all times, as well as the specific plans for executing that strategy. For example, if you plan on using a lot of champions, you'd better be mining gold.

One of the most exciting aspects of a scenario in *The Conquerors* is how it changes and evolves through time, forcing players to alter and modify their tactical approaches. These "mini-games" are a true challenge, and skilled players must be able to manage their economies to best support shifting tactical goals.

> **Tip** If you can spare the manpower, put a few villagers on gold and stone mining early in a scenario. This can help you build up a nice reserve when you click into an advanced age and need to burn through these resources quickly.

How do you do this? As is often the case, the first tool is knowledge, and that means studying the technology tree of your civilization and the production costs. Get to know your civilization and your goals at any given moment, so that your economy can be growing to meet that objective in a way that takes maximum advantage of your civilization's strength.

Always try to think at least one move ahead in the game. Sculpt your economic machine to meet your primary goal first, but be sure to position yourself for a graceful shift to the next task.

This is easiest to see in the early stages of a game. More often than not, a player's first goal is to reach the Feudal Age as rapidly as possible (see the "Out of the Gates" section in this chapter for specific advice), while the next will be to develop a strong military presence. As you set yourself up for the push to the Feudal Age, keep in mind the military structures, resources, and technologies needed for your next step. Keep the areas for your military buildings clear, and be sure to also save room for marshalling troops. Begin to research some of the technologies you'll need, and prepare your villagers to construct your buildings as soon as you enter the new age.

Resource Management

The key to cultivating a civilization is a steady influx of precious resources. While there are often more than enough resources to go around, the effective retrieval of them can be a game in and of itself. Advancing through the ages requires a significant stockpile of resources, and the player who advances quickly can gain a decided advantage as the game progresses.

The sections below detail each of the resource types and discuss how to maximize gathering techniques.

Food of Life

Clearly, the most important resource is food. Most units you create require food to be trained, and moving into a new age requires a well-stocked larder. Food is easy to find and is rarely the source of contention between rival civilizations, so defending the resource isn't as important as maximizing production and gathering.

Food can be gathered, hunted, fished, or farmed and is available in many forms (see Table 1.1). Gathered items like berries and sheep will be your preferred source of food early in the game. Each regular map will provide at least six forage bushes and eight sheep or turkeys near the player's town center.

Table 1.1: Food values per food type

Food Type	Value	Food Type	Value
Deer	140	Forage Bush	125
Fish (Dorado)	225	Great Fish (Marlin)	350
Fish (Perch)	200	Sheep	100
Fish (Salmon)	225	Shore Fish	200
Fish (Snapper)	225	Turkey	100
Fish (Tuna)	225	Wild Boar	340

Berry bushes are a great staple food source early on; be sure to deplete them before moving on to farming. Each bush provides 125 units of food, so the six bushes provide a total of 750 food units. The most important aspect of forage bushes is the time it takes to transport the food they hold back to the drop-off point. Place a mill in the vicinity to increase drop-off speed (see Figure 1.2).

Figure 1.2:
Building a mill near forage bushes will increase drop-off speed and prepare you for the eventual move into farming.

> **Note** Sheep and turkeys are worth 100 food, but they decay once slaughtered. A single villager will only be able to gather about 60 percent of this total. To maximize the supply, assign at least four villagers to a single carcass.

Sheep and turkeys are another source of food early on. They begin as gray-colored "gaia" units and will be converted once one of your units moves close. Once converted, you can herd and move them just like any other unit. Move them to your town center and use a villager to slaughter them.

Becoming a great *Age of Kings* player requires that you become adept at hunting, which requires micromanagement. Deer and wild boar are a great source of food, and villagers can carry more food units in a single trip to the drop-off point (35 units as opposed to 10 for berry bushes). On the other hand, these food sources can be difficult to locate and require effort to kill.

Deer should be hunted by at least four villagers at a time. Multiple hunters will drop a deer in its tracks, and four hunters are enough to carry all of one deer's meat back to a mill or town center. Boars have 70 hit points, as well as the ability to attack, so multiple villagers are needed here as well. It's best to send one villager out to lure a boar to a pack of hunters. Position them near a town center or mill to cut down on transport time once they make short work of the boar. Also, like sheep and turkey, wild game will decay over time. Exhaust other food resources before hunting wild game, unless you luck out and find some grazing near a drop-off point that you've already built.

Fishing is a great source of nonrenewable food that can be exploited early in the game. The easiest type of fishing is shore fishing—when fish are in the first water tile near the shoreline, you can order a villager to begin fishing with a casting net. It's generally most effective to assign one villager per shore fish resource. If you have multiple shore-fishing spots, fill them out with fishermen as soon as possible.

Deep-water fishing requires a dock (which serves as the drop-off point) and at least one fishing boat. The amount of food found in the sea is significant, but you'll want to optimize the travel times of your fleet. It's generally a good idea to build at least three ships and begin fishing the area right around the dock. If you fish out the stock nearby, build another dock where fish can be found (always try to keep your fleet fishing in the same general area to maximize efficiency).

Tip While farms are a great renewable source of food later in the game, be sure to utilize all of the found food resources in the early game, as setting up a robust farming system will cost a lot of wood.

Farming is the foundation of your food supply and will become your primary source of food production in the Feudal Age and beyond. Before you can farm, you'll need to build a mill, which should have been done to harvest berries. Build farms right up against your town center and mill to minimize the walking time for villagers.

Farm food production escalates through the ages (to reflect the advances in agrarian technology, see Table 1.2). Once their food supply has been harvested, the ground turns fallow. You can reseed by building another farm on the same location, but the best way to avoid this micromanaging is to queue up farms for reseeding. Click the mill and then the farm icon—this will immediately deduct the 60 points of wood from your stockpile for each farm, but your villagers will immediately reseed a fallow farm if one is in the mill queue (see Figure 1.3).

Table 1.2: Farm output through the ages

Age	Basic Farm Production
Dark	175
Feudal	250
Castle	375
Imperial	550

Figure 1.3:
Use the farm queue option to prepay for farms and have them automatically reseeded.

The Lumber Trade

Wood is the foundation upon which you'll build your civilization. Nearly all buildings—and many units—require some wood to construct, and during growth spurts, you'll be sure to find your stockpile dangerously low.

Wood gathering is a fairly easy affair, with each tree delivering a set amount (100 – 125 units) of wood before it is consumed. The real key in wood gathering is the location of your main lumber operation. Of course, when the game starts, you'll want to set some villagers clearing the "straggler" trees near your town center, but you should quickly determine the location of your primary lumber camp (or camps).

Trees have the tactical advantage of obstructing movement, so your main forest might also be a good tactical barrier. If that's the case, be sure to limit clear-cutting. Ideally, you'll want to find a large grove of trees that isn't tactically important from a defensive point of view. Build a lumber camp and set your villagers to work with enough spacing so they can move to and from the camp without bumping into each other.

> **Tip** Once villagers are about seven tree stumps from the lumber camp, build a new one to minimize walking.

Wood retrieval can generally go on autopilot after that, but always make sure that you have enough villagers chopping wood so that you always have the resources needed to grow and expand.

Mining

You can mine stone and gold in *The Conquerors*. Stone is used to build towers and fortified walls and becomes important when you want to build more town centers, fortify a defensive stance, or place offensive towers and castles. If you are a mobile, offensive player (or playing a civilization like the Huns true to form), you may not even need stone.

Stone is gathered from stone deposits and can be dropped off at either the town center or a mining camp (see Table 1.3). As a general rule, you won't really need to begin serious stone mining until the Castle Age (though you may want enough in reserve when you hit Castle Age to enable you to build town centers and a castle immediately).

Gold, on the other hand, is an absolutely vital resource and one that always seems in short supply near the end game. More advanced military units require gold to train, and building up a formidable late game army will drain your coffers dearly.

Like stone mining, gold can be dropped off in mining camps or at the town center (see Figure 1.4). Unlike stone, gold is a valuable asset to all players and is vulnerable to enemy attacks. While farms can be placed in protected surroundings wherever you wish, gold mines are part of the map and you must go to them. As a result, you'll need to protect them with towers or, after reaching Castle Age, town centers.

Since gold is crucial late in the game, you'll need to quickly locate additional veins beyond those near your town center at the beginning. Quickly identify the general positions of your enemies and then locate additional gold resources in uncontested areas of the map. If you can find veins sufficiently off the beaten path, you just may be able to enjoy hassle-free gold mining for the duration of the game. It's also worthwhile to commandeer deposits near your enemies, as you'll then deprive them of the resource.

Relics are another gold source. Select a monk and right-click a relic. Once the monk retrieves it, right-click a monastery. The monk will garrison the relic inside it, and you'll earn 45 gold units per minute.

Table 1.3: Mining values

Mine Type	Value Per Deposit	Deposits Near Town Center
Stone	350	10
Gold	800	14

Figure 1.4:
If you're lucky, you may have stone and gold mines close enough together that you can construct a single mining camp to service both materials.

Trade, Tribute, and Market Play

In addition to physically collecting resources on the map, you can employ other means to build your stockpiles. Trade allows you to generate an income stream of gold into your coffers with little effort on your part. On land, trade requires you to build a market and then one or more trade carts. Sea-borne trade requires a dock and one or more trade cogs.

To trade, select a cart or cog and right-click another player's market or dock (that player can be an ally, neutral, or even an enemy). The trade vehicle will then travel to that destination and return, dropping off an amount of gold in your treasury when it gets back. The amount of gold is determined by the distance between your location and the other player—the longer the trade route, the larger the payoff (but also the longer the turnaround time).

In general, it's better to use multiple trade carts or cogs over a shorter route than fewer over a longer route as the production speed is increased and the risks are minimized. Trading with an enemy isn't a good idea, since you'll need to defend your merchants with military units that could be better utilized elsewhere. It's also advantageous to be on the receiving end of a trade route, since your treasury keeps 10 percent of the gold earned by a trading player using your docks or markets (consider it a processing fee).

Tribute is another way to send or receive resources from another player. You will first need a market, and then you can use the Diplomacy button on the menu bar to send or request resources. Early in the game, the tributing player will pay a 30 percent fee on resources sent to another player. This high cost makes tribute an unattractive means of commerce. Only use tribute to send or receive resources in immediate need by a player (such as one under attack who needs gold to quickly marshal a defensive force). You can research coinage and banking later in the game to eliminate this processing fee.

Finally, you can purchase or sell resources directly from your market (see Figure 1.5). This form of commerce allows you to spend gold to purchase wood, food, or stone, or to receive gold by selling those resources. The game has a small "commerce engine" that manages the prices for all of the goods, and it will reflect the trading ebb and flow (for example, if a lot of players sell stone, the price of the resource will drop). You can monitor prices to get an idea of what your opponents are selling and buying, which can be an indication of their strengths and weaknesses.

Figure 1.5:
The market interface, located in the lower right when you click your market, allows you to quickly buy and sell goods for gold.

Working the market costs an initial 30 percent transaction fee, but this can be reduced (though not eliminated) by researching the guild's technology. In general, the market is the least desirable source of resources because of the high fees and the fluctuating prices. Avoid it unless you need a quick influx of a scarce resource.

Maximizing Your Resources

Resource management is crucial to building a strong economy, and the key to maximizing those resources is to roll up your sleeves and dive deep into the game. Many players can perform very well by just playing on the surface of the game and not wringing out every possible advantage, but truly talented players realize that there are advantages to be had in every game and every scenario.

The first advantages can be found within the technologies your civilization can research. Technologies are skills that allow your people to do new things, train new units, or increase efficiency in certain areas. If you thumb through the technologies available in the game, you'll see that these upgrades come at a steep price. Still, consider

this an investment in your future. If you have built a strong, basic economy, you should have the resources needed to conduct your research without taking too much of a growth hit.

Look through the *Age of Kings* and *The Conquerors* manuals, as well as Chapter 8: New Technologies and Units to get a handle on all of the technologies available to your civilization. Remember that you don't need to research each and every technology; look only at those that will best support your current and long-term economic goals.

> **Tip** The Technology Tree item in the main game menu is the best source of civilization and technology information in the game. With this display, you can learn about each and every unit or technology in the game, the path needed to create it (shown in white), and the upgrades that will enhance performance.

In addition to the standard suite of technologies, each civilization has a number of advantages in the way that it manages resources. For example, the Aztecs receive a bonus on relic gold, which allows garrisoned relics to earn 60 gold units per minute rather than the standard 45. This makes gathering multiple relics a key bonus for that civilization. As another example, the Huns do not need houses for their units. While they begin a scenario with −50 wood, the Huns receive an advantage by not having to house their units as their civilization grows.

Refer to the tech tree appendix in the manual for *The Conquerors* and turn to Chapter 7: Civilization Strengths and Weaknesses to learn about each civilization's unique economic advantages.

Out of the Gates

The opening moments of a scenario, either single player or multiplayer, is crucial to your success. What you do in the initial seconds (both right and wrong) can become inflated into a large advantage or disadvantage well into the game.

In nearly every scenario you play, moving through the ages rapidly is a primary goal, and this "game within a game" is often set into motion within the first minute of play. Your goal is to get your economic machine humming along nicely as fast as possible. That means that you should be creating an uninterrupted stream of villagers until you advance to Feudal Age. While specific expert starts are presented for each civilization in Chapter 7, the following basic plan can be applied to most civs.

1. Click your town center and create four villagers (the hotkeys are H, C, C, C, C, with H selecting the town center and C creating a villager).

2. Assign your existing villagers to build two or three houses while you send your scout (or eagle warrior) in a circle around the town center looking for your first four sheep or turkeys (see Figure 1.6).

Figure 1.6:
Scout the terrain surrounding your town center as soon as the scenario begins.

3. Move sheep or turkeys to the middle of your town center and have at least four villagers begin harvesting meat from one of the animals. If all four villagers are created before you have the 50 food needed to create another, manually have your villagers deposit the food they have (select the villagers and right-click the town center or mill) or research loom.

4. Send another villager to your berry bushes, build a mill, and have that villager plus three others begin harvesting berries.

5. Assign the next eight or so villagers to chopping wood, starting with the straggler trees near your town center. Once you have 100 wood, build a lumber camp and move your choppers to trees next to the camp.

6. By now, your scout will have hopefully discovered the other four sheep or turkeys lurking in pairs near your town center. Again, send them to the middle of the town center.

7. When your original food sources expire, lure the two boars near your base to the town center. Also, consider hunting deer, depending on their distance from a mill or town center. When those sources are exhausted, build farms.

8. Continue expanding your villager population until you have 25 to 30 (don't forget to build houses). Assign a couple to gold mining and split the rest equally between cutting wood and gathering food. With this balance, you

should reach the magic threshold to advance into the Feudal Age in around 14 minutes. After that, construct two of the required buildings so you can advance to the Castle Age (and create two more villagers during the construction).

9. While your civilization is growing, continue to have your scout cavalry or eagle warrior explore the map, using waypoints to plot an ever-expanding course around your base. You might also want to pull a few villagers from stone duty to create some more houses.

Building a Strong Army

Throughout history, great nations first stood strong on the economic mastery of their rulers. True greatness was achieved only when they unsheathed their blades and entered into battle. Conquest was the one true litmus test of medieval civilizations, and in The Conquerors, you must beat plowshares into swords if you wish to vanquish your foes.

The chapter that follows will help you assess your enemies and craft a potent offense. You will also learn a host of tactical tips and tricks that will provide an edge on the field of battle. Finally, you'll learn how to defend yourself from the pretenders to your rightful crown.

Threat Assessment

The first chapter of this book helped you to grow a thriving economy—but to what end? To build an army, of course. Whether your army will be dug-in and defensive in nature or charging into conflict, you'll need to use your finely tuned economy to produce the military force that best suits your playing style and civilization.

Begin each scenario with a goal and a general plan of how you will reach it. From a military point of view, that means that you must make a threat assessment of your enemies. In a campaign game, this might involve entering the mission and trying it out a few times to ascertain what you're up against and what military resources are at your disposal (which may be finite in a set-piece scenario).

In a single-player mission against one or more computer players, you can begin to develop fairly accurate threat assessments after several play sessions. The computer players will proceed very systematically at the early ages of the game, rapidly researching technology, but not doing much militarily until later in the Feudal Age. At this point, they will focus immense resources on building a varied, though not that tactically enlightened, military force. When assessing the computer players, you don't have to think about attacks in force until all civilizations are in the Feudal Age. Start worrying when you reach the Castle Age, as computer players will almost always begin their major offensives then.

In a multiplayer game, your best ally is information. Scout units and observation posts are absolutely vital in multiplayer games to allow you at least a slight glimpse into the threat on the other side of the fog of war. Scout early and scout often.

Just what is a "threat assessment?" It's an educated guess at the nature and force of any threats against your civilization, as well as an inventory of your assets and advantages. Assessing the threat to your civilization is a key factor in determining the speed of your military buildup and the makeup of your offensive or defensive forces.

Some key components in a threat assessment exercise include the following:

- ♦ Knowing the strengths and weaknesses of the military units in your civilization
- ♦ Knowing the strengths and weaknesses of the military units in your enemy's civilization
- ♦ Assessing the distribution of resources all over the map, especially gold
- ♦ Understanding the technologies and research paths that are needed to train your most advantageous units
- ♦ Knowledge of the terrain surrounding your civilization and any possible "choke points" (see later in this chapter)
- ♦ Knowledge of your enemy's location of the obvious (and not-so-obvious) paths into the hearts of their civilizations

- 🛡 Considering your enemies' growth behaviors
- 🛡 Learning more about your enemies' unit production and tactical approaches

While this may seem like a daunting task, experienced players will tell you that it becomes almost second nature. Stated simply, a threat assessment is "going in with both eyes open." Once you perform your threat assessment (and it's a very good idea to keep tabs on your enemies as play progresses, to see if things have changed at all), you can determine the best possible approach to building a strong, task-focused army.

Offensive Approaches

Very rarely has one civilization utterly erased another in a single battle. More often, two civilizations waged a war over several battles until one side gained an advantage and pressed it to a conclusion over time. *The Conquerors* models this approach very well, and a skilled player should think in these terms rather than try to marshal an overwhelming army to obliterate an opponent in one fell stroke.

Think for a moment about what you want to do as a player. This thought process will give you great insight into building an effective offensive strategy. Strive to collect resources, explore the map, advance through the ages, and build a powerful army. These goals provide the key offensive strategies to skilled players. If you can stop or slow down opponents, you create a situation balanced in your favor.

> **Note** Variations in fighting forces are the most diverse in the Imperial Age. More units are available and variations in player tactics lead to the development of very different armies.

More often than not, the deciding battles in *The Conquerors* take place in the Castle and Imperial Ages, once all civilizations have advanced to a level when they can muster powerful fighting forces. If you can set yourself up to be stronger than the other players at the endgame (more resources, more territory, first to the Imperial Age, etc.), the final battles can tip in your favor.

All of the offensive goals touched on above can be distilled into one simple rule: Damage your opponent as early as possible while remaining undamaged yourself. If you can continually wound and hamstring the enemy while keeping on track in your economic and military growth, you'll set yourself up for a powerful and victorious conclusion to your game.

17

While tactics play an important role in an offensive game (see later in this chapter), strategy is key as well. In order to damage your opponent, you'll need to adopt a flexible strategy incorporating ongoing offensive strikes that will hopefully wound your opponent(s) as you move toward victory.

As mentioned in Chapter 1, begin with your end goal in mind (this will help you to best coordinate your economic and military growth). As your economy grows, begin sowing the seeds for your offensive strikes. Remember, most military action does not occur until you reach the Feudal Age and doesn't escalate to all-out war until the Imperial Age (see Figure 2.1).

Figure 2.1:
The Aztecs prepare for a powerful Imperial Age attack with a fighting force of nearly 50 of their most powerful units.

Scouting your terrain is one of the most useful strategies you can adopt—learning the map during the early Dark Age will provide you with vital information before scouting becomes a risky affair. Scout to learn the following:

1. Starting positions of opposing players and locations of their initial resources (lumber camps and mines).

2. Advantageous tactical routes to your and your enemy's strongholds.

3. The location of key resources, such as gold mines.

Once you have an understanding of the map, you can build military structures away from your town center. Your goal is to expand your area of influence (and to facilitate easy, harassing attacks upon the enemy) while you put yourself in the best position to secure gold mines and other resources in the late game.

Depending on your overall strategy, you can set yourself up in the Feudal Age with one or more solid strike forces comprised of archers and men-at-arms and attack your enemy's resource outposts, particularly wood choppers, as there tends to be many of them. Archers are your best bet against enemy villagers, with men-at-arms in reserve in

case enemy troops break into pursuit. Don't strive for a full assault in the early stages—concentrate on eliminating villagers and controlling gold and stone mines near the enemy. An ongoing guerilla campaign distracts opponents and damages them enough that they will need to play catch-up to reach the Castle and Imperial Ages. Once you reach the Castle Age, guard towers, fortified walls, and castles make village raids more difficult but still valuable. If you can't raid their town, raid their initial expansions to continue to keep them off balance.

> **Tip** In the Castle Age, a force of scorpions makes a great clean-up tool. Assault with a raiding force, and once the enemy military engages you, pull back to your line of scorpions and let them go to work. Pass-through damage (the weapon passes through units causing damage to all units in its path) and the range of these siege weapons have been increased in *The Conquerors*, making them even more effective against charging foot soldiers.

Remember that your general goal is to damage their economy (so they must constantly play catchup) while you sprint toward the Imperial Age and build your "finishing" force. Remember to act quickly once you reach the Imperial Age—if you've played well, you'll have set yourself up for a rapid military "boom" of research and production rather than a complete force assembly. Your enemies will catch up if you wait too long in the Imperial Age, so press your advantage as soon as possible.

Logistical Tips

A solid offensive strategy begins not on the battlefield, but in the barracks and the armorer's shop. A skilled field commander prepares his troops for battle before raising the flag and signaling muster. The following tips will help you maximize military planning and development:

- Don't build military units until you reach the Feudal or Castle Age—in the early game, their cost is high and their effectiveness low.
- Build a military to suit your purposes. This goes hand in hand with scouting and knowing civilization strengths and weaknesses.
- Build enough forces to defend your economic infrastructure. A host of archers garrisoned in your town center is particularly effective.

Chapter 2: Building a Strong Army

🛡 Prepare your resources and ready your villagers so that you can quickly erect a castle the moment you reach the Castle Age. This will provide you with access to special units and technologies, and protect your civilization (building it within range of a town center is good thinking).

🛡 Construct a varied attack force, but always keep in mind the strengths and weaknesses of your enemy. If you play the Spanish against the Aztecs, for example, build up a large cavalry force, and use speedy hit-and-run tactics to tear up their foot-only troops.

🛡 Don't restrict your military buildings to the vicinity of your town center. A battle camp near the enemy is more effective and can serve as a diversion to assaulting enemies (see Figure 2.2).

Figure 2.2:
Building military structures near an enemy town is a great way to launch consistent harassing attacks and keeps the battle away from your economy.

🛡 Always maintain a reserve force behind your front lines. Nothing is worse than losing your entire army in a massive battle when victory was just within your grasp.

🛡 Never forget the offensive punch of castles and town centers, especially when built right next to an enemy's resources. Use a team of villagers to build the structures rapidly.

🛡 Before launching a major attack, take a few seconds to tend to your infrastructure and queue up your farms, inspect gold mines, and line up additional troops at military buildings. You might be at your population limit, but establishing a queue of your military units will ensure that fresh troops will be trained the moment others fall in battle.

Tactical Tips

You enter pure tactical mode once your troops move within sight of the enemy. Gone are the larger issues of victory conditions and economic growth—now, you must command your troops to the best of your ability on the field of battle. The following tips should give you an offensive leg up on your competition:

- In small battles, superior numbers often have the edge over superior strength. With four swordsmen attacking a knight, the swordsmen can get off more attacks in a melee round.

- Allow your groups to settle into formation, which will maximize their offensive punch. Also have a good understanding of counter units—don't send three knights into a pack of pikemen, for example.

- Use siege weapons sensibly. Siege weapons can be very powerful, but they can also collapse quickly under an onslaught. It's best to use them against a specific goal (scorpions are great defensive stay-at-home weapons against attacks), and guard them carefully as they attack.

- Rams are now an even more powerful tool. Battering, capped, and siege rams can now garrison up to four units (see Figure 2.3). Garrisoning units increases the speed and assault strength of these building smashers, and once the ram is destroyed, your units will be available for continued assault.

Figure 2.3: Garrisoning units inside rams not only improves their speed, but increases their attack effectiveness.

- Press your advantages relentlessly. For example, if you play as the Mayans, exploit cheap archery units and your Plumed Archer to craft a devastating long-range force with tons of reserves queued up when you go into battle.

- Remember to add a group of monks to any assault or late-game raiding force. They're great for healing damaged units, and with the theocracy technology, you can more rapidly and effectively convert enemy units to your cause.

- Seek to control enemy resource locales. Kill all the villagers you can, and build towers, a town center, or castles near lumber camps and mines.

- Attack from multiple fronts at the same time and alternate advance and retreat maneuvers on both fronts, confusing the enemy units (this works best against computer players).

- Arrange your army into attack groups of the same sort of units: pikemen, archers, cavalry units, etc. Use the group functions to quickly and effectively bring them into the most advantageous battle situations (like pikemen against enemy mounted forces, for example).

- Never be afraid to retreat. In fact, retreating is a powerful offensive tool, since it will spread out the enemy force due to differences in unit speed. You can then concentrate on destroying the isolated units, one by one.

- Be ruthless and set traps. Hide significant, powerful forces in the trees and strike out with a small, nimble force. Engage the enemy and then retreat, luring opposing troops to an ambush (this works well against both computer and human opponents).

Note Remember that in *The Conquerors*, you can quickly and easily command computer allies to do everything from give you gold to attack opponents. The manual thoroughly explains how it's done.

Defensive Approaches

Considering the offensive goals outlined above, you can clearly deduce your prime defensive goals: Keep your economic machine intact and keep your military efforts on target. Other players will be seeking to disrupt you, and your main defensive goal is to thwart them in their efforts. A good defense means being prepared for the attacks before they come (you want to act, not react) and continuing an early and aggressive offensive push (which will limit an opponent's ability to harass you).

The two key factors in a successful defensive strategy are knowledge and force. Knowledge is knowing what's coming, and in *The Conquerors*, that is accomplished with forward scouts or observation points (such as towers). Force is having the counter units available to deal with whatever attack is coming your way. Generally, it's a good idea to keep a defensive army close to your home base to react to raids. The better observation and early warning system you have set up, the easier you can move your defensive troops into an intercept position to cut off foes before they reach their target.

Defensive Tips

The following tips should give you an edge in protecting your home turf:

- Houses can be invaluable as both walls and observation points. Use them to cut off access to your base and build them in anticipated thoroughfares to act as lookout towers.

- Build town centers all over the map at gold mines and other resources so that it can do double duty as a base and a resource drop-off point. If your original settlement comes under attack, you've already got the start of another base in place.

- Construct your defensive structures to create "choke points," which force attackers to approach your village along a particular line. Then set up ambushes and defensive structures at these locations.

- Garrison your reserve forces in military structures, town centers, and castles. This will provide a raiding army with a nice surprise once it reaches the heart of your civilization, and it will keep the enemy from knowing the size and nature of your force.

- Have a grouped force of fast infantry or cavalry units on hand to destroy siege weapons coming to attack.

- If you build up a larger town area, place some onagers behind the walls to chew up any attacking forces attempting to breach your fortifications (see Figure 2.4).

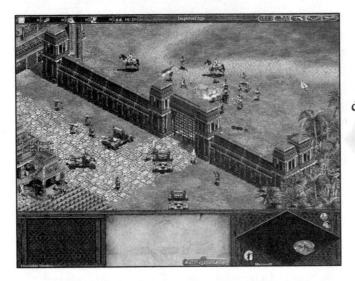

Figure 2.4:
Onagers are a great defensive force to keep at home, safely protected by a fortified wall, they can stop nearly any frontal attack from behind the wall.

- If all looks hopeless, take some of your forces and villagers and run. A quick retreat can give you a second chance.

- If under a massive attack, take some of your military units and break through the attacking line. Retreating behind enemy lines will scramble their organization, giving your other forces a chance for a safer retreat.

Attila the Hun

Gaining control of the Huns in 433, the ferocious King Attila helped advance his people through Central Asia and Europe, sacking Persian and Roman towns along the way. Attila's dominance was so profound that the Roman Empire paid a tribute to him, hoping to keep the Roman cities safe. Attila's eventual death, in 453, threw the Huns into disarray and caused people throughout Western Europe to breathe a sigh of relief.

In this chapter, you'll find a complete walkthrough for The Conquerors' Attila the Hun campaign. The Huns' cavalry-heavy forces don't require houses to support population, allowing them to quickly generate a military force that ensures furious combat against the Roman Empire.

Attila 1: The Scourge of God

Initial Objectives

- Attila must survive.
- Attila must make sure Bleda is killed and then return to the Huns' camp.

Forces

	Their Stance	Your Stance
Bleda's Huns	Ally	Ally
Scythians	Enemy	Enemy
Persians	Enemy	Enemy
Romans	Neutral	Enemy

Map Highlights

Your starting location, also Bleda and Attila's base, lies in the northwest section of the map. In the southeastern corner of the map is a well-guarded Persian stronghold that rests across a large section of river that runs through the center of the map. To the southwest you'll find the Eastern Roman Empire's town at the end of a long road flanked by watchtowers. The Scythian camp is positioned in the northwest area of the map.

Battle Plans

The scenario begins in the northeast when Attila and Bleda enter on horseback arguing over control of the Huns. Bleda issues a challenge—whoever can defeat the iron boar that inhabits a forest to the north shall lead the Huns in battle.

Attila accepts the challenge, but not without some words of advice from one of his trusted Hun commanders. What if Bleda had an "accident" during the boar hunt? With that in mind, you gain control of Attila the Hun with your first objective: eliminate Bleda before returning to camp.

The easiest way to dispatch your rival is to follow him north to the boar. Approach the iron boar to trigger its attack and observe Bleda coming to assist. When the boar targets Attila, select the Diplomacy menu and change your stance with Bleda from ally to enemy. Then attack Bleda by shifting your blade from the boar to your rival's steed. Attila will take damage from the boar, but he heals himself at about one hit point per second and should have enough hit points to survive that attack and then kill both it and Bleda.

26

With Bleda defeated, move Attila back to the village and watch as the Huns praise your accomplishment. Moments after you arrive, however, a small band of archers, allied with Bleda, emerges from the northern forest. Having witnessed your act, the archers attempt to convince the others that you shouldn't be trusted. Despite their claim, most of the Tarkans (the Huns' unique unit) side with Attila. As soon as you gain control of the cavalry units, engage the treacherous archers and Tarkans. When Bleda's units have been defeated, move through the base and gain control of the structures and peasants. You'll also receive a sizable tribute from Bleda's former constituents (see Figure 3.1).

Designer's Notes

There are three ways to respond to Bleda's challenge: you can help him kill the Iron Boar and then suffer the ambush, you can just kill Bleda outright, or you can refuse his challenge altogether and ride off to establish a new Hun tribe, which makes the rest of the scenario play very differently. The Iron Boar (like Ornlu the Wolf) is a fabrication. Of course, there were a few interesting playtests when we got the I.D. for the boars mixed up and accidentally placed Iron Boars on random maps. It was pretty hysterical the first time someone lost over 10 villagers trying to lure the boar to their town center!

— *Greg Street*

Figure 3.1:
Assassinate Bleda to gain control of the Huns and you'll receive a tribute from your new subjects!

🛡 **New Objective:** Defeat two of your remaining enemies (the Scythians, Romans, and Persians).

After Attila gains control of the Huns, you're offered a new mission objective to eliminate two of the remaining enemies. Thankfully, this daunting task can be made easier by forming an alliance with the Scythians. The Hun military is extremely weak at the outset, so don't engage your foes too early. Remain inside the Hun camp and strengthen your economy and army. You should try to get to Feudal Age quickly as you can't train troops till then.

> **Tip** The narrow river to the west of the camp contains plentiful fish, both along the shore and in deeper waters. Consider building a dock and fishing boats to hasten your acquisition of food, the main resource needed to strengthen your military.

Select the town center and continue to produce villagers until you have 15 to 20 villagers. Assign half to forage the food resources near the Hun mill, adjacent to the town center. You'll find foraging bushes, shore fish, and deer to add to your food reserves. Cycle through the idle villagers and place a third on wood and the others on the small patch of gold at the southern end of the camp. When you no longer need wood for new structures and archers, shift the lumberjacks over to mine the gold.

Then advance to the Feudal Age and purchase the military upgrades available at the barracks, archery range, and blacksmith. Begin producing infantry and organize your troops into preset groups; assign the cavalry and infantry to your first two groups and the archers and spearmen to a third. Use the scout cavalry to explore the surrounding area, but don't venture too far just yet. Many Scythian, Persian, and Byzantine patrols wander about the map, so stay close to home until you've accumulated a substantial military.

When food and gold become scarce, you can build farms for food, though available land is tight inside the Hun camp. Alternatively, you can scout the northern area (just over the bridge to the west) of the map and you'll locate a Hun stable. Just west of the barracks lies an open field filled with foraging bushes and deer. Scythian cavalry patrol here, so be sure to bring military units to protect your villagers.

To acquire additional gold, use the market to trade wood or stone. Also, there's plenty of gold ore southeast of the Hun camp behind a Persian wall protected by a tower. It's extremely difficult to conquer and exploit this gold. Destroying the wall and tower is only half the battle, as Persian ships bombard the area from the wide river southeast of the Hun camp.

🛡 **Optional Objective:** Rescue Hun captives from the Roman fort to the south.

> **Tip** If you make sure you don't provoke the Persians by building a mining camp inside their former grounds and watchtowers by the river, and refrain from attacking Persian fishing boats, the Persians completely ignore this area and you can get away with mining the gold.

After 20 or 30 minutes of game time (F11 displays elapsed time), you should have advanced to the Castle Age and trained a sizeable army of 30+ infantry and cavalry and 20+ crossbowmen. Now you're ready to explore the map. Continue to produce infantry, cavalry, and crossbowmen as resources become available. Never leave the Hun camp completely defenseless because you'll occasionally be raided by Roman and Scythian forces.

Begin by heading southwest across the bridge to the west of the Hun camp. Eliminate the Scythian patrols here and continue south across the river crossing. Follow the road, flanked by Byzantine watchtowers, toward the southwestern corner of the map. If you spot Byzantine infantry and archers headed for the Hun camp, cut them off and overwhelm them with greater numbers.

🛡 **Optional Objective:** Free the Scythian scout from the Byzantine fort.

> **Tip** Almost every attacker approaches from the same route. A castle built on their approach, right next to the southern-most Hun watchtower, will snuff out any threats.

Upon reaching the Byzantine town, another objective presents itself: the Scythian scout promises a reward if he is freed. The imprisoned Hun villagers and Scythian scout are located in the southern part of the Byzantine town. Your present forces should be enough to wipe out the Byzantine defenses. Defeat any surviving Byzantine forces, then free the scout as soon as possible to precipitate the alliance.

Work your way through the Byzantine camp, destroying military structures first (destroy them all and they will be formally defeated). Free the Hun villagers and Scythian scout trapped in the south (see Figure 3.2). Keep the Hun villagers nearby for now, as once you've allied with the Scythians, you can begin mining the gold and stone just south of their base.

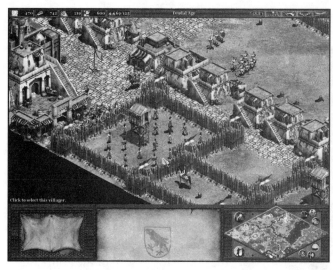

Figure 3.2:
Destroy the palisade around the Hun captives and Scythian scout.

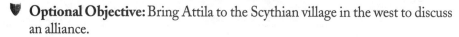

Optional Objective: Bring Attila to the Scythian village in the west to discuss an alliance.

Once the Scythian scout is freed and heads back to his camp, you'll receive another optional objective, this time to bring Attila to the Scythian village in the west to discuss an alliance. Move Attila northwest into the Scythian village and locate the scout. As you approach, the Scythians offer an alliance and will now engage the Persians and remaining Byzantines on sight. This optional treaty makes the level significantly easier.

It's safe to explore the northern and northwestern area of the map once allied with the Scythians. If you haven't already, acquire the Hun stable just west of the Hun camp, build a mill, and begin foraging the bushes and hunting the deer nearby. Use the freed Hun villagers to mine the gold and stone north of the Roman base (just south of the Scythian base). Advance to the Castle Age and consider constructing a castle to produce the Hun unique unit, the Tarkan, once you've mined enough stone.

Optional Objective: Send 10 horses to the flagged Scythian palisade.

Before you mount an offensive against the Persian stronghold, located at the south-eastern area of the map, explore the Scythian base. Take specific note of the circular palisade surrounding flagged posts. When you approach, the Scythians request 10 horses in exchange for additional military assistance. Completing this optional objective rewards you handsomely.

Though the map, especially the western side, is littered with wild horses, you'll need to locate 10 standard horses and move them inside the Scythian camp (see Figure 3.3 for the location of all horses). You'll find three horses already in the Hun camp, two horses to the east, two to the southwest, two to the northwest over the bridge, one resting west of the bridge, two west of the Byzantine base, and another pair east of the Byzantine base. Move at least 10 horses into the flagged Scythian palisade and your new allies will give you 20 cavalry archers. As the horses can be killed, avoid battles while rounding them up.

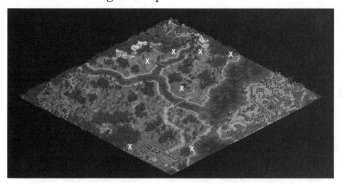

Figure 3.3:
Find horses at these locations.

Warning Don't engage the Persian town center alone. The garrisoned troops can inflict plenty of damage on your infantry, archers, and cavalry archers. Wait for the Scythian forces to engage the town center, then assist. The combined attack will destroy the town center much more quickly and result in fewer casualties. You could also build a dock and some warships to defeat the Persian war galleys. Controlling the river is of great help in conquering the Persian city.

By now, you'll be about an hour of game time into the scenario. You'll likely notice Scythian troops engaging the Persian troops and base in the southeast (see Figure 3.4). Assign your units to preset groups (and continue to produce more military units with available resources) and move them toward the Persian stronghold to the south. Assist the Scythians with your military units and donated cavalry archers. Use Tarkans (extremely effective against buildings), battering rams, and petards against the Persian military structures. Defeat any hostile units or military structures first. Stay away from the river, as the Persian fleet will bombard your troops should you wander too close.

🛡 **Optional Objective:** Keep 10 horses in the flagged Scythian palisade so the Scythians can supply Attila with soldiers.

At some point during your attack on the Persian base, the Scythians announce that their horses are stampeding and have gotten loose from the flagged palisade. Returning them to the palisade is another optional objective that nets you extra cavalry archers. Shift your view over to the fleeing horses and select them. Move the horses back into the Scythian camp to receive the additional troops.

Figure 3.4:
Completing the mission becomes much easier once Attila allies with the Scythians.

Attila 2: The Great Ride

Initial Objective

⚑ Raid the Byzantine villages. Once you have enough resources to build a forward base, you can field an army against the Byzantines.

Forces

	Their Stance	Your Stance
Sofia	Enemy	Enemy
Naissus	Enemy	Enemy
Adrianople	Enemy	Enemy
Dyrrhachium	Enemy	Enemy
Thessalonica	Enemy	Enemy
Eastern Roman Empire	Enemy	Enemy
Scythians	Ally	Ally

Map Highlights

The Hun army (a mixture of Tarkan and cavalry archers) enters in the northeastern section of the map. The Sofia village lies west of the player's start point, while you'll find the Naissus lumber camp toward the southeast. The town of Dyrrhachium, complete with castle and walls, lies south of the Sofia village. Head southeast of the Dyrrhachium castle to encounter the Thessalonicans.

At the southern edge of the map you'll find the Adrianople village. It is accessible either from the Naissus lumber camp or east from the Thessalonican fishing village. Finally, your Scythian allies possess a tiny village in the center of the map. You can reach the Scythian outpost by entering the forest just east of the Byzantine city.

Battle Plans

You gain control of the Hun army in the northeastern section of the map. Select your Tarkans and assign them to one group, then select your cavalry archers and assign them to another. When you encounter enemy infantry, pull back your cavalry archers and keep them safe against attack. As the enemy pursues the cavalry archers, attack with your Tarkans.

Designer's Notes

An early design for The Age of Kings called for the Celts, Mongols, and Vikings to be "raider civilizations" that had to capture villagers and resources from their enemies. For various reasons, we could never give this feature the attention it deserved and so it was eventually cut. Scenarios such as this one are intended to reinforce the point that raiders like the Huns succeeded at the expense of their neighbors. In this scenario, the different Roman towns can each offer a different resource (food, wood, gold, stone, villagers, and soldiers). There are also some Scythian witches living in the forest who can assist the Huns...for the right price.

— Greg Street

Proceed west until you reach Sofia. Keep your cavalry archers back and pummel the infantry defenders with your Tarkans. As you enter the town, you're informed that razing the Sofia town center will net valuable resources. Ignore the other structures and target the town center. Be sure to engage any remaining hostile infantry before continuing the town center assault. Demolishing it places food in the Hun reserve and Sofia is officially defeated (Figure 3.5).

Figure 3.5:
Razing the Sofia town center nets the Huns extra food. Return later in the mission to mine the gold just south of Sofia.

> **Note** When completing the destruction of the logging camp, you hear the locals speak of "wild Scythians" nearby. As established in the first mission, the Scythians are now your ally, so it's wise to seek them out. You'll enter the Scythian forest village just south of the Naissus village. The rewards you gain from the visit assist in the final assault against the Romans—so save your encounter with the Scythians for later in the mission.

Head back to the start location and proceed southeast along the edge of the map. Here you'll encounter the Naissus logging village: a small group of houses and lumber camps. You're invited to demolish the lumber camps to deprive the locals of their lumber. There are four lumber camps in total, placed on the perimeter of the village. Destroy all four and receive 900 wood in the Hun reserve, then demolish the trade workshop so that the village declares defeat.

One entrance to the Roman city lies south of the Naissus camp, but as there's no way to survive the encounter with the Roman forces at this point, ignore it for now. Return to your starting position and head west through Sofia. Continue to the western corner and the town of Dyrrhachium, which boasts a castle surrounded by stone walls.

> **Tip** Depending on your forces, you may wish to storm the palisade later. It must be done to make Dyrrhachium acknowledge defeat.

As you near Dyrrhachium, you're informed that several Huns are held prisoner within the castle. If you can demolish the structure, you can free your comrades. Explore the area carefully and defeat any hostile units you encounter. Just north of the town's stone walls you'll find an octagonal palisade containing archers and a mangonel. Eliminate the archers and the siege weapon.

Break down the gate or a portion of the wall surrounding the Dyrrhachium castle. Enter the base and engage any hostile infantry or archer units first. With the base clear, assault the castle. You'll notice that the Hun captives will assist. You'll incur some heavy casualties during the assault, but don't worry, as you'll soon be constructing a base of your own.

With the Hun captives freed, proceed south from Dyrrhachium (leave the structures—especially the farms—intact) until you encounter the Thessalonicans by a narrow river. You are advised to demolish the Thessalonican houses to gain access to

their villagers. Organize your military and assault the homes around the Thessalonican market (beware the monk trying to convert your soldiers). Once all the homes are destroyed, you're provided with several villagers to begin resource gathering and construction of your town and army.

New Objective: Train an army and defeat the Romans by leveling their town center.

By now, you'll probably be 20–30 minutes into the game (F11 shows elapsed time). Build two town centers near the conquered Thessalonica and Dyrrhachium. Construct one town center near the shore; it's here you'll build the military structures to produce an army. Erect another town center inside now-desolate Dyrrhachium. Build a mill around the planted farms with at least four villagers, as only those who build the mill can work the farms. Produce around 10 villagers at each town center. Use the northern villagers on the Dyrrhachium farmland (see Figure 3.6) and assign the southern villagers to chopping wood and mining gold from the nearby resource. There are also many deer around, providing an additional food source.

Figure 3.6: Leave the Dyrrhachium farms intact. Once you have villagers, work those farms to increase the Hun food supply.

You're already in the Castle Age, so you only need to start building structures in order to begin producing a formidable Castle Age army. Construct a barracks, archery range, stable, and siege workshop near your southern town center. The Byzantine stronghold, in the eastern corner of the map, is accessible from there. Furthermore, Byzantines like to attack along the southern edge of the battlefield, so it's wise to organize your army here. Produce a mixture of infantry, archers, and cavalry. You may also want to construct some siege units.

There's one more village to raid before you assault the Byzantine city. Proceed east along the southern edge of the map until you reach Adrianople village. Here you'll raze the mining camps to acquire gold and stone. As you enter the village, beware of the monks waiting just inside, as they'll waste no time in converting your units. Eliminate the monks quickly and destroy the monastery. Watch out for watchtowers to the east, and use your siege units to eliminate them. Destroying the mining camp places 550 gold and 220 stone in the Hun reserve.

> **Tip** You'll find plenty of gold ore south of the Sofia base you raided in the beginning of the mission. Should you require more gold, send over some villagers and defending infantry. Construct a mining camp and begin gathering gold.

Optional Objective: Give six villagers to the Scythians' Wild Women in return for their assistance.

Continue to produce a mixture of military units until you've hit your population maximum. Head east past the Adrianople village, but before entering the Byzantine city, turn north along the eastern edge of the map. Locate the path leading west into the forest. Here you'll find the Scythian forest village. Wild Women await your arrival and request six villagers; the women promise assistance should you complete the task (see Figure 3.7).

Escort six villagers from your northern or southern base into the Scythian forest camp. Be sure to protect your villagers with a small band

> **Tip** You can also take out the camps before you even start building, right after Thessalonica. As long as you limit yourself to destroying the mining camps and monastery, things are easy. The acquired gold enables you to launch the attack on Naissus much earlier than it would be possible otherwise.

of infantry. When the villagers reach the Scythian women, you're told a reward awaits you just north of the Scythian camp. Here you'll find 14 hunting wolves and 12 petards for use against the Byzantine stronghold. The petards are best used against the guard towers and siege workshop (to stop production of Roman siege units). Use the wolves to assist against enemy infantry and archers.

Figure 3.7:
Locate the Scythian forest camp just northwest of the Roman stronghold. Do a favor for the Wild Women to receive bonus units.

Tip The Byzantines will periodically send an attack group consisting of infantry, cavalry, scorpions, and battering rams along the southern edge of the map into your southern base. Scout the area thoroughly and attempt to assault the Byzantines while they're trapped within the forest that runs along the southern river. Attack here and you can avoid most of the damage from the Byzantines' siege units.

After boosting your troops' abilities (research all attack and defensive bonuses—you should have plenty of resources), you'll be about an hour to 90 minutes into the scenario: time to attack! It's best to wait until the Byzantines send out their military and siege units before venturing inside the cramped city. Eliminate the hostile units and destroy the gate or wall enclosing the Byzantine city. You can completely eliminate all resistance and military structures, or you can just focus on the town center as its destruction ends the scenario in victory.

Attila 3: The Walls of Constantinople

Initial Objective

- Stockpile 10,000 gold in tribute from the Byzantines.

Chapter 3: Attila the Hun

Forces

	Their Stance	Your Stance
Constantinople	Enemy	Enemy
Marcianopolis	Enemy	Enemy
Philippopolis	Enemy	Enemy

Map Highlights

You'll locate the Hun camp in the northeast section of the map. Marcianopolis is just east of the Hun start location. To the far west lies Philippopolis. Finally, Constantinople, as shown on the mini-map, can be found in the far southeastern corner. Thorough exploration of the map will reveal two relics, each of which can be taken to a monastery for extra gold. You'll find one relic north of Philippopolis and the other to the northwest.

Battle Plans

Select your military and the nearby monk as soon as the mission begins. Within moments, a small band of Marcianopolis cavalry and infantry units enters from the north and attacks your structures. Move your military to engage, and use your monk to attempt unit conversion and heal your troops.

> **Tip** As you produce your army and gather resources, Marcianopolis will send over infantry and cavalry units to attack your villagers and structures. Position your monk near Marcianopolis and convert troops as they approach your base. Terminate remaining hostile troops with your organized groups of infantry, archers, and cavalry units.

Marcianopolis is just southeast of the Hun village (if you scout just a short distance, you'll spot the Marcianopolis walls). You begin the scenario with an ample supply of resources. Produce 10 to 15 villagers and begin farming and chopping wood. You again begin in the Castle Age, so construct the necessary military buildings and research attack and armor bonuses at the blacksmith. It won't take too many troops to eliminate Marcianopolis. Produce a moderate-sized mixture of infantry, archers, and cavalry and head east from the Hun camp.

Approach Marcianopolis and enter through the front gate when Marcianopolis units exit. Alternatively, you can simply destroy the gate. Don't worry about the structures or villagers. Eliminate all hostile infantry and cavalry units first; you won't face much opposition from Marcianopolis (see Figure 3.8).

Figure 3.8:
Raze Marcianopolis as soon as possible. Its weak defenses shouldn't offer much resistance.

Once you've cleared the enemy units, attack the town center. Destroying the Marcianopolis town center extorts 3,000 gold from Constantinople. Leave the farms intact, as you can construct a mill here and use the farms yourself. Also, escort your monk over and convert the Marcianopolis villagers and use them to farm or chop wood.

Designer's Notes

Attila the Hun desperately wanted to be taken seriously as a world power and not just as a barbarian nomad. He thought that conquering a metropolis such as Constantinople or Rome would buy him credibility. Unfortunately, the Hun siege weapons just weren't up to the task of penetrating the famous walls of Constantinople. Those great walls remained impregnable for hundreds of years, until the Turks finally managed it in 1453.

—Greg Street

From the demolished town center, head southeast along the shoreline to the Marcianopolis docks. Raze the two docks to extort an additional 1,000 gold from the Byzantines. Clear out the remaining structures if you wish, then move your military back to the Hun base. Philippopolis will send over pikemen and crossbowmen at some point, so don't leave the Hun base unguarded. Also, leave a few military units in Marcianopolis to protect working villagers.

Philippopolis, located in the western part of the map, boasts much stronger defenses and many more military units. Don't scout or assault the town until you've

generated a substantial military and maximized your population with military units. Position your organized military groups on the western side of the Hun base to intercept any Philippopolis raiding parties.

Even with maximum population, queue additional infantry, archer, cavalry, and siege units to continue to produce military units after the assault commences. Organize your military into preset groups and proceed west towards Philippopolis. Proceed with caution and eliminate any hostile units you encounter.

Pikemen and crossbowmen pour out of Philippopolis as you approach. Return their attack with archers against the pikemen and cavalry and infantry against the crossbowmen, then work your way to the Philippopolis town center. Eliminating the town center not only extorts gold from the Byzantines, it demilitarizes the Philippopolitans. It's in your best interest to demolish the town center as soon as possible. Keep producing military units and send them to Philippopolis to reinforce your attack. Destroying the town center extorts an additional 3,000 gold from Constantinople.

> **Tip** A river runs south along your path to Philippopolis. Spot the Philippopolis trade cart heading toward Constantinople and destroy it before it escapes to extort 500 gold from the Byzantines.

> **Tip** Also try attacking Philippopolis first. It has few defenses save a couple of watch-towers and a weak army. Raiding Philippopolis (and targeting villagers) right from the beginning can result in their resignation after about 17 minutes of game time.

Explore Philippopolis and eliminate any remaining military units. Locate and destroy the Philippopolis market to extort an additional 500 gold from Constantinople. Go south through the town and find the dock. Destroy it for an additional 500 gold tribute from the Byzantines. Scout around Philippopolis to locate two relics, one to the north and one to the northwest. Take these relics back to your monastery for bonus gold.

If you've followed the walkthrough and eliminated all targets of opportunity, you've now extorted 8,500 gold from Constantinople. Organize your military and proceed south from the desolate Philippopolis base until you locate a bridge leading to the east. Continue east until you encounter a Byzantine monastery. Demolish it to further distress the Byzantines, and they'll send you an additional 1,000 gold in tribute.

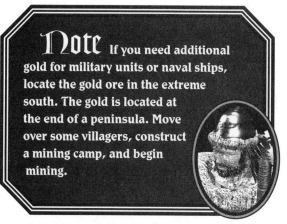

Note If you need additional gold for military units or naval ships, locate the gold ore in the extreme south. The gold is located at the end of a peninsula. Move over some villagers, construct a mining camp, and begin mining.

Keep moving cautiously to the east until you're along the outer perimeter of the Byzantine capital. As you approach, you're told assaulting Constantinople will be nearly impossible; however, attacking the docks, positioned along the southeastern shore of the city, might scare the Byzantines enough to offer additional tribute.

While you can construct docks anywhere along the southern shoreline, perhaps the best route of attack lies from the northeast corner of the map. Move villagers along the eastern shore past the remnants of the Marcianopolis, then construct multiple docks to hasten your production of war galleys (be sure to research the war galley advancement). You should have plenty of food, wood, and gold to support a large fleet. Organize your naval fleet (approximately 10–25 ships should be sufficient, but more would be even more effective) and head southeast along the shoreline until you encounter the Byzantine stronghold (see Figure 3.9).

Figure 3.9:
Use your remaining resources to build war galleys and attack the docks along the southeastern shoreline.

You'll find one dock behind a river wall and gate. Destroy the gate and defending ships inside, then concentrate your firepower on the Constantinople docks. Be wary of the monks that walk along the shore and attempt conversion. Back off your fleet or eliminate the monks. Demolishing the eastern dock extorts another 1,000 gold.

Note Moving a unit within spotting range of Hagia Sophia (the wonder in Constantinople) extorts another 1,000 gold in return for not destroying the wonder.

You should now have enough tribute to complete the level. However, if you've missed one of the targets of opportunity, you can extort more gold by destroying the remaining two docks located to the south of Constantinople. Move your fleet along the shore toward the southwest area of the map. The docks here, like those of the eastern dock, are positioned behind a river wall and gate. Blow apart the defending ships and then the gate. Expect the Byzantines to send over archers, crossbowmen, and even siege units to counter your attack. Wipe out both southern docks for an additional 2,500 gold tribute from the Byzantines.

Attila 4: A Barbarian Betrothal

Initial Objectives

- Defeat Orlèans.
- Defeat Metz.
- Defeat Burgundy.

Forces

	Their Stance	Your Stance
Burgundy	Enemy	Enemy
Metz	Enemy	Enemy
Orlèans	Enemy	Enemy
Western Roman Empire	Enemy	Enemy

Map Highlights

The scattered Hun army starts in the eastern corner. You'll find the Burgundy village just west of the Hun start location, and Metz to the northwest. Finally, the city of Orlèans can be found northwest from the Hun start location. Though there are several gold ore sites in the Huns' southeastern corner, you'll find even more inside and west of the Burgundy village.

Battle Plans

The Hun army begins to spread out in the eastern corner of the map. You aren't in immediate danger, so use scout cavalry to reveal the terrain and search for a suitable spot to build a town center. Thorough scouting reveals several patches of gold and stone in the southeastern corner. Place the town center in an open clearing to provide area for farms and military structures.

> **Tip** Locate the stone in the southeastern corner and mine at least 650 in preparation for an optional objective later in the mission.

Use your current food storage to produce more villagers. Begin constructing farms around your town center, and then build a mill nearby and surround it with more farms. Assign some villagers to chop wood in the adjacent forest and others to mine gold at the nearby gold deposit.

Burgundy, positioned west of the Hun camp, has crossbowmen and infantry placed around the perimeter of its village. It's likely some of these guards will wander into your base, so be prepared and erect a barracks, archery range, and stable as soon as possible. You'll also want a blacksmith to research attack and armor bonuses. Also, if you construct two Castle Age buildings or a castle, you can advance to Imperial Age. Be sure to set up adequate defenses—blocking access with stone walls is especially easy and effective—before you divert resources to age advancement, though (see Figure 3.10).

Figure 3.10: Produce military units to defend your villagers and structures before you advance to the Imperial Age.

Metz, located north of the Hun camp, and Orlèans, positioned to the northwest, will also send scouts and raiding parties (featuring infantry, cavalry, and even some siege units and battering rams) from time to time, so produce an adequate defensive army consisting of infantry, archers, and cavalry. You may also want to erect and upgrade walls and towers to place on the northern side of your base.

Burgundy isn't too strong at the outset, but it builds up a moderate army of infantry and archers if left alone for too long. As soon as you've produced 20–30 military units, organize them into groups of infantry, cavalry, and archers, and push an offensive into Burgundian territory. You'll encounter the guards along the perimeter first. Defeat these hostile units and push into the main area of their base and attack the town center. But don't eliminate Burgundy because your show of force convinces the village that an alliance might be in order.

It's best not to hurt Burgundy more than absolutely necessary. Destroying just the town center results in Burgundy being a much more valuable ally.

🛡 **Optional Objective:** Give Burgundy 500 gold tribute and form an alliance.

The Burgundians are willing to join you if you can convince them that you are trustworthy. Burgundy first requests a tribute of 500 gold. You'll need a market to send the tribute, done through the Diplomacy menu. You should also be mining stone at this time (there are several quarry sites in your part of the battlefield) to prepare for the next optional objective.

🛡 **Optional Objective:** Build a castle within Burgundy town limits.

After your tribute of 500 gold, Burgundy requests that you build a castle inside its village to protect it against attacks from Metz and Orlèans. You have 10 minutes to build the castle, which should be plenty of time if you've already mined some stone. If you haven't, divert several villagers to stone mining, then move them inside the flags that mark the Burgundy town boundary and construct the castle (see Figure 3.11).

> # Note
> Though Burgundy doesn't assist much in your battle with Metz and Orlèans, it's still imperative that you seek the alliance. It isn't very costly—only 500 gold and a castle—and the castle is useful for producing Tarkans and trebuchets when you advance to Imperial Age. Also, you gain access to the plentiful gold ore scattered throughout the Burgundy base.

Once allied with Burgundy, you should immediately move over villagers, scout the perimeter of the base, and begin mining all available gold. Reseed your farms (and

queue up more at the mill) and continue to chop wood. If you haven't already—and still have an adequate defense—advance to the Imperial Age to gain trebuchets, better infantry and cavalry, and stronger attack and armor bonuses.

Position your military on the northern side of your base and scout the area between Metz and the Hun base. Metz will periodically send over attack groups consisting of cavalry, infantry, siege units, and battering rams. Produce a mixed army with infantry, cavalry, archers, and siege units. Build trebuchets for long-range artillery attacks and produce some battering rams (and research the capped ram) for an assault against the Metz structures. Research additional attack and speed bonuses and begin advancing north once you've gained a sizable force. You have a large population that can support many military units, so garrison infantry in your battering rams to increase their speed and damage, and support your siege units with a large mixed army. Place some monks in your force for unit conversion and healing.

Figure 3.11:
Ally with Burgundy by sending a 500 gold tribute and constructing a castle within their base.

Advance north and engage the Metz army first. Though the town possesses a moderately sized army, its defenses are much weaker than those of Orléans. Attack hostile units and structures first, then assault the town center. Unpack your trebuchets within range of Metz's structures and protect them with infantry and cavalry units (the Guard command is useful here). Once the Metz town center falls, the town resigns from the conflict. Ignore the remaining structures, but finish off any remaining Metz military units.

Orléans is a much more difficult foe. Two castles lie along the outer perimeter of the city, and you'll find the town center and military structures protected by stone walls. Also, beware of Orléans monks at the monastery east of the town; kill them quickly to prevent unit conversion (see Figure 3.12).

Figure 3.12:
Demolish the monastery and the monks positioned on the eastern side of the Orlèans base or you'll find your units switching sides.

The trebuchets should assist greatly in knocking out the outer perimeter of the Orlèans base; however, expect Orlèans to send its own siege units to retaliate. Protect your trebuchets with infantry units and engage the Orlèans military. Continue to produce your own military units and send them into the conflict. Also, it's possible you might run out of gold during the long, expensive assault against Orlèans. Use your market to sell wood, food, or stone for more gold resources.

Designer's Notes

One can only imagine what would have befallen poor Honoria if Attila had been able to steal her away to the Hunnic settlement on the Danube. It remains unclear if Honoria merely longed for a life of adventure and wanted to stun her aristocratic friends by pledging herself to the barbarian king, or if Attila actually did have some kind of correspondence with the Roman princess. In retrospect, Honoria probably never realized how grateful she should have been that her marriage to Attila was never consummated.

—*Greg Street*

Advance against one castle at a time and use siege weapons to knock them down. Once you bust through the Orlèans walls, take out the siege workshop and stables as soon as possible to prevent more scorpions and cavalry units from being built. Use your trebuchets against the town center, but don't forget to protect your powerful siege units with some infantry.

♥ **New Objective:** Defeat the Byzantine army.

When Orleans concedes defeat, the Western Roman Empire sends in an army of cataphracts and champions. The Byzantines enter from the northwestern forest and pour into the remnants of Orlèans. Engage the Byzantine army and continue to produce and send military units into the conflict. Seek out any remaining Byzantine troops by scouting the surrounding area. The Byzantines only send one army.

Once you've defeated Orlèans and the Byzantine reinforcements, the mission concludes in victory.

Attila 5: The Catalaunian Fields

Initial Objective

♥ Defeat the Romans, Alans, and Visigoths.

Forces

	Their Stance	Your Stance
Ostrogoths	Ally	Ally
Western Roman Empire	Enemy	Enemy
Visigoths	Enemy	Enemy
Alans	Enemy	Enemy
Franks	Enemy	Neutral

Map Highlights

You begin at the Hun camp near the southeastern corner, toward the center of the map. The Ostrogoths, an ally, start just to the northwest. The nearest enemies, the Visigoths, are in the south corner of the map, southwest of the Hun base. Just north of the Visigoths are the Franks, who won't pose a problem in the mission. To the north of the Franks you'll find the Alans. The Byzantines, the toughest opponent here, lie east of the Alans in the northeastern corner. Scout north of the Hun camp and the Ostrogoth base for additional supplies of gold. You'll also find gold concealed by a forest northeast of the Visigoth village.

Battle Plans

Construct a town center and produce a hefty quantity of villagers. Use the sheep provided for food, and send other villagers to the nearby gold and forest to gather resources. The Hun camp isn't in imminent danger, though the Ostrogoths require extra defense against Byzantine and Alan raiding parties. Not long after the mission begins, the Ostrogoths remind you of the alliance and request support (see Figure 3.13). Position the Hun Tarkans in the northern section of the Ostrogoth base and set them on aggressive stance.

Tip A viable option is to build stone walls across the passes in the forest. You're given tons of stone at the mission's start, and it's possible to completely close off your half of the battlefield with stone walls in just over 10 minutes of game time—before any attacks from the Byzantines and the Alans.

You begin the mission with plentiful resources, so start producing military units as soon as possible. Select a villager and construct a barracks, archery range, stable, blacksmith, monastery, and siege workshop. Though it's tempting to quickly advance to the Imperial Age, be sure to produce adequate defense forces before doing so. Research attack and armor bonuses at the blacksmith and upgrade units at the barracks, archery range, and stable. Position scouts around the perimeter of both your base and the Ostrogoth camp to remain abreast of incoming raiding parties.

Position your military on the western side of the Hun base (though keep the Tarkans in the Ostrogoth camp) as most of the enemy forces will enter from that direction or from the Visigoths in the south. Once you've converted all the sheep to food, build a mill and begin planting farms.

Figure 3.13:
Place your initial military inside the Ostrogoth base to protect your ally from Byzantine raiding parties.

The Visigoths should be your first target; they don't offer much resistance, so it's wise to clear them out as soon as possible, as they will persist in rebuilding castles and troops. If you have an adequate defense and enough reserve resources, then advance to the Imperial Age. Research attack and armor bonuses and upgrade your infantry, archer, and cavalry units. Gather enough stone to build a castle and construct trebuchets for your assault against the Visigoths.

Organize your military into infantry, archer, cavalry, and siege unit groups. Use your siege factory to construct battering rams to use against the Visigoth castle, town center, and other structures. Petards and Tarkans also work well in weakening and taking down the Visigoth structures. Maximize your population limit, but make sure you're still producing units and gathering gold, wood, and food so reinforcements arrive as soon as possible. Also, position a small defensive force in the northwest section of your base in case the Alans or Byzantines send down a raiding party while you're assaulting the Visigoths.

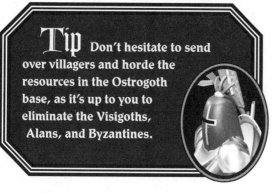

Tip Don't hesitate to send over villagers and horde the resources in the Ostrogoth base, as it's up to you to eliminate the Visigoths, Alans, and Byzantines.

Designer's Notes

Recreations of actual field battles are hard to manage in *The Age of Kings*. If you start the player off with only soldiers and no villagers, very little decision-making is required and the scenario ends in a few minutes. This scenario was our attempt to capture the rapid pace and downright chaos of a large-scale battle. While the Ostrogoths are trying to defend your flank, the Romans and their barbarian allies are attacking from three directions at once. If you avoid building castles everywhere (which the computer player has difficulty attacking), this scenario can be quite challenging.

—Greg Street

Cross the bridges west of the Hun camp. You'll encounter Visigoth knights, archers, and huskarls. Concentrate your forces on the hostile units before moving against the structures. Unpack your trebuchets to pummel Visigoth structures from a distance, and keep several infantry units nearby to defend the fragile artillery units. Send in your battering rams once you've cleared out most of the defending units.

The Visigoths initially possess two castles and a town center that need to be destroyed. Eliminate military structures first, specifically the stable and barracks, but divert your forces to any hostile units that approach. Continue moving west through the base and eliminate the town center and castles. Garrison units inside the delicate battering rams for added protection.

Warning The persistent Visigoths will attempt to keep their civilization alive by building a new town center or castle. Spread your military throughout the Visigoth town and attack any villagers you spot, especially those constructing new buildings.

Once the Visigoths resign, send your military units back to the Hun camp and heal as necessary. Restore any casualties and make sure you have an organized mixture of troops before planning an attack against the Alans. Battering rams and siege units work especially well. Use your military units against any hostile defenders while the garrisoned battering rams and siege units destroy the structures (see Figure 3.14).

Figure 3.14: Use trebuchets to assault the Alan and Byzantine cities.

Keep resource stockpiles high. With the Visigoths gone, explore the forest northwest of their destroyed base and locate a patch of gold obscured by trees; build a mining camp and begin mining. If you haven't already, mine the gold inside, and just north of, the Ostrogoth town.

Assault the Alans next. Attack them from the decimated Visigoth base, but be sure not to enter or assault the Byzantine base just yet. Once you've organized your attack force, send it west over the bridge and into what's left of the Visigoth village. Head north and past the harmless Franks.

Use tactics against the Alans similar to those you utilized against the Visigoths. Target siege units on the perimeter structures, and when defending units charge out, eliminate them with your infantry, archers, and cavalry. Send in the garrisoned battering rams once you've cleared out a majority of defenders. Raze military structures as soon as you spot them and eliminate the castle and town center to force the Alans to resign.

The Byzantines offer the most difficult target on the map. Plentiful and extremely tough infantry and cavalry units coupled with numerous towers, siege units, and trebuchets make them tough foes. Assault the Byzantines from the east, as this allows you to simultaneously attack them as well as defend against raiding parties sent into the Ostrogoth and Hun camps.

Cross the river to the north and head west into the Byzantine city (see Figure 3.15). Defeat the defenders on the outer perimeter and slowly send your mixed force toward the Byzantine structures. Unpack your trebuchets and protect them against attackers. Keep your garrisoned battering rams safe and behind your military. Knock out the towers with the trebuchets and keep pushing forward until you encounter the Byzantine castle and the nearby town center.

Figure 3.15:
Assault the Byzantine city from the eastern side of the map. Cross the river just west of the Ostrogoth base.

Pummel the Byzantine castle and town center with battering rams and move your trebuchets closer so they can assist in the assault. Use the monks to heal your military while also converting the enemy. Beware of Byzantine siege units that enter from the west. Send cavalry units to intercept them or use your monks to convert them. Keep pushing west, destroying all Byzantine defenders, villagers, towers, and military structures along the way. Once the Byzantines resign, the mission concludes in victory.

Attila 6: The Fall of Rome

Initial Objectives

- ♦ Defeat Milan, Padua, Verona, and Aquileia, so that you may parley with Rome.
- ♦ Attila must survive.

Forces

	Their Stance	Your Stance
Aquileia	Enemy	Enemy
Milan	Enemy	Enemy
Verona	Enemy	Enemy
Padua	Enemy	Enemy
Western Roman Empire	Ally	Ally

Map Highlights

The Hun camp starts in an extremely tight area of the map, the northern corner. The town of Milan lies to the southwest, while Aquileia can be found to the southeast, along the eastern shore. Padua is due south of the Hun starting position. Just south of Padua you'll find Verona. Finally, Rome can be found in the southern corner below Padua and southwest of Verona. There are two important resources of note: a large patch of gold in the northwest corner of the map (follow the northern edge of the battleground southwest from the Hun base), and an equally big patch of stone in the northeast (follow the northern edge northeast from the Hun base).

Battle Plans

You begin in the northern corner of the map with a group of Tarkans (including Attila), heavy cavalry archers, and trebuchets. Organize your Tarkans and cavalry archers and prepare to defend the Hun camp. Milan and Padua are your closest neighbors; expect attack groups from both cities to begin assaulting the Hun camp about four minutes into the mission. Raiding parties from Milan will attack from the southwest, while groups from Padua enter from the east. Aquileia and Verona will also attack.

> **Note** Quick, mixed cavalry raids (within the game's first 10 minutes, and periodically thereafter) on the farms outside Milan and the lumber camps northwest of Aquileia can significantly stunt their military production.

Working in the extremely tight valley poses one of the biggest challenges in the mission. Initially, resources appear quite scarce. Scout along the northern edge of the map to the northwest and northeast corners and you'll find plentiful gold in the northwest and patches of stone in the northeast. Either place protective walls and towers around your miners and resources or position some infantry units nearby for protection. Food is another problem. Immediately surround your town center with farms and, if you can handle the micromanagement in this hectic mission, hunt the boars to the southwest and northeast of your town center (see Figure 3.16).

Use your starting food to produce more villagers—immediately fill the town center queue, as you'll need at least 30 in this mission—and assign them to wood, farms, and mining.

Construct a monastery and military structures southeast of the Hun camp in the clearing, and front it with a castle. You're already in the Imperial Age, but still need to research attack and armor bonuses and upgrade infantry and cavalry units at their specific structures. Especially important are crossbowmen (to man the towers and castle) and upgraded cavalry (to take out enemy siege units).

If you haven't built stone walls, keep scouting the perimeter of your growing camp to alert you of incoming attacks. Use monks to keep your forces healed and convert incoming troops.

Figure 3.16:
Bolster initial food supply by luring the nearby boar to your town center.

Within the first 10 minutes, one of your opponents (usually Padua) starts a wonder. It will take a while to construct, as there are only one or two villagers working on it. Once the wonder goes up, though, you have 350 years (approximately 10 minutes) to eliminate it before the mission concludes in failure. Remember that researching Atheism adds 100 years to wonder victory time.

Warning Milan tends to send champions, paladins (fewer if you destroy the farms outside their base early), crossbowmen, onagers, and trebuchets. Padua likes longbowmen, pikemen, scorpions, and trebuchets. Aquileia initially fields knights and pikemen, then cavaliers, light cavalry, halberdiers, scorpions, and galleons. Verona has the toughest army and sends paladins, elite throwing axemen, pikemen, monks, and trebuchets.

The Paduans aren't especially strong; the difficulty with them lies in protecting the Hun base from raiding parties from the other cities. Padua is close enough that you could retreat units back to your base if you're threatened (especially if you managed to build a castle near the city). Trebuchets work well against the Padua base, but you must protect them from attack and repair them should they get damaged. Knock out the front gate of Padua and send cavalry to eliminate the trebuchets inside, set up to retaliate against your own trebuchet attack.

> **Tip** Aquileia, located in the northwest area of the map, usually sends its attack groups along the northern edge of the map by the patches of stone you scouted early in the mission. Plug the alley northwest of your base with walls and towers and prevent Aquileia's infantry, cavalry, and siege units from reaching your base. Alternatively, simply position a defensive force and scouts to the northwest and eliminate the units as they approach.

Demolish Padua, keeping an eye on fleeing villagers, as they will attempt to rebuild near Verona. Monitor the other cities and rotate your front to any raiding parties headed your way. Pour over the Paduan walls and advance your trebuchet group to pummel structures. Knock out Padua's castle and military structures first, then eliminate the town center and wonder-in-progress. Petards can be of great help storming cities, especially when using other units to distract defenses so that the petards have a clear run at their target.

Monitor your resource gathering and keep producing units to bolster the Hun camp's defensives and to send reinforcements into the current battle. The Paduans will likely place a town center in the southern town of Verona, so you likely won't be able to finish them off until you engage Verona. Padua won't pose a threat as you battle other cities, though.

> **Tip** An aggressive strategy is to attack Padua and Milan simultaneously, focusing on Milan. Eliminating that city gives you two attack fronts on Padua.

Two other cities—usually Aquileia and Milan—start wonders soon after Padua. Also, Verona, located along the southeastern edge of the map, starts wonder construction soon after the northern cities. The Aquileia wonder is placed against the eastern shore behind protective walls. The Milan wonder is more vulnerable, though expect plenty of opposition as you assault the Milan base. Milan is a wiser second target for two reasons: First, a patch of gold lies just south of the town. Second, Milan is the only enemy city on the western shore of the lake in the center of the battlefield. With Milan conquered, you control the whole western side of the map and can construct docks on the coast, as well as fish the lake (see Figure 3.17).

Figure 3.17:
Milan's shoreline offers an easy source of food—just defeat its defenses before you send over the villagers.

Mount an assault against Milan after healing and reinforcing your attack groups from the Paduan attack. Build battering rams and research capped and siege rams if you haven't already maximized your population, then advance your attack group against Milan. Eliminate hostile units first and use trebuchets to destroy the surrounding wall and towers before proceeding inside the base. Send the battering rams against the military structures and protect your siege units. Destroy the wonder and eliminate any villagers you spot constructing additional buildings in Milan.

Tip During your assaults on the three northern cities of Padua, Milan, and Aquileia, Verona will send tough raiding parties into the Hun camp. Verona is Frankish and has the mission's toughest military, with plenty of paladins. Don't leave your base unguarded. By now you should have plenty of resources, so if you didn't at the outset, consider building a wall around your camp and protecting the perimeter with guard towers.

Once Milan has been cleared, construct docks along the western shore and build fishing boats if you don't have enough farms to sustain your military production. Send

villagers to the gold resource located south of the vacant town and build a mining camp. Use the additional resources to reinforce your army and proceed against Aquileia, which may be nearing completion of their wonder.

Finish off Aquileia with the same tactics you employed against the other cities. Smash through the city walls with siege rams and use trebuchets to knock out the outer buildings. Eliminate the castles, town center, and wonder positioned along the eastern shore (see Figure 3.18). Once you demolish Aquileia, build docks along the shore to gather more food if needed.

Figure 3.18:
Aquileia protects its wonder behind a wall. Finish off the wonder, and then Aquileia itself, with your well-protected trebuchets.

Push your forces down the eastern side of the map until you reach the outer perimeter of Verona. If you have the stone, consider building a castle and other military structures between decimated Padua and tough Verona. Knock out the houses and structures outside the walls, and it's likely the defending forces will exit the walled base and attack. Eliminate the hostile units—which include tons of paladins and trebuchets—and continue to push your siege units forward and assault the front gate and towers. Move inside Verona and use siege units against military structures. Knock out the Padua and Verona town centers as you fend off any remaining hostile units.

🛡 **New Objective:** Attila must meet with Pope Leo I outside the gates of Rome.

As soon as the last of the four enemy cities concedes defeat, Pope Leo I asks to speak with Attila. You'll find his holiness just outside the Roman gates on the southwestern area of the map.

Locate and select Attila and escort the Hun leader down to the gates of Rome. Once you reach Pope Leo I, the mission and campaign concludes in success.

Designer's Notes

We had a few scenarios in *The Age of Kings* where the player needed to destroy a wonder (such as the third Genghis Khan mission, "Into China"), but the Huns are so good at wonder-bashing with their Tarkans, accurate trebuchets, and Atheism, that I thought it might be fun to try and knock down five wonders! This scenario is much more challenging on the harder difficulty levels—on Standard, the Romans wait patiently in their cities, but on Moderate or Hard, they counterattack as well. It is true that no one knows what the Pope said to Attila, or why the mighty Hun king turned away from Italy on the brink of his greatest triumph.

—*Greg Street*

El Cid

Rodrigo Díaz, also known as El Cid, begins the campaign by impressing the distrustful King Sancho and receiving command of the Castilian army. El Cid's overwhelming popularity soon leads to his exile, though. The proud warrior sets up camp in various Moorish and Spanish towns, continues to fight, and hopes to return to his former home.

This chapter features a complete walkthrough for The Conquerors' El Cid campaign. Since El Cid inhabits several different cities during the campaign, your technology tree and unique unit changes between Spanish (missions 1, 2, 5, and 6) and Saracen (missions 3 and 4).

El Cid 1: Brother against Brother

Initial Objective

🛡 Become King Sancho's champion in a trial by combat.

Forces

	Their Stance	Your Stance
King Sancho	Ally	Ally
King Sancho's Champion	Enemy	Enemy
King Alfonso	Enemy	Ally
King Alfonso's Army	Enemy	Enemy
Serfs	Ally	Ally

Map Highlights

The player's starting location is in the tournament grounds on the southeast section of the map. Though buildings belonging to King Sancho cover most of the land, you'll find the majority of them along the eastern side of the map. King Alfonso's castle lies to the north. Serfs, who will side with El Cid, possess a small farming village in the map's center. Several monks, relics, and a monastery are located in the northwest corner.

Battle Plans

El Cid enters the tournament grounds and King Sancho sends in his champion. If El Cid can defeat the champion, he can assume control of the Castilian army in a mission to capture King Alfonso.

Tip As soon as you can, send El Cid to the northeast corner of the map. Here you'll find a group of monks surrounding relics and a monastery. The monks will join El Cid if he approaches. Have the monks put the relics in the monastery to receive a steady influx of gold.

When King Sancho's champion enters, simply select El Cid and attack the aggressive opponent. El Cid will easily eliminate the champion. Once he is defeated, King Sancho issues another challenge—a battle against a knight on horseback. Sancho then offers a steed to El Cid. Approach the stable north of the tournament grounds if you wish to battle on horseback. You'll emerge victorious no matter how you choose to fight.

Acquire the steed after the battle if you haven't already. King Sancho now outlines your mission—to capture King Alfonso from his castle in the north. The Castilian army assembles southwest of

the tournament grounds and you're provided with Conquistadors (the Spanish unique unit), knights, pikemen, long swordsmen, archers, and villagers (see Figure 4.1).

Figure 4.1:
El Cid receives the Castilian army after defeating King Sancho's champion and knight.

Designer's Notes

We needed a good way to kick off the campaign while establishing El Cid as a heroic fighter, so we used the tournament from the 1961 movie. This was also a great place to showcase the new ability of hero units to heal damage. The idea for the ornery serfs came from a multiplayer playtest, where I watched a bunch of villagers placidly labor while a battle raged all around them. I remember thinking that if I were a villager, I'd give those military types thrashing my fields what for! It was a real treat to hear people laugh when they ran across them in playtests.

— *Karen Sparks*

♦ **New Objective:** Take command of the Castilian army in order to capture King Sancho's conniving, ambitious brother, King Alfonso.

The first order of business is to find a suitable location for a town center. You aren't under immediate pressure from King Alfonso's troops, so scout the area thoroughly before committing to a particular location. You'll find more pikemen and conquistadors ready to join El Cid near the center of the battlefield.

Escort your army and villagers southwest to the river. Once you reach the river, head northwest until you locate a patch of gold. Though King Sancho's men are already mining here, position your town center near the resource. Once construction is finished, build houses to maximize your population. Also, King Sancho will send a moderate tribute as soon as the town center has been built. Move one villager southeast into the open clearing and begin building houses. Assign other villagers to chopping wood to keep up with house production.

Continue constructing houses until you reach a population limit of 100. As your limit rises, produce 10 to 15 more villagers to increase resource production. Begin mining the gold adjacent to the town center. Escort some villagers west over the bridge and past the serf village, and use the open clearing here to build a mill and plant surrounding farms. Scout the river and build a dock and fishing ships to fish the river. You can also assign villagers to shore fish.

You should soon have enough wood to build a barracks, archery, stable, and blacksmith. Use resources to research attack and armor bonuses and upgrade units. When you have enough food and gold, advance to the Castle Age. Don't feel rushed into assaulting King Alfonso's base, which lies inside the northern corner of the map. Continue to amass resources and produce a formidable army.

Mine the gold west of your farming area once you've exhausted the eastern supply. Now that you've advanced to the Castle Age, it's time to construct El Cid's castle. You'll find a sizable deposit of stone in the upper northeast corner of the map, just above King Sancho's base. Here you'll also encounter more gold and foraging bushes. Build a mining camp and a mill and move villagers to the

> **Tip** Once you acquire the forces in the center of the map, save the game and try attacking. It is possible to successfully defeat King Alfonso's troops by attacking at around the 10-minute mark, right after you've set up your infrastructure.

> **Tip** Escort El Cid west over the bridge to a small farming and lumber village. Upon seeing him, the serfs there will join your cause and you'll gain access to their structures and villagers. Use the villagers to chop wood north of the former serf village. An adjacent lumber camp serves as an excellent drop-off point. This spot is another good one for your town center—if you research town watch, you can see the enemy castle from here.

corner to acquire the resources. King Alfonso may send units over to investigate, so guard your villagers and structures with a small band of infantry and cavalry units.

Once you've acquired enough stone, build a castle and produce Conquistadors (see Figure 4.2). Also, you'll want to produce a squad of petards for use against King Alfonso's castle. If you haven't already, construct a siege workshop and chop enough wood to produce enough rams and mangonels to pummel King Alfonso's surrounding wall and towers.

Figure 4.2:
Mine enough stone to build a castle and produce petards and Conquistadors.

With your population maximized with military units (a mixture of infantry, archers, cavalry, siege units, and petards), advance north from the middle of the map. Use the rams against the walls and mangonels against the towers while making sure to defend the siege units against any counterattack. If you continue to advance into King Alfonso's base, you'll soon spot his castle at the center of a four-way bridge.

Though you should demolish the towers and military structures in front of the castle, don't assault the castle from this position. King Alfonso's siege factory and scorpions lie to the west and will attack if you assault from the south. Once you've knocked out the barracks, towers, and southern structures, reinforce your army and head up the eastern side of the base until you spot the enemy monastery. Enter King Alfonso's base here.

Use the rams or mangonels to demolish the wall and send your infantry, archers, and cavalry against the nearby structures. Send in your squad of petards and ram the castle with their demolitions. Follow up the petard attack with your military and siege units. Once the castle falls, King Alfonso will surrender to El Cid's control.

🛡 **New Objective:** El Cid must bring the captured King Alfonso to King Sancho's tournament grounds.

King Alfonso appears in the rubble of the castle. Escort El Cid to King Alfonso's base, then select both men and move them to the southeast corner of the map. Once you've ascended to the tournament grounds, the mission concludes in victory.

El Cid 2: The Enemy of My Enemy

Initial Objective

🛡 Find a way to stop the rebellion in Toledo.

Forces

	Their Stance	Your Stance
Toledo	Ally	Ally
Spanish Rebels	Enemy	Enemy
Moorish Rebels	Enemy	Enemy
Motamid Monk	Ally	Ally
The Imam	Ally	Ally

Map Highlights

El Cid and the Castilian army enter from the northwest section. The Spanish and Moorish rebels occupy Toledo in the southern corner of the map. You'll find the Motamid Monk east of El Cid's start position. The Imam, who knows how to quell the rebellion in Toledo, is situated across a lake in the northern corner. Gold reserves can be found along the western and eastern sides of the map.

Battle Plans

The Castilian army begins in the northwest. Advance forward to spot fleeing Toledo villagers with a message for El Cid.

🛡 **New Objective:** El Cid must meet with the Imam and find out how to quell the unrest in Toledo.

Though the Spanish and Moorish rebels will soon send raiding parties against you, the Castilian army is relatively safe in the early moments of the mission. Send your army and villagers to the western edge of the map and locate the gold resource there. Then use your villagers to construct a town center nearby.

Take your scout cavalry and El Cid and scout three areas. First, scout just east of the start location to find the Motamid Monk (see Figure 4.3). The Motamid Monk will heal anyone placed next to him, as well as tell you where to find the Imam and

stone. Continue east to the northern corner and locate the transport along the lakeshore. Send El Cid inside and cross to the monastery and the Imam. Visiting the Imam reveals how to complete the primary mission objective: recovering four relics from inside Toledo.

Figure 4.3:
Locate the Motamid Monk; he'll help you on your way.

New Objective: Recover the four relics from the rebel leaders and return them to the Imam.

Tip Don't ignore the Motamid Monk's tip about the stone (and the fact that you start the mission with enough for two town centers). Use the transport to take villagers to the eastern edge of the map. Unload, send the villagers to the two stone piles in the southeastern corner, and build a town center. This is a good spot for a forward base, so consider building military structures and a castle here.

The Imam tells El Cid that if you can recover four relics from inside Toledo, now under control of the Spanish and Moorish rebels, the Imam should be able to end the rebellion. The third area to explore with your scout cavalry is south of the start location. Here you'll find a herd of sheep. Escort them back to your town center and use them for a food resource. Be sure to capture the sheep quickly, or you may lose them to the Spanish rebels.

Spend the early part of the mission gathering resources and constructing houses. Build enough houses to support your population limit of 75. Locate the forest in the northwest corner and build a lumber camp, assigning several villagers to chop wood. Use your town center to produce more villagers and upgrade their ability by researching the wheelbarrow. As you gain more wood, build military structures, a blacksmith, and a monastery.

There are several options for food. You can build a mill along the stream south of your town center and shore-fish the narrow brook, then plant farms. Another important source of food is the lake surrounding the Imam in the northern corner. Move a villager over and use the transport to reach the Imam's side of the lake, then build a dock, produce fishing ships, and start fishing. With an excellent economy rolling, produce more military units, research attack and armor bonuses, and upgrade infantry units at the barracks. Build a siege workshop and produce battering rams to use against the rebellious city of Toledo.

The Spanish and Moorish rebels will soon send raiding parties from the bridge in the center of the map. Also, expect some troops to emerge along the river south of your town center. Defend these spots and be especially aware of Spanish battering rams that accompany some assaults. Produce monks to heal your army and convert enemy knights and camels.

Designer's Notes

Medieval noble families often fought ruthless wars of succession—not just between families but within families. After his death, Ferdinand I's children were no exception. Dissatisfied with ruling only Castile, Sancho set out to rule León as well. He sent Rodrigo Díaz de Bivar, later known as El Cid, to capture his younger brother Alfonso, who ruled the territory. Sancho then exiled the captive Alfonso. When Sancho was killed (some say assassinated) as he laid siege to his sister's city, Zamora, Alfonso returned from exile and took the crown of Castile and León for himself. El Cid was needed to lead the reluctant nobles to swear fealty to their new king. And so it was in no small part that Alfonso owed his crown and rule to El Cid. An embarrassing proceeding to be sure, and one that poisoned the relationship between the ambitious king and his most charismatic knight.

—*Karen Sparks*

Once you possess a solid military, advance through the center of the map and across the bridge (see Figure 4.4). Eliminate the towers and advance slowly into the various small Moorish rebel lumber and farm camps. Expect camel, infantry, and archer units to retaliate. Pull your attack away from the enemy villagers and resource structures to deal with any hostile units. Heal with your monks before advancing further.

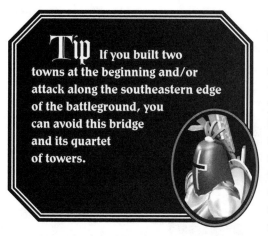

Tip If you built two towns at the beginning and/or attack along the southeastern edge of the battleground, you can avoid this bridge and its quartet of towers.

Continue to produce military units to reinforce your army and replace casualties. Assault the rebels from the eastern side of the map and take out the tower at the base perimeter. Then slowly advance your infantry, archers, cavalry, siege units, and battering rams. Destroy enemy military structures as you progress. You'll find relics inside the three monasteries positioned near the middle of the rebel-controlled town. Beware of enemy monks near the monasteries—they might convert your units as well as run off with a treasured relic.

Figure 4.4:
Rebel towers protect the bridge in the map's center.

Tip The Moorish rebels send in war galleys once you put the first relic in lmam's monastery, so keep relics in your monastery (earning you gold) until you have them all. Otherwise, you need to build naval defenses.

Bombard the monasteries, send in monks to recover the relics, escort them to your monastery, and prepare your assault to gain the fourth.

You'll find the fourth relic within a Moorish rebel castle in the southern corner of the map (see Figure 4.5). Reach the castle by heading west from the demolished monasteries and follow the bridge to the south onto the small island containing the castle and other rebel structures.

Figure 4.5:
Raze the rebel castle to acquire the fourth relic.

> **Note** Most of the gates inside rebel-controlled Toledo still belong to the Toledo people. Since Toledo is allied with El Cid, the gates will open when your units approach. Alternatively, you can simply click the gate (and other allied structures) and press the Delete key to demolish it.

Destroy the towers and cross the bridge, then demolish the castle and have your monk pick up the relic positioned behind. Ungarrison the relics in your monastery, have a transport pick up the four relic-toting monks, and unload on Imam's island. Once all four relics are in Imam's monastery, the Imam quells the rebellion and the mission ends in victory.

El Cid 3: The Exile of El Cid

Initial Objectives

- El Cid must survive.
- El Cid must find a new city in which to live and a new lord to serve.

Forces

	Their Stance	Your Stance
King Alfonso's Army	Ally	Ally
Motamid	Ally	Ally
Count Berenguer	Enemy	Enemy

Map Highlights

El Cid starts within King Alfonso's territory in the northwestern corner of the map. King Alfonso also possesses a castle blocking the entrance to Zaragoza, the Motamid city to the southeast. Count Berenguer's camp lies mostly in the northeast, though he has scattered camps along the eastern side of the map. El Cid can gain troops inside King Alfonso's territory and acquire structures in the southwest corner of the map. In this battle, El Cid leads Saracen forces.

Battle Plans

You start with a single unit, El Cid, in King Alfonso's village in the northwest. Select El Cid and approach Alfonso's gate to the southeast. As you near the entrance, a soldier reminds you to retrieve your steed from the stable. Move El Cid back to the northwest corner and approach the stable to mount the horse. Return southeast through the gate.

Head east to leave town. When you walk by the northern edge, King Alfonso orders the town guards to attack (see Figure 4.6), prompting an assault by nearby archers. Keep moving east and engage the long swordsmen. Try to move out of archer range to stop taking damage from the ranged units.

Continue east until you're nearing the edge of town. As you approach, a squad of knights and pikemen join El Cid. Locate the valley to the south and proceed through with caution—three long swordsmen and two scorpion siege units loyal to Alfonso await you. Send knights to knock out the scorpions while everyone else concentrates on the swordsmen. Advance south and rendezvous with four camels to be invited to Zaragoza in the southeast.

- **New Objective:** Join Motamid of the Moors at his castle in Zaragoza.

If you attempt to reach Zaragoza by heading east, camel units will report that Count Berenguer's base blocks the way and you'll need to find a different route. King

Alfonso possesses a castle to the south, and if you can demolish it, you can safely reach Zaragoza. The camel units also speak of something important in the south, which turns out to be a small village consisting of military structures and houses.

Figure 4.6:
King Alfonso orders archers to attack El Cid. Keep moving and get out of archer range.

▼ **New Objective:** Destroy King Alfonso's castle, so that you may continue to Zaragoza.

Position your troops along the western wall and start heading south. As you move down, you may spot Alfonso's watchtower and wall-enclosed castle to the east. You don't have the troops to take down the walls, castle, and troops inside, so keep moving.

Head to the village in the southern corner of the map. As you approach, you'll gain use of the buildings, which include military structures and houses. You'll also acquire line of sight into Zaragoza (via watchtowers). Although Zaragoza is under attack from Berenguer, don't bother moving units to assist—Zaragoza can fend for itself for the time being. Motamid sends a tribute once you reach the southern village. You'll find a stable, barracks, archery range, and siege workshop ready for use.

Construct two or three rams and use additional resources for knights, crossbowmen, skirmishers, and long swordsmen. Once you've exhausted resources and reached your population limit, advance north toward the walls surrounding the castle. Lure the troops inside—four pikemen and four archers—and weaken them from long range before taking them out with your melee attack.

Next, use the rams to demolish the front gate. Then pour inside and assault the castle with your troops and rams. As soon as the castle falls, King Alfonso calls for a truce with El Cid. Leave a small force behind in the village (see Figure 4.7). Count Berenguer sends raiding parties of infantry, archers, and battering rams to the southern base—consider walling off the area from the destroyed gate to the edge of the

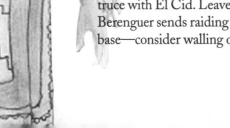

battlefield—and an enemy monk may attempt to recover the relic there. If you locate the town center as recommended by a narrator in the game, the raiding stops. Proceed east with the remainder of your force into Zaragoza. The gates automatically open for your troops, and you receive some cavalry archers, a camel, and villagers.

Figure 4.7:
Protect your southern base from Berenguer's raiding parties.

Head toward the north section of Zaragoza and approach the castle. As soon as Motamid contacts you, the town comes under attack from Berenguer's forces from the north.

New Objective: Defend Zaragoza by destroying Count Berenguer's siege workshop nearby.

Motamid requests your help. You'll spot the Berenguer forces assaulting the gates and towers on the northeast section of the base. Don't pour your troops out of the gate immediately. If you can afford it, build mangonels and use them to weaken the enemy troops, which consist of cavalry, infantry, archers, and battering rams.

Then send out your troops and finish off the Berenguer attack force. Locate the siege workshop just to the northeast, and demolish it and the surrounding pavilions.

New Objective: Defeat Count Berenguer.

It's suggested you build a town center north of Zaragoza, which is a good locale as it has resources and allows you to easily intercept enemy troops exiting the castle to the north (see Figure 4.8). Also head south of the town and locate the gold resource below the river. Build a town center adjacent to the gold. Chop wood at the small forest to the west. Build houses along the southern edge of the map until you have enough to support your population limit of 75. Construct a mill east of the town center and plant surrounding farms. You may also wish to build a dock and fish the river.

Figure 4.8:
Locate additional stone and gold resources just north of Zaragoza.

> **Tip** In the southeastern corner of the map, you'll find a relic. Build a monastery as soon as possible and place this relic, as well as the one located in your first village in the southwest, inside to receive a steady gold bonus.

You have military structures in the southwest, so you don't need to rebuild them at your new base. However, be sure to protect the southwestern village, as Berenguer sends raiding parties—consisting of infantry, archers, cavalry, battering rams, and structure-converting monks—down the western side into the base. Build a blacksmith to research attack and armor bonuses and a monastery to produce monks to heal injured units. When you have enough resources, advance to the Imperial Age to gain its research options and the ability to produce trebuchets.

Continue to produce military units and mine stone so that you can build a castle and trebuchets at your northern base. Once the castle is up and you have four to six trebuchets, assemble your military and assault the Berenguer base from along the eastern edge of the map. Unpack your trebuchets within range of the gate and structures just inside. Berenguer retaliates with infantry, archers, and cavalry. Counter the attack with your own force and protect the fragile siege units (bring some villagers to repair them should they get damaged).

Advance your army slowly into Berenguer's base and prioritize your attack on military structures. Don't send your military at the castle until you've eliminated the nearby ground forces. Demolish the castle and raze all other structures, including the town center and another castle located in the west.

Berenguer villagers are persistent and will continue to replace buildings. Clear out the villagers with your troops while you finish off the base with the trebuchets. Once Count Berenguer resigns, the mission ends in victory.

Designer's Notes

Alfonso's fear and resentment of Rodrigo Díaz's popularity and charisma grew steadily. After he had been accused of keeping a portion of a tribute due Alfonso, the king foolishly exiled his most capable knight. Díaz, ever pragmatic and somewhat mercenary, wandered Spain gathering warriors and soldiers as he went. He fought for many rulers, Christian and Moslem alike. At one point he swore allegiance to the Moorish prince, Al-Motamid, whose lands were threatened by the Count of Barcelona, Berenguer Ramon II. Díaz successfully battled the Berenguer and others while in service of the Moslem emir. Al-Motamid himself was not eagerly anticipating the arrival of Yusuf's Black Guards. Moslem culture was quite refined at this point (and Al-Motamid quite established), so he did not relish the ruthlessness and lack of civility of Yusuf's forces, nor what would become of the lands they conquered. Al-Motamid in fact attempted an alliance with Alfonso but was later captured by the Black Guards as they overran almost all of Moslem-controlled Spain.

—Karen Sparks

El Cid 4: Black Guards

Initial Objectives

- Follow the knight in order to rescue King Alfonso.
- El Cid must survive.
- King Alfonso must survive.

Forces

	Their Stance	Your Stance
King Alfonso's Army	Ally	Ally
Black Guard Army	Enemy	Enemy
Yusuf	Enemy	Enemy
Black Guard Navy	Enemy	Enemy

Map Highlights

El Cid's army starts in the northern corner. You'll find King Alfonso's village to the northwest and the Black Guard stronghold in the south. The Black Guard army inhabits the northern section of town, while the Black Guard navy occupies the middle and south along the shore. To the southeast you'll find Yusuf's camp.

Battle Plans

You begin in the northern corner. El Cid's army consists of Conquistadors, knights, pikemen, swordsmen, monks, and scorpions. Begin by following King Alfonso's knight to the southwest.

🎗 **New Objective:** Escort King Alfonso to his camp in the west.

You'll soon reach a large battle between King Alfonso's army and the Black Guard. Go east of the battle with El Cid and intercept King Alfonso, then begin moving to the northeast to find the monarch's land. While you can use your monks to try to convert some of the Black Guard camels or knights, you're best off to move quickly to the east—as the narrator says, there are a lot of enemy troops on the way. Once the Black Guard army is defeated, Yusuf's troops move in to finish off King Alfonso's remaining forces (see Figure 4.9).

Figure 4.9:
A huge battle ensues at the mission's start. Locate King Alfonso and escort him to his western base.

Once you locate King Alfonso's base, send King Alfonso and El Cid's army inside toward the town center; you'll receive the buildings and villagers within the town walls. King Alfonso also presents a new mission objective.

🛡 **New Objective:** Destroy the eight Black Guard docks.

Tip As soon as possible, send El Cid west. You'll discover the Black Guard mosque and will be asked to spare it. In return, the Black Guard monk will offer tips on how to defeat the Black Guard, and if you send a monk over, you'll gain all monastery techs at no cost, which will save you tons of gold.

King Alfonso asks El Cid to cripple the Black Guard navy by destroying the eight docks. Select idle villagers and put them to work chopping wood, shore fishing, and mining gold. Use the town center to produce more villagers, and build homes to reach a maximum population limit of 75. Construct a mill near your town center and plant farms to keep food supply high. If you can afford the wood cost, you should also start producing fishing boats and gather fish from the body of water surrounding your base.

Attacks from the Black Guard army and Yusuf soon come from the west, so keep your troops behind the gate and use scorpions to eliminate attackers as they attempt to penetrate the city walls. A vulnerable area of King Alfonso's base lies on the western side, where a single pavilion blocks a ramp entrance. Expect enemy troops to assault this ramp to avoid the base's durable front gate.

Prepare for a huge attack that comes about 20 minutes into the mission. If you attack first, their attack is much weaker. There's a Black Guard city directly south of your village, with four watchtowers protecting the quarry and army camp north of its walls. Your initial forces, bolstered by a battering ram, can destroy the enemy quarry and the watchtowers, and your scorpions can fire right into the city. While the attack at 20 minutes will still come, Yusuf's camels won't be accompanied by Black Guard cavalry archers. Once you've fended off this big attack, you're on the way to winning this mission—it's a long slog with lots of buildings to destroy, and the sooner you start on it, the better. Remember to quickly start mining the stone so that you can build a castle just west of your base's front gate and another between the mosque and the Yusuf town. Also consider walls to block off the whole northwestern part of the battlefield. By doing so, you also gain a small gold deposit and a great site for another town, in the far western part of the battleground (just north of the mosque).

Build a siege workshop and monastery, then advance to the Imperial Age once you possess the resources. Use the blacksmith to research attack and armor bonuses and upgrade your archers and infantry using the archery range and barracks, respectively. When you exhaust the gold resource inside King Alfonso's base, locate another just south of the base. Move villagers there, build a mining camp or town center, and begin gathering. Protect the camp with military units.

Designer's Notes

It was time for Díaz to save Alfonso's bacon one more time. Facing defeat at the hands of Yusuf's Black Guards, the king desperately appealed to the exiled Díaz to fight for him once more. There is more than one interpretation of what happened next. One account says that Díaz successfully rallied Alfonso's forces and beat back the Black Guard tide. Another says that he failed to join Alfonso and, in anger, goaded by Díaz's detractors, Alfonso had Díaz's family imprisoned and his property seized. We chose to depict Díaz as a hero riding to Alfonso's rescue. Our ever-volatile Alfonso exiles him again after victory is assured. Imagine a boss that literally owes his job to you, fires you, begs you to come back, fires you again, and takes your car, your house, and your family to boot. You can imagine how El Cid might have felt.

I borrowed a device from the first scenario of the Joan of Arc campaign—encountering a battle underway. One of the things that changed along the way was that the Black Guard navy (yellow) defended its town with lots of cheap units. The town was continually peppered with skirmishers and pikemen that sniped at the flanks of El Cid's forces. We later opted to have them defend with more expensive units—scorpions, camels, and trebuchets—that were slower to train and more satisfying to smash (in addition to the cheap counter-units).

—*Karen Sparks*

> ### Tip
> A sneaky tactic is to research chemistry, then have villagers build a bombard cannon near the two enemy docks on the south shore. The cannon will take them both out.

The Black Guard docks lie along the shore south of the Black Guard base. Attempting to destroy the entire Black Guard base to reach the docks will prove difficult, so instead position your army in the northeast corner and work your way down the eastern side of the map until you locate Yusuf's base (see Figure 4.10). If you demolish this base, you can gain access to the river and build war galleys and galleons to take out the Black Guard navy and then the docks.

Advance your army slowly toward the southeastern corner and Yusuf's base. Stick close to the rocky wall to the east so you disturb the Black Guard as little as possible. Unpack the trebuchets as you near town, making sure to defend the siege weapons with your military. Demolish the towers just before Yusuf's gate, then knock out the gate itself and advance the trebuchets inside to take out the military structures, town center, and castle.

Send villagers into the town and build a dock along the southern shore. Defend the dock with your trebuchets and archer units until you're able to produce warships. Expect the Black Guard navy to send war galleys and demolition ships from the east. Knock out the demolition ships first. Use villagers to repair damaged ships before sending them back out to battle.

Figure 4.10:
Destroy Yusuf to gain access to the river.

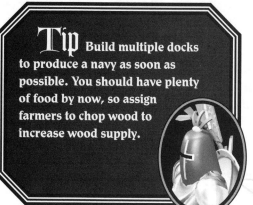

Tip Build multiple docks to produce a navy as soon as possible. You should have plenty of food by now, so assign farmers to chop wood to increase wood supply.

Produce a large fleet of galleons—approximately 20 to 25 vessels—and build a university to research technologies to increase missile damage. Send the galleon fleet west and attack the Black Guard docks. Concentrate fire on hostile ships before attacking the docks. Continue west demolishing docks and Black Guard navy vessels until you reach the southwestern side. Clear out all the docks along the river, and the mission will conclude in success.

El Cid 5: King of Valencia

Initial Objectives

- ♦ El Cid must survive.
- ♦ El Cid must once again find a new city in which to live.

Forces

	Their Stance	Your Stance
Berenguer	Enemy	Enemy
Denia	Ally	Ally
Lérida	Ally	Ally
Valencia	Ally	Ally

Map Highlights

El Cid starts upon his horse in the west. You'll find the town of Denia just east of the start location. The small Lérida village waits for El Cid just south of Denia, and the largest of the allied cities, Valencia, is on the Mediterranean shore toward the southeastern side of the map. To the north you'll find Count Berengeur's base.

Battle Plans

You'll find El Cid, once again without a home, on the western edge of the map. Proceed through the forest to the east and encounter three Berenguer swordsmen at the river crossing. The powerful El Cid should have little trouble defeating the three warriors.

Continue east to the town of Denia. As you enter, El Cid acquires the structures inside as well as a small squad of swordsmen, skirmishers, and villagers in the southeastern section of town.

♦ **New Objective:** Defend Denia from Count Berenguer.

To stay in Denia and receive support, El Cid is asked to defend the town from Count Berenguer's attacks. These assaults come from the northwest and are too large for even El Cid to defend against (see Figure 4.11). Though you can use the villagers to work the farms around the mill, don't produce additional military units or structures, though researching squires and creating a few monks is helpful. Berenguer's force of infantry, archers, cavalry, battering rams, mangonels, and trebuchets will easily overwhelm El Cid's force.

Assemble your army and villagers to the south and prepare to exit when Berenguer's attack force arrives.

♦ **New Objective:** El Cid must flee and establish a new base.

Berenguer's attack cues El Cid's exit from Denia. El Cid must then find a new city in which to mount an army against Count Berenguer. Continue southeast from the Denia walls, ignoring the carnage brought on by Berenguer behind you. As you head southeast, you'll encounter the small Lérida camp and a band of knights who will join El Cid's cause.

Figure 4.11:
Berenguer's assault against Denia is too large to hold off.

Tip Send El Cid scouting due east from the southern point of Denia. Here you'll find a monastery and a Missionary (another Spanish unique unit) that will join El Cid. Keep the speedy Missionary in your military group to heal injured units.

Keep advancing to the south until you encounter more Lérida structures, camels, and villagers. You don't acquire the structures, but the villagers and military units join El Cid. They recommend heading to Valencia to help defend the city from Berenguer's attack groups. Go north along the Mediterranean coast until you locate the walls that surround Valencia. Enter the town to acquire its structures.

 New Objective: Defend Valencia from Berenguer until its wonder is completed.

Valencia is currently constructing a wonder in the eastern part of the city. Move El Cid and his army inside the city gates and position them near the gates that provide access to the wonder. Move your villagers to the town center and start converting the nearby sheep into food. Consider constructing walls to cut off the route from Denia

(block off the bridge), cut off access to the monastery plateau, and enclose the big gold deposit just west of city walls.

Designer's Notes

Exiled, stripped of family, land, wealth, and title, Rodrigo Díaz began his military actions again. Known for his bravery and brilliance, it was not long before he had an army at his back. Valencia, recently conquered by the Moors, presented a ready target for the canny Díaz. He took the town after a short siege and claimed it as his kingdom. It was here, as king of Valencia, that he began to be known as El Cid.

In this scenario, it is possible, though difficult, to largely hold off Berenguer's attack on Denia (green) if you wall off the small pass to the north of the town. It is awe-inspiring to see Berenguer's force mill idly across the river, desperately trying to figure out how to get into Denia and then suddenly—smash!—turn the destructive force of trebs and rams onto the wall. Can you make enough units in the time it takes for them to tear the wall down? Berenguer is relentless; the longer the scenario goes, the tougher he gets. So it's not necessarily best to hold on to Denia, but I'd venture a guess to say that the inhabitants would appreciate it.

—Karen Sparks

Locate the gold and stone deposits within the city walls and begin mining them (see Figure 4.12). You should also build your stone reserve as high as possible, so you can repair walls and also build towers near the city gates to further protect the town from Berenguer's attack. You have a population limit of 75, and Berenguer's busy destroying Denia's housing, so make sure you have enough houses.

Start producing additional military units, research attack and armor bonuses at the blacksmith, and upgrade your infantry at the barracks. Once you've exhausted the supply of sheep, build farms around a mill or the town center. You can also use Valencia's dock and fishing ships to gain food from the bountiful Mediterranean.

Wood is scarce, however. It's so rare that the Valencians send a tribute of wood to El Cid moments after he arrives at the city. There are some palms scattered within the city walls, but eventually the supply runs dry and you'll have to venture out of town to locate more lumber. The best place to scout is along the eastern edge of the map just above the Mediterranean shore. There are plenty of palms here, and you can erect a mill and shore-fish the Mediterranean for additional food. If you can afford the stone expense, build a town center instead of a mill to serve as a gathering center for both lumber and food.

Figure 4.12:
Mine the gold and stone within Valencia as soon as possible. Use the stone to repair walls and construct towers.

Tip You'll likely need more gold to reinforce your military and build expensive siege units. Locate the valuable resource due west of the northern section of Valencia. Be sure to protect villagers and the mining camp here with a squad of units and towers, or just wall it off.

Though it's tempting to advance to the Imperial Age to receive its research tree and ability to build trebuchets, the resources required could be put to better use—namely, for more military units and defenses. As your lumber supply grows, build a siege factory and produce mangonels or scorpions to assault Count Berenguer's infantry, cavalry, and battering rams that approach close to the Valencia gates. You'll also need some cavalry to take out enemy trebuchets.

Berenguer sends a series of assaults from his northern base. Attack groups include infantry, cavalry, archers, monks, battering rams, mangonels, trebuchets, and, later in the mission, bombard cannons. Fending off the assault takes both a great deal of patience and the resources to build towers along the Valencia walls and gates. Monks or Missionaries are also needed to convert enemy units and keep El Cid's military healed. The patches of stone located inside the Valencian walls should provide enough resources for plenty of towers. When you can afford castles, build them close enough to the Valencian walls to repel Berenguer's attack.

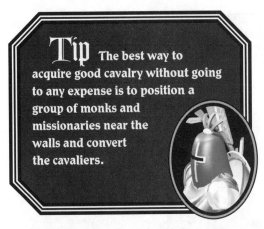

Tip The best way to acquire good cavalry without going to any expense is to position a group of monks and missionaries near the walls and convert the cavaliers.

When Berenguer begins to assault the wonder with trebuchets and bombard cannons, send your military out through the city gate and engage the enemy (see Figure 4.13). Knock out the siege units as soon as possible and use villagers to repair any damage to the wonder. When you're engaged with the Berenguer army, keep your own military structures producing units so you'll have immediate reinforcements in case enemy infantry or cavalry storm through the Valencia gates.

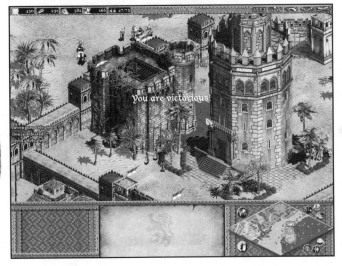

Figure 4.13:
Protect the wonder against Berenguer's trebuchet and bombard cannon assault.

Save your game after each Berenguer attack so if you fail, you can jump back to the previous battle and attempt to reduce your casualties. As soon as the Valencians complete the wonder, the mission ends in victory.

El Cid 6: Reconquista

Initial Objectives

- Defeat the armies of Yusuf so that Valencia will remain free.
- The body of El Cid (near the castle) must come to no harm, lest the people of Valencia realize they have lost their leader.

Forces

	Their Stance	Your Stance
Body of El Cid	Ally	Ally
Black Guard Army	Enemy	Enemy
Black Guard Navy	Enemy	Enemy
Yusuf	Enemy	Enemy

Map Highlights

Valencia and the body of El Cid are found near the center of the map, just north of the Mediterranean. The Black Guard army now covers the northern edge of the map, and to the west is the Black Guard navy. Yusuf's base can be found in the far southeastern corner of the map. Powerful defensive towers protect their shoreline, and you must cross the Mediterranean in order to assault Yusuf's stronghold. The Black Guard army's base contains valuable gold and lumber resources, so you should deal with them as soon as possible.

Battle Plans

Defeating the powerful Black Guard navy and Yusuf requires carefully balancing the most needed resource at the particular moment. For instance, when you're attempting to control the Mediterranean, you'll need copious amounts of gold and lumber to build war galleys and, eventually, galleons. But when you're trying to protect your base from ground assault, you'll need an ample supply of food to match your wood and gold.

> **Tip** A neutral monastery can be found just southwest of the Black Guard army's castle. If you acquire it quickly enough, you can also claim the relic nearby. Also create a Missionary to convert attacking units and heal your injured ground forces.

Your first concern is an attack from the Black Guard army, which enters from the west (see Figure 4.14). Locate your knights, camels, and swordsmen at Valencia's northern section, then place them in a single group and prepare to retaliate against the Black Guard army's attack.

The Black Guard sends cavalry, archers, battering rams, and trebuchets at you. Though your towers should be able to fend off the cavalry and archers, it's important to eliminate the battering rams and trebuchets before they break holes in Valencia's walls or, worse, start demolishing important structures that you'll have to rebuild.

Two friendly villagers start near the stone and four more surround the town center. Your current ground force is sufficient to hold off early attacks, so start gathering

lumber with the four villagers surrounding the town center and gold with the two adjacent to the stone. Select your town center and produce as many additional villagers as you can. You can increase your population limit to 85 by building additional homes. Locate your lone dock west of the town center and use the fishing ships to start harvesting.

Figure 4.14:
Organize your military quickly; the Black Guard army attacks early in the mission.

> **Tip** Aggressive players can use the starting forces to assault the Black Guard castle west of the city, eliminating the trebuchet threat.

Though you shouldn't spend time mining more stone, use your reserve to build towers either on the western side of the base, or along the walls facing the sea.

When the first Black Guard army attack arrives, send out your military and eliminate the trebuchets as soon as possible. With the siege units out of the way, move close to Valencia's walls to engage the Black Guard army's cavalry, archers, and battering rams. Fight close to your own towers for added offense and damage.

The next step after defending against the Black Guard army attack is to start production of a significant naval force. The Black Guard navy and Yusuf send wave after wave of galleons, cannon galleons, fire ships, and transports to demolish Valencian docks, walls, and interior structures. Unfortunately, the supply of wood in Valencia is rather limited. Scout east along the Mediterranean until you find a desolate Black Guard army base, an ample supply of lumber, and a new source of gold.

Tip After the initial assault, the Black Guard army will rarely bother you again—it becomes more of a nuisance than a significant threat. However, you should still strive to demolish its castle and siege workshop as soon as possible to cease production of trebuchets and battering rams.

Send the majority of your villagers east to the edge of the map and along the Mediterranean shore (the rest should be mining the gold resource inside Valencia). Build a lumber camp and start chopping wood. Select the lumberyard and research enhancements to improve the speed at which you acquire wood resources. Keep a few military units nearby in case enemy troops investigate this position, and erect towers to protect the structures and the shore. Build a second dock here, start producing war galleys, and upgrade to galleons. You'll need food in order to upgrade to galleons, so start farming around your town center or build more fishing ships to use the fish farms already built for you.

The Black Guard navy and Yusuf will soon attack both the dock west of Valencia and your new camp along the eastern edge of the map. Protect both with an ample naval fleet. Repair damaged ships by sending them against the shore, then select a villager and right-click the ship to repair the vessel (see Figure 4.15). You can save large amounts of wood and gold by taking the time to repair damaged ships.

Figure 4.15:
Repair your ships with villagers to cut down on wood and gold expenses.

The large amount of stone in the Valencia base should be used to fortify your perimeter walls and build towers. Save enough wood to construct a university, and

research chemistry to improve your galleons and gain the ability to build bombard cannons to further protect the perimeter of Valencia. Concentrate your bombard cannons along the sea wall.

After finishing off the Black Guard army with ground troops and trebuchets, your second target should be the Black Guard navy. Cease shipbuilding and save up wood for additional siege units. You're likely to have a large stash of gold by now, so divert the gold miners to planting farms to increase food production. Maximize your population with additional military units. Exit Valencia to the northwest and prepare your assault against the Black Guard navy by organizing your assault group into infantry, archer, and trebuchet groups.

Follow the Mediterranean shore to the south. Consider using villagers to advance towers and cannon towers toward the Black Guard navy base for further offensive support. Stick close to the coastline and use your fleet of galleons to guard your assault. Ignore civilian structures, such as houses and resource yards, and advance south into the heart of the Black Guard naval base. Take out military structures and docks, then assault the town center and castle. Use monks and Missionaries to heal troops and convert enemy cavalry and archers.

Eliminating the Black Guard navy base should provide relief from most of the attacks. Yusuf will continue to send over small fleets of galleons, cannon galleons, fire ships, and transports, however. Scout the sea thoroughly and intercept transports before they reach your shores. Locate additional gold and lumber within the Black Guard navy base.

> **Tip** Position your western navy fleet along the Black Guard navy's shoreline. Not only can you fire at enemy structures, you can also damage their ground units advancing toward Valencia. Monitor the situation, however, and divert fire toward enemy ships if they enter the area.

> **Tip** Before mounting your invasion of Africa, locate the small island roughly in the center of the sea, and build a tower on it for ship-spotting purposes.

Take control of the sea and begin bolstering your military with ground troops and trebuchets. Build three or four transports to hold your assault group. If you have the resources, use your docks to research technologies to enhance the speed and cost of naval units and increase the size of transports.

Send your transports down the western side of the map into the southern corner. Move your naval fleet south toward the western edge of Yusuf's base. A powerful tower rests here on a rock, and there are two others positioned toward the west. Divert the first tower's fire from your transports (simply order a galleon to circle around the tower), and then unload your transports at the western side of the base. Unpack your trebuchets and assault the powerful tower, which should fall easily to your bombardment. There's also a good spot at the other end of the shore from which you can shell enemy structures with bombard cannons or trebuchets.

Move your naval units along the shore and fight Yusuf's troops as close to your naval ships as possible. The combined offense should wipe out Yusuf's units as they approach, but beware of enemy monks converting your ships and troops. Then unpack the trebuchets and assault nearby structures (see Figure 4.16). Advance to the east, laying waste to units and structures in your path.

Figure 4.16:
Destroy Yusuf's buildings with trebuchets while protecting the siege weapons with your infantry.

Tip The Black Guard navy's monastery includes a relic. After destroying the monastery, use a monk to escort the relic back to your own monastery to receive a steady bonus of gold.

Most of Yusuf's military structures can be found in the southeastern corner. Continue to produce infantry, archers or hand cannoneers, cavalry, and trebuchets or bombard cannons. Keep villagers gathering food, gold, and wood, and protect your shore with towers in case Yusuf sneaks in a transport (which holds cavalry, infantry, and battering rams). Once Yusuf falls to your forces, the mission and campaign concludes in success.

Designer's Notes

The Moslems had controlled the lion's share of Spain for centuries. It was with victories like El Cid's at Toledo and Valencia that the Christians slowly reconquered Spain. Over the course of the next five centuries, the Moslems slowly gave ground in battle after battle until they were driven not just from Spain, but from all of Europe. Echoes of the intertwined Arab and European culture still mark Spain today, down to one of its greatest heroes—Rodrigo Díaz de Bivar, El Cid Campeador.

—*Karen Sparks*

Montezuma

The arrival of the Spaniards threatens the Aztecs' homeland. The Spaniards' powerful weaponry, including horseback and gunpowder units, confuse Montezuma, the emperor of the Aztecs. Are these strangers conquerors or gods? The Aztecs soon discover the answer and must battle the Spaniards and their Central American allies to retain control of their lands.

In this chapter, you'll find a complete walkthrough for The Conqueror's Montezuma campaign. The Aztecs' lack of cavalry and gunpowder units provides a challenge for players relying on powerful paladins, hand cannoneers, and bombard cannons. Instead, the Aztecs must combat enemies with their impressively powerful and quick foot soldiers, Jaguar and eagle warriors. Monks are extremely useful for converting the powerful Spanish units.

Montezuma 1: Reign of Blood

Initial Objectives

- 🛡 Capture the four shrines (monasteries) sacred to Quetzacoatl.
- 🛡 Place a sacred relic in each of the four shrines (monasteries).

Forces

	Their Stance	Your Stance
Tlatiluco	Enemy	Enemy
Xochimilco	Enemy	Enemy
Tepanaca	Enemy	Enemy

Map Highlights

Your small Aztec village is near the southeastern corner of the map. Plentiful lumber, gold, and stone resources are scattered around the outskirts of the camp. To the west you'll find the Tlatiluco base. It's weakly defended and should be the first target. The better-defended Tepanaca can be found just north of the Aztec base. To the northwest is the Xochimilco base, the toughest of the three enemy cities. The four shrines (monasteries) are revealed at the mission's start. Two are located just west of the Aztec camp, while one is positioned between the Tepanaca and Xochimilco bases, and another can be found in the far northwestern corner over a river, protected by a jaguar.

Battle Plans

You begin with three eagle warriors and a handful of peasants. Start the peasants foraging in the bushes near the mill, then select your barracks and produce two militias. Have one of your eagle warriors scout to the west and he'll soon locate eight turkeys (they're like sheep). You'll find four in two locations along the road that leads west. Lead the turkeys back to your town center.

While you're collecting the turkeys, an eagle warrior might hear jaguars, as four of the big cats head to your town center from the north. Position your eagle warriors and militia north of the town center and intercept the beasts before they reach your vulnerable villagers. As you gather food, start producing villagers and assign most to food gathering and the remainder to lumber and house construction. Use the recently acquired turkeys, the bushes around the mill, and the two shore-fishing spots in the pond just east of the Aztec town center (see Figure 5.1). You should also build additional militia to help fend off the early attacks.

With a sizable quantity of villagers produced, you can attempt to defend your town by forming a combination of infantry and skirmishers to counter the enemy infantry and archers, but it's easier to build walls and towers around your city. Assign villagers to chopping wood and obtaining gold and continue to harvest food (then create farms). You'll find lumber and gold resources in abundance northeast of the Aztec base along the eastern edge of the map, and there are two sizable stone patches east and southeast of your base.

Designer's Notes

For this first scenario, we wanted to introduce players to the new architecture of the Mesoamericans, as well as to the new rainforest terrain complete with macaws, javelinas, and turkeys. Just to make sure players didn't assume this scenario played just like a random map, we added a few scripted events, such as the early jaguar attack and the Mayan eagle warrior ambush at one of the shrines.

Why did we add turkeys to the expansion pack? Well, sheep aren't native to Central America. The Aztecs raised mostly turkeys and dogs for meat, and we figured hunting dogs might not go over so well in certain parts of the world!

—*Greg Street*

Figure 5.1:
Locate the flock of turkeys to the west for an excellent early food source.

Walls only cost five stone per section, so you can begin construction before you've even assigned villagers to mine stone. Build one wall just north of your base, between the forests that flank the road. Build another west of your base enclosing the two patches of gold (you'll definitely want these for later).

> **Tip** It's likely your army will take damage after each small, early skirmish with enemy troops. While waiting for the next attack, garrison your military inside the town center. This allows your units to heal in time for the next encounter.

Trying to manage everything early on can be tough, especially with your three enemies constantly sending raiding parties into your base. The attacks will continue to escalate in severity until they merge into combined assaults by all three enemies. Furthermore, the Xochimilco will send scorpion siege units, offering a tough challenge for your infantry and archer units.

Once you have enough stone, start building towers along both walls. Place as many as resources will allow—while saving at least 650 stone for a castle—and monitor the towers' strength from time to time. Assign villagers to repair damage to the towers or the wall as needed.

> **Tip** Remember that garrisoned towers have increased attack strength. Ring the town center bell when enemies approach so that villagers working near the towers will automatically garrison.

Now that you're walled in and have some protection from towers, you need not worry about attacks from the three enemy cities. You may have to repair damage from time to time, but you shouldn't lose walls or towers unless you're careless. Xochimilco will produce scorpions, but it's the only enemy siege unit you'll encounter, and it doesn't do significant damage to walls or towers.

Concentrate on your economy now that you're safe from attack. Plant farms around your town center and mill, and research horse collar and heavy plow to improve farming. Use your town center to research wheelbarrow and food cart to further enhance resource acquisition. Mine the gold east and west of the Aztec base, and continue to chop wood in the sizable forest area located to the east.

As soon as you have enough resources, advance to the Castle Age. Construct a castle near one of the walls, specifically your northern wall, to bolster your defense (see Figure 5.2). Build all available military and civilian structures, and remember to enhance your attack and armor strength at the barracks and upgrade units at the barracks and archery range. Finally, build a siege workshop to produce battering rams.

Start training Jaguar Warriors (the Aztecs' unique unit), long swordsmen, crossbowmen, and battering rams, and gather them to the west of your base inside the city

walls. Produce twice as many infantry as crossbowmen and include at least five battering rams in your assault group. If resource stockpiles are high, consider deleting some villagers in order to increase the size of your army.

Figure 5.2:
Place the castle carefully and use it as a defense against enemy attack.

Tlatiluco, which lies west of your base, offers the easiest initial target. Go west until you reach the southwestern area of the map. Send your infantry and crossbowmen against hostile units while you move in battering rams for use against military structures. Locate a Tlatiluco barracks and archery range in the southwestern corner of the map and work your way towards them, destroying the town center and all military structures along the way. Destroy them, kill all villagers, and Tlatiluco will resign.

Once Tlatiluco is finished off, regroup and reinforce your military. Gold and stone resources are located west of the Aztec city wall and just before the river crossing; move villagers there and resume your gathering efforts. Your next target should be Tepanaca, located just north of the Aztec base. Enter the town from along the eastern edge of the map, using battering rams to break through the walls.

Chapter 5: Montezuma

Tepanaca sends infantry, eagle warriors, plumed archers, and skirmishers to intercept your force. Use your ground forces against the hostile units while you send battering rams to hammer the Tepanaca military structures. You'll find the Tepanaca castle along the eastern edge of the map on a slight elevation. Send in your battering rams first, followed by your ground forces. The castle's defenses won't inflict much damage on the battering rams, so victory here should come easily.

Once you've forced Tlatiluco and Tepanaca to resign, only Xochimilco remains in the northern corner. Reinforce your troops and proceed northwest from Tepanaca toward one of the shrines. Capture this monastery as you travel to Xochimilco, and be prepared to defend it. Tepanaca eagle warriors will attack from the north once you've "tainted their shrine." Fortunately, you should have a sufficient military force to fend them off.

To defend this shrine, move up some villagers and construct a castle and town center adjacent to it. If you possess additional stone reserves, consider erecting a wall or additional towers to prevent enemy attack. Use the monastery and produce a monk to escort the relic inside, then have him heal your military units. Proceed west to the Xochimilco base.

As you did in razing the other two cities, concentrate on military units and structures first. You'll find the Xochimilco castle and town center in the southern part of the town. Eliminate both with your battering rams, then target the Xochimilco military structures and kill off the villagers.

Once Xochimilco resigns, all you have left to do is to capture the remaining shrines. Two are located just west of the Aztec base (see Figure 5.3). Send over villagers or infantry units to capture the monasteries. Produce a monk and place the relics into their corresponding shrines.

The last shrine is located in the northwest corner of the map across a small river. Move up a villager and build a dock and two transports. Then send over a monk and nine infantry units. Head west slowly, watching for the vicious jaguars awaiting your arrival. Use your infantry against the jaguars. Approach the shrine and have the monk put the relic inside. Once all four monasteries are captured and all four relics are inside their respective monasteries, the mission ends in victory.

Figure 5.3:
Two monasteries can be found along the road west of the Aztec base.

Montezuma 2: The Triple Alliance

Initial Objectives

- Deliver the summons of war to the Texcoco town center.
- Deliver the summons of war to the Tlacopan town center.

Forces

	Their Stance	Your Stance
Tlaxcala	Enemy	Enemy
Tlacopan	Ally	Ally
Texcoco	Ally	Ally
Cortéz	Neutral	Neutral

Map Highlights

The Aztec messengers start in the southern corner of the map. Head northwest to locate your nearest ally, the Tlacopan. The Texcoco, your other ally, lies east of Tlacopan and northeast of the Aztec start position. To the northwest corner you'll find Tlaxcala. The Spanish arrive, on ships and horseback, from the northern corner of the battlefield at the end of the mission.

Battle Plans

You begin in the southern corner of the map with a group of eagle warriors sent to deliver a message to potential allies, the Tlacopan and the Texcoco. Head northwest along the road. Be prepared for some fighting as you'll encounter jaguars along the way. Continue north over the river ford until you spot the outskirts of Tlacopan, colored yellow on the mini-map. Scout the Tlacopan town and locate the town center just north of the water.

Approach the Tlacopan town center with your eagle warrior messengers to complete the first objective. Tlacopan joins in your battle against the Tlaxcalans. Now you must seek out Texcoco and send the second summons. Head north out of Tlacopan and then east when you reach a path. Don't venture too far north or you'll trigger an attack from Tlaxcalan troops at their base located just north of Tlacopan.

Continue east and you'll soon spot Texcoco units in an open clearing. Keep moving until you're approaching the eastern edge of the map and locate the Texcoco town center (see Figure 5.4). Approach it with your eagle warriors to deliver the summons and complete the mission's second objective. Like Tlacopan, Texcoco allies itself with the Aztecs in their battle with the Tlaxcalans.

Figure 5.4:
Deliver the summons to the Texcoco town center to complete the mission's initial objectives.

💜 **New Objective:** Defeat the Tlaxcalans by destroying their four town centers.

With both Tlacopan and Texcoco allied with you, the mission objective switches to eliminating Tlaxcala by razing its four town centers. A transport loaded with four villagers appears at the southern corner of the map. Move the transport to the eastern shore and unload the villagers, then move them into Texcoco to start constructing an Aztec town.

> **Tip** Sizable patches of stone are located southwest of Texcoco and southeast of Tlacopan. Use this stone to build a castle and towers inside Texcoco and Tlacopan. Later in the mission, when Texcoco and Tlacopan become enemies, the towers attack the enemy structures and provide a line of sight into their towns. Placing petards next to important buildings will result in a quick victory once they switch alliances.

There's no major rush to eliminate Tlaxcala. If you build your town within Texcoco, its units will help protect your town. Build a town center with room for farming. Produce additional villagers and start chopping wood and mining gold, both located to the southeast. The water behind the Texcoco base to the northeast contains shore-fishing opportunities. If you can control the waterway, you can build a dock and fishing boats to reel in the plentiful fish along the eastern edge of the map. The Tlaxcalans will send over war galleys, however, so be prepared to protect your fishing boats from attack.

West of Texcoco are three Tlaxcalan barracks and two archery ranges, as well as a monastery with three relics. The earlier you eliminate them, the better.

Keep building your economy and research all related upgrades, including farm, town center, mining, and lumber production enhancements. Should you need more gold, scout north along the eastern shore and south inside the dense forest. Since both allies will turn on you after Tlaxcala falls, hoard as much resources as possible so you have plenty of reserve for units late in the mission.

Build a full complement of military structures—barracks, archery range, and blacksmith—and research all military upgrades. Locate the stone reserve southwest of Texcoco, and mine enough to prepare for the Castle Age. Once you've advanced, cycle through military structures and research any newly available upgrades. Build a monastery for monks to heal your troops and a siege workshop for battering rams to help annihilate Tlaxcala.

Produce an army consisting of Jaguar Warriors, crossbowmen, elite skirmishers, and garrisoned battering rams. North of Tlacopan offers an excellent area for your initial offensive, as three of the four Tlaxcala town centers are located in the northwest corner of the map. It's a long way, but well worth the effort.

Advance north from Tlacopan and assault the Tlaxcala camp. Concentrate on the military structures first, staying along the western edge and using battering rams against the town centers. Clear out the entire northwestern corner, leaving one Tlaxcala town center—the one located just east on a small hill.

🛡 **Optional Objective:** Bring 10 Jaguar Warriors to the Temple of Tlaloc.

Just northwest of Tlacopan you'll find a bridge leading to a gate protecting a temple. Tlaxcala towers also protect the temple inside. Break open the gate with battering rams and destroy the towers inside. Approach the monastery inside to trigger an optional objective: Bring 10 Jaguar Warriors to this temple to increase their hit points.

> **Tip** You probably won't need to build a new town if, as suggested above, you place petards near Tlacopan and Texcoco castles and town centers.

Before you finish off the Tlaxcalans, send your villagers to the northwest corner and build a new town center, military structures, and castle. If you don't have the resources, or many still remain in the southeast, consider waiting to bolster your reserves even further. You'll need this new town once the final Tlaxcalan town center is razed, as the Tlacopan and Texcoco will turn on you.

With your new town erected, send your military east and finish off the final Tlaxcalan town center. Guide your forces back to the northwest corner, and use monks to heal infantry and archer units and villagers to repair battering rams.

🛡 **New Objective:** Defeat your former allies, the Tlacopan and Texcoco.

Since you're now located north of Tlacopan, its southern town should become your next target. Reinforce your military and siege units until you have four to six battering rams and approximately twice as many infantry and range units as you started with. If you have an ample supply of resources, consider deleting villagers so you can produce more military units.

> **Tip** Build another barracks or castle on the outskirts of Texcoco. Since you're very far from your current base in the northwest corner, the new structures will be needed to provide timely reinforcements.

Head south into Tlacopan and attack military units and structures first (see Figure 5.5). Bring monks along to convert Tlacopan units. Send your battering rams against the town center, barracks, and archery range. Finally, use your Jaguar Warriors to eliminate the scattering villagers.

Once Tlacopan resigns, heal and reinforce your military and battering rams. Proceed east and assault Texcoco from the northern side of the settlement. The Texcoco castle protects its

military structures, so you should eliminate it as soon as possible. Use your military to escort the battering rams inside, protecting them from enemy infantry. Once your battering rams reach the castle, you should be able to raze the stone structure within seconds.

Clear out the Texcoco town with your military and siege units. Once Texcoco resigns, the map shifts to the northern corner. Cortéz, a new Spanish arrival, enters on boats and horses. Watch the concluding cutscene, and the mission ends in victory.

Figure 5.5:
Destroy your former allies, the Tlacopan.

Designer's Notes

We went back and forth quite a bit trying to figure out how much foreshadowing of the eventual betrayal was too much in this scenario. If the players knew that their allies would turn on them, then the event would not be as much fun. However, if the players were taken totally by surprise, then they might feel compelled to restart a long scenario in order to better plan their defenses against enemies to the front and the rear. The hidden shrine of Tlaloc was used to demonstrate the new trigger to change object hit points, as well as to give me another cheap opportunity to work Ornlu the Wolf into yet another scenario.

—*Greg Street*

Montezuma 3: Quetzalcoatl

Initial Objective

⚉ Defeat the Tlaxcalans.

Forces

	Their Stance	Your Stance
Tlaxcala	Enemy	Enemy
Cortéz	Enemy	Enemy
Tabasco	Ally	Ally

Map Highlights

The Aztecs start with a southern established base. The village of Tabasco, a small Aztec ally, lies near the northern corner of the map between the two enemy camps: Tlaxcala to the west and the Spanish to the east. Tlaxcala can be found in the northwestern corner, while the Spanish are located along the eastern side of the map. The Spanish horses play an important role in the mission. You'll find access to three horse corrals in the southeastern corner, and a fourth to the northeast.

Battle Plans

Locate your town center in the south corner and use the nearby villagers to work the farms. Produce five more villagers and get them started on the trees to the west and the adjacent gold (construct a mining camp by the gold). Produce more villagers and build another mining camp near the stone resource north of the Aztec town. As in the first mission of the Aztec campaign, it's important to build defensive walls to keep the Tlaxcalans and Spanish out of your town (see Figure 5.6).

Select a villager and begin building thick walls in the forest exits that lead northwest and east from the Aztec base. There are two paths to the east wall. Before you enclose the path to the north, explore and locate a second gold and stone mine. As the gold mine near the Aztec base is rather small, you'll need to control this second mine if you are to succeed against both Tlaxcala and the Spanish. You can also place monks and convert enemy units as they approach.

An additional food source lies east of the Aztec base, where a mill is surrounded by many berry bushes. Order a villager to build houses along the southern edge of the map until you can support the maximum Aztec population.

⚉ **New Objective:** Prevent the Aztec allies in Tabasco from being defeated.

While you're busy gathering resources, Tabasco comes under attack from the Spanish and the Tlaxcalans. Though you could hold off their attack for a time, it's best to leave them to their sad fate. Concentrate instead on enclosing the clearing north of the Aztec base so you have access to the stone and gold mines.

Figure 5.6:
Plug forest paths with stone walls to keep Spanish and Tlaxcalan units away from the Aztec base.

🛡 **New Objective:** Capture 20 Spanish horses and return them to the flagged pen in the Aztec camp, or defeat the Spanish.

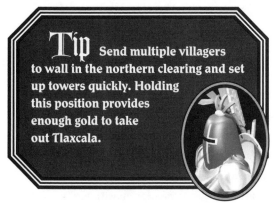

Tip Send multiple villagers to wall in the northern clearing and set up towers quickly. Holding this position provides enough gold to take out Tlaxcala.

Once Tabasco falls, Tlaxcala and the Spanish form an alliance. You're told by the Aztec narrator that if the Spanish horses could be stolen, the Spanish would be weakened and victory could be achieved. Three horse corrals are located in the southeastern corner, and the fourth is positioned to the northeast just beyond the river.

Spanish long swordsmen, paladins, bombard cannons, and Conquistadors offer quite a challenge for the Aztec military. Once you're enclosed with walls and have towers protecting the Aztec perimeter, build a monastery and siege workshop, and save enough stone to build a castle. As soon as you possess the resources, use the town center to advance to the Imperial Age.

Begin producing military units for your assault against Tlaxcala. You'll encounter Tlaxcalan eagle warriors and archers, so produce Jaguar Warriors and elite skirmishers to counter. Upgrade attack and armor bonuses at the blacksmith and consider upgrading the Jaguar Warriors to Elite Jaguar Warriors. Manufacture battering rams and trebuchets to fill out your mixed assault group.

Advance northwest from the Aztec base and approach Tlaxcala. Assault the city from long range with your trebuchets, making sure to protect the fragile weapons with

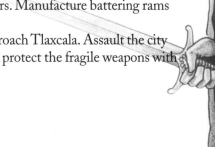

your Jaguar Warriors and elite skirmishers. Concentrate your fire on military structures first. Include monks in your attack group to heal wounds and convert enemy units. You may also want to take along a villager to repair any damage to the trebuchets.

> **Tip** This mission is made much easier if you build a monastery early, place at least a pair of monks on every path leading to your town, and convert approaching enemy units. Research monastery technologies, first block printing (increased conversion range), then redemption (necessary to convert cannons). You should be able to gather about 20 enemy units (conquistadors, knights, and bombard cannons) before the Spanish research heresy at around the 30-minute mark.

Continue through the Tlaxcala base. Send in the battering rams and use the Jaguar Warriors against infantry and the elite skirmishers against the archer units (see Figure 5.7). Reinforce your military by continuing to produce units at the castle and archer range in the Aztec base.

Designer's Notes

The Aztecs make sense for *The Conquerors Expansion* since they were both conquerors and conquered. The Tlaxcalans represent one of many other nations that were conquered by the Aztecs. The other members of the Triple Alliance were engaged in an uneasy cold war with the Aztecs. Cortéz could never have defeated the gigantic armies of Aztec warriors were there not so many Aztec enemies eager to throw their lots in with him.

— *Greg Street*

Raze the Tlaxcala base (the castle and town center can be found near the northwestern corner of the map) and begin to harvest uncollected resources. A gold and stone mine can be found southeast of Tlaxcala just before the river crossing. Additional gold mines are located east and northeast just beyond the Tlaxcalan monastery. Send Jaguar Warriors to escort the villagers to these positions, as you can expect the Spanish to protect these mines. Once you've seized the mines, build walls and towers to protect the mining villagers.

Figure 5.7:
Use battering rams
against the Tlaxcalan
structures.

Tip The Aztec unique technology, Garland Wars, can be researched at the castle. It's an extremely expensive technology but significantly enhances the strength of Jaguar Warriors and other infantry. If you have the gold, research it before or during your assault on Tlaxcala.

An important decision awaits when only the Spanish remain. To win, you can free 20 horses and escort them to the holding pen just northwest of the Aztec base, or you can assault the Spanish base. While it's easier to mount hit-and-run attacks against the horse pens than to destroy the Spanish town, collecting 20 horses is difficult, as you must get the horses from all four pens to meet victory conditions.

Destroying the Spanish town takes careful military strategizing and specializing your troops even further. Research pikemen at the barracks for use against the Spanish Conquistadors and paladins, and be prepared to micromanage infantry units (include speedy eagle warriors in your group) to intercept the powerful Spanish bombard cannons (or use monks to convert them). The Spanish also possess cannon galleons patrolling the river. Keep your distance and use spread skirmishers or arbalests to terminate the naval vessels.

If you choose to capture the horses, approach from the south. Avoid using trebuchets to destroy the palisade walls protecting the pen—you don't want to accidentally kill any horses. Send infantry to destroy the fragile wooden walls, then move an infantry unit inside the pen to capture the horses. Move the horses back west toward the Aztec holding pen.

> ## Warning
> When moving the horses out of the Spanish pen and toward the Aztec base, be careful to monitor their route. You may wish to set waypoints and micromanage them so they don't stray from your intended path and end up targeted by Spanish bombard cannons and the Spanish castle. Though the Spanish possess more horses than you need, it's wiser to take the time to escort the horses back to Aztec territory safely.

The Spanish bombard cannons are your biggest concern, as the immense power of these siege weapons can obliterate a group of infantry or range units in a single blast. Use the spread formation and attack the cannons with eagle warriors or Jaguar Warriors on sight.

Three Spanish horse pens are accessed from the southern route (see Figure 5.8). You're dangerously close to the Spanish siege workshop here, though, so eliminate the workshop and the bombard cannon it produces before advancing to the pens. One is located against the eastern edge of the map. You must cross the shallow river in order to reach the horses. You'll need to eliminate the cannon tower protecting the entrance to the pen with battering rams or trebuchets before moving inside.

Figure 5.8:
The southeastern corner of the map contains three Spanish horse pens in close proximity.

Once you've razed the Spanish town or captured 20 horses and led them to the Aztec holding pen, the mission ends in victory.

Montezuma 4: La Noche Triste

Initial Objective

🛡 Destroy the Spanish wonder to end Cortéz's influence in Tenochtitlan.

Forces

	Their Stance	Your Stance
Cortéz	Enemy	Enemy
Conquered Aztecs	Enemy	Enemy
Tlaxcala	Ally	Ally

Map Highlights

The player's lone Jaguar Warrior starts in the southwest section of the map. The Spanish begin construction of their wonder immediately, and it's revealed in the northeast. Tlaxcala occupies the northern edge of the map, and Cortéz and the Spanish can be found surrounded by water in the middle. Conquered Aztecs also occupy the middle of the map and use war galleons to harass Aztecs attempting to liberate Tenochtitlan.

Battle Plans

You begin with just a single Jaguar Warrior, Cuauhtemoc, the story's narrator. He has an attack of 10+22—don't lose him! Explore the landscape to recruit additional troops. Start by heading to the northwest and meeting an eagle warrior. He states that transports can be found to the northwest, but they're guarded by Tlaxcala patrols. Tlaxcala holds Aztec prisoners up north, and the transports are key to reaching them.

🛡 **New Objective:** Rescue the Aztec warriors held prisoner by the Tlaxcala.

Tip Approach along the western edge of the map. The transports lie on the western side at the shoreline. If you venture too far east, you'll encounter Tlaxcalan Jaguar Warriors at the bridge. Though you could defeat them, it's unwise to risk taking casualties at this point. Save your troops for battles later in the mission.

Don't head further northwest. Though it's possible to defeat the enemy eagle warriors protecting the transports, it's much safer to travel south and recruit additional troops first. Proceed toward the southern corner of the map. Here you'll encounter two houses, six elite skirmishers, five pikemen, and five eagle warriors (see Figure 5.9).

Assign your infantry units to one group and the elite skirmishers to another, then return north to the transports and defeat the eagle warriors on guard along the shoreline.

Move the transports north along the western edge of the map until you reach the next shoreline. Unload the transports and you'll encounter two Spanish Conquistadors. Eliminate them and continue along the western edge of the map until you reach the northwest corner. Your men spot a Tlaxcalan priest just to the west. Assaulting the priest would risk unit conversion, so listen to the clue provided by your men and inspect the jaguar pen adjacent to the priest. You're in control of the palisade wall enclosing the jaguars, so delete a section of it and cause the jaguars to scamper out and attack the Tlaxcalan priest.

Figure 5.9:
Aztec reinforcements to the south help in your battle to reach the transports.

Designer's Notes

It is important to remember that the Spanish had not taken Tenochtitlan by force, but were invited in by Montezuma. Thus, when a gigantic army of highly trained and pretty upset Aztecs finally did fight back against the Spanish, it was virtually a rout, with the Spanish attempting to flee with as much gold as they could carry. We wanted players to become familiar with the complicated city of Tenochtitlan in this scenario, since they would be defending the same map in scenario six. The most fun part of it for me to make is when the jaguars break out of their pen to attack the Tlaxcalan priest. In order to make progress move slower on the Spanish wonder on easier difficulty settings, I periodically delete the lone builder and force the Spanish to train another.

— *Greg Street*

Proceed east and you'll acquire an onager, a powerful siege weapon and upgrade for the mangonel. Cautiously continue east and use the onager to weaken approaching Tlaxcalan Jaguar Warriors. Then finish them off with your elite skirmishers and infantry. You'll gain nine additional eagle warriors here; the reinforcements come just before you reach the outskirts of the Tlaxcalan camp. Battle more Tlaxcalan troops and a tower here, but don't waste time with the other structures.

- **New Objective:** Travel across Lake Texcoco, where you may safely gather resources.

- **New Objective:** Release the Aztec prisoners, locate the Spanish docks, and steal transports to travel across the lake to a stretch of land on the southern edge of the map.

> ## Warning
> **Beware the Conquered Aztec war galley before charging across the bridge toward the Spanish docks. Use your elite skirmishers to assault the naval vessel, then follow up the spears with a volley from your onager to finish it off quickly.**

Release the Aztec prisoners, consisting of Jaguar Warriors, eagle warriors, and elite skirmishers. Assign each to the infantry and range groups you have already formed. When you release the prisoners, additional Tlaxcalan units attack your rear flank from the west. Use the onager to weaken the approaching Jaguar Warriors and crossbowmen. Send infantry against the Jaguar Warriors and use your skirmishers against any crossbowmen not eliminated by your siege weapon. Beware of Tlaxcalan scorpions also. Be sure to spread your troops out and send a Jaguar Warrior or eagle warrior to intercept the powerful weapons.

The toughest part of the mission is reaching the stolen transport ships safely. Though it's not vital to save as many troops as possible, it's extremely cost-effective, as you won't have to spend resources to train replacements when you reach the southern corner. Saving this initial force also helps protect your base from early ground attacks from the Spanish and Tlaxcalans (see Figure 5.10).

Spanish troops patrolling around the docks are tough, but your biggest problem is the Spanish mangonels positioned south and southeast of the docks. Keep your force spread out and north of the city and docks. Micromanage your Jaguar and eagle warriors and send them at the mangonels. Your attack should force them to retreat. Use the diversion to send your troops onto the transports.

Figure 5.10:
Carefully guide your Aztec force through Spanish-occupied territory.

> **Tip** Skilled players will find that it's possible to complete this mission in about 30 minutes with just the upgraded troops you have and the monks to heal your guys and convert enemy units. There are just two gates between you and the wonder, whose destruction wins you the mission.

Select your ships and head due east. Spanish cannon galleons patrol here, so if you take a direct route to your destination to the south, you might come under naval attack. Maneuver around the enemy ships and sail to the southeastern corner. Unload your troops and scout the nearby territory until you encounter a small village with houses, a monastery, and monks.

You don't possess any villagers, so you must use Aztec monks to convert Tlaxcalan or Spanish villagers. Though it's tempting to spend gold to produce more monks and convert more villagers, it's more cost-effective to use one or two monks and a few converted villagers to begin the new Aztec town. Heal your infantry and elite skirmishers before you head into Spanish-occupied territory.

Escort the monks across the bridge, located southwest of the Aztec camp, toward Tenochtitlan. Convert an enemy villager as quickly as possible and use your infantry and ranged units to hold off any counter-attacks. Don't get too greedy, as the Spanish will retaliate heavily with Conquistadors and other ground units. Send the villager back to the Aztec camp and locate an open clearing northwest of the monastery and build the town center.

Tip The monks speak of a rumored island filled with gold and protected by jaguars. You'll find this land in the northeastern corner of the map. If you need additional gold to defeat the Spanish wonder later on, use transports to send villagers and infantry to this rich land. Protect your mining with towers and war galleys.

Once your town center is built, produce additional villagers and begin converting nearby turkeys into food so you can produce more villagers. Begin chopping wood and mining gold. You should also construct a dock as soon as possible and build a small fleet of war galleys to protect your shoreline from bombard attack. You might also want to start mining stone to construct walls, a gate, and a tower at the bridge. Expect the Spanish naval fleet, located west of the bridge, to assault the stone structures, however.

Build the full complement of military structures—barracks, archery range, blacksmith, siege workshop, and castle— and research available bonuses to attack and armor strength and upgrade infantry and archer units. Additional gold is located on the southern tip of the Aztec island; if you need more, migrate your miners there or use the jaguar island in the northeast corner of the map. Bushes along the eastern edge of the map provide an additional food source, so build a mill nearby and plant farms to keep food production high (see Figure 5.11). Use wood to build houses until you can support the population limit.

Figure 5.11:
Don't neglect your available food sources. Use a mill to gather the berry bushes at the new Aztec base.

Since you're attempting to eliminate the Spanish wonder, you're on a timetable. Should the wonder be built, you'll have 350 game years (about 10 minutes) to destroy it before the mission ends in failure. You have a few options regarding your assault of the Spanish wonder. Though you could cross the bridge into occupied Tenochtitlan, the Spanish naval fleet positioned west of the bridge will tear your military apart. Instead, use transports to deliver troops to the southeastern corner of Tenochtitlan. Escort transports with war galleys as both Spanish and Conquered Aztec ships will be defending the shore.

Remember that you don't need to raze all the Spanish and Conquered Aztec structures—destroying the wonder alone satisfies the victory conditions. Assemble a mixed force of Jaguar Warriors, arbalests, pikemen, battering rams, and petards. Trebuchets also work well in clearing a path to the wonder, though the expensive siege weapon must be protected from enemy attack or you'll waste valuable resources. Divert enemy forces with your infantry and ranged units while you send battering rams and petards against the Spanish wonder.

Spanish mangonels pose a threat to your assault group. Also, two Conquered Aztec castles just northeast of the Spanish wonder help defend your intended target. When assaulting the wonder, lead with a few infantry units to divert the castles' fire while you send in the battering rams and petards. Use infantry units to eliminate any villagers repairing the wonder and defend your battering rams against enemy infantry attack. Once the wonder falls to Aztec forces, the mission ends in success.

Montezuma 5: The Boiling Lake

Initial Objective

⚜ Defeat the Tlaxcalans and the Spanish.

Forces

	Their Stance	Your Stance
Tlaxcala	Enemy	Enemy
Cortéz	Enemy	Enemy

Map Highlights

The Aztec bases are located on the southern edge of the map. The military portion of the bases can be found on the southeastern side, complete with barracks, archery range, and castle. Look to the southwest for the Aztec farming community and town center. Both Aztec bases include docks. Tlaxcala and the Spanish stronghold are located along the northern and eastern edges of the map. Spanish horses and trade carts filled with gunpowder can be captured to produce cavalry and bombard cannons. You'll find trade

carts in the southeast and northwest sections of the map, as well as inside the Spanish base to the northeast. Horses are located inside wooden and stone pens to the east and northwest, and inside the Spanish base to the northeast.

Battle Plans

The mission begins with a large battle between Jaguar Warriors, eagle warriors, and crossbowmen located in the south, and the Spanish infantry, Conquistadors, and archers from the north. Quickly select the Jaguar Warriors and eagle warriors and assign them to your first group, then select the crossbowmen and assign them to a second.

Designer's Notes

Karen did a great job with Lake Texcoco for this map. I really like the way the battle starts in a full rout with the Spanish fleeing. Of course, if the Aztecs pursue for too long, they may run into more Tlaxcalans than they can hope to defeat. The huge lake allows for some naval engagements, but there are also enough shallows for soldiers to run back and forth across the water. At the same time, land is scarce and the player may have to fight for real estate on which they can farm. If you advance too much on one side (or across the middle of the lake) you open yourself to attacks from the other.

— *Greg Street*

Advance slowly against the retreating Spanish army. Push the Spanish units back north, but try not to suffer too many casualties. It's cost-effective to save as many military units as possible. Eventually, the Spanish military will flee to the north. When you spot the pen of horses to the west, stop your advance. It's impossible to continue on into the Spanish base without taking heavy losses.

 Optional Objective: Bring captured Spanish units to the plaza and create new units.

Bringing horses will create cavalry. Bringing trade carts full of gunpowder will create bombard cannons. So before you assault the stone wall around the Spanish horses, send a unit into the southeastern corner. Here you'll discover and capture two Spanish trade carts. Send the carts to the Aztec castle (inside the flags just in front) and they'll be instantly converted into bombard cannons (see Figure 5.12).

Send one bombard cannon to your military positioned near the Spanish horse pen. Attack a section of the stone wall there with the bombard cannon. Once destroyed, escort the horses back to the Aztec castle and gain elite Tarkan cavalry units. Tarkans are the Huns' unique unit and are extremely effective against structures.

Figure 5.12:
Capture Spanish trade carts and convert them into Aztec bombard cannons.

Warning Protect your bombard cannons well, as the Aztecs have no means of constructing their own cannons.

Retreat your military forces and place some units on guard at the western Aztec base. Have the rest protect the northern end of the eastern base. Though vast, Lake Texcoco contains shallow swamplands allowing passage across each section.

Protection against Spanish naval attacks should be your first priority. Use remaining gold and wood resources to build war galleys, and prepare to counter attacks at both the western and eastern Aztec base. Produce more villagers at the town center and chop wood south of the town center. Assign other villagers to gold mining and a few to stone mining, and then place towers around the perimeter of both bases to protect villagers from Tlaxcala and Spanish raiding parties. Build houses to support the maximum Aztec population.

Controlling Lake Texcoco is vital to long-term success. The Spanish use war galleys and cannon galleys. Build enough Aztec fire ships and war galleys—maintain a fleet of at least 10 to 12 vessels—to counter any Spanish naval attacks. Use villagers to repair damaged ships to conserve wood and gold.

Concentrate on base defense first. Don't send war galleys north to attack the Spanish shoreline, as bombard cannons protect the shore and will rip apart the fragile Aztec ships. If you approach from the west, you can destroy the docks without losses. But don't attack at the expense of the Aztec shore. Position fire ships and war galleys

near erected towers for further defense. Upgrade military units via the barracks and various military structures, and research chemistry at the university to improve the war galley's offensive capabilities.

> **Tip** An island filled with gold is located northwest of the Aztec base. The island is dangerously close to the Spanish and Tlaxcalan shoreline, however, making it difficult to protect both the island and your southern base. Build another fleet of war galleys and fire ships to protect a mining camp there. Use remaining stone resources to cover the island with towers.

Produce additional Jaguar Warriors and ranged units to complement the troops that survived the initial battle with the Spanish. Don't bother with siege units just yet—your next objective is to migrate your forces to the northwest corner of the map. Additional Spanish horse pens can be found there, as well as trade carts and gold.

It takes many troops to hold the northwest position. Send the majority of your military force along the western side of the map to the northwestern corner. Move villagers and build a town center just north of the gold resource. Tlaxcala will soon send infantry, ranged, and siege units to force you out of the northwestern corner. Be prepared with a strong military presence. Also consider erecting a castle and towers as soon as possible to supply further defenses.

> **Tip** Four more Spanish trade carts can be found along the northern edge of the map just east of your northwest forward base. Capture the trade carts and escort them carefully to the Aztec castle. Tlaxcalan and Spanish units will attack the carts, so you must protect them or lose the resulting bombard cannons. Note that monks can heal carts.

Hold off the Tlaxcala attack and escort villagers from the southern base to your new position in the northwest. Build a barracks, archery range, and siege workshop at the northwest base, then produce new troops here to quickly move them into battle.

Scout north and northwest of the gold resource here for two Spanish horse pens. Break open the pen walls with bombard cannons or your elite Tarkan cavalry. Send the horses to the southern edge of the map and then east to the Aztec castle, avoiding

Chapter 5: Montezuma

Spanish troops and naval units. You'll receive additional elite Tarkan cavalry once the horses reach the castle.

Organize your military into infantry, cavalry, ranged, and siege (upgraded battering rams, trebuchets, and bombard cannons) units. Begin advancing into the northeast section of the map. You'll encounter Tlaxcalan structures first. Keep battering rams back and use trebuchets to raze Tlaxcalan buildings from a distance. Protect siege units with your ground troops.

Scout ahead with Tarkans to spot Spanish bombard towers along the shore protecting the gated entrance to the Spanish section. Hold your military units back and destroy the towers with trebuchets and bombard cannons (see Figure 5.13). As you lose units, reinforce your army with the forward base built in the northwest.

Figure 5.13:
Advance cautiously into the Tlaxcalan and Spanish base to avoid the bombard towers.

Don't worry too much if rogue Tlaxcalan and Spanish units attack the Aztec base to the south. You have everything you need in the northwest section of the map (though make sure you have enough houses to maximize the Aztec population), and it's more important to continue your assault against Tlaxcala and Cortéz in the north. When you reach the Tlaxcalan and Spanish town centers and castles, move in upgraded battering rams. Micromanage Jaguar Warriors to intercept infantry units attacking the battering rams.

Additional Spanish horses and trade carts are located in the northeast corner, but are well protected by Spanish structures. It's unlikely that you'll need more elite Tarkans and bombard cannons to finish off your enemies, though you can send captured horses and trade carts back to the southern castle to receive cavalry and siege reinforcements.

Once you destroy their town centers, Tlaxcala and the Spanish are forced to resign, and the mission ends in victory.

Montezuma 6: Broken Spears

Initial Objectives

- Defeat the Tlaxcala, the Spanish army, and the Spanish navy.

- Prevent Tenochtitlan's wonder from being destroyed in order to keep the morale of your troops high (optional).

Forces

	Their Stance	Your Stance
Cortéz's Navy	Enemy	Enemy
Cortéz's Army	Enemy	Enemy
Tlaxcala	Enemy	Enemy

Map Highlights

The Aztecs have regained Tenochtitlan and currently occupy a large, established base on the map's central island. Bridges connect Tenochtitlan to the other surrounding civilizations. To the north you'll find the Spanish army, consisting of paladin and Conquistador cavalry. The Spanish navy is located along the southern edge of the map, and is made up of galleons, cannon galleons, and fire ships. The bridge heading west from Tenochtitlan leads to Tlaxcala and is protected by Jaguar Warriors, eagle warriors, and scorpion siege weapons. There's a small island northwest of Tenochtitlan that has all the gold you need for the entire mission. There's even a mine there, already built for you—just don't build towers on the island or lead an enemy ship to it. Enemy forces won't discover the island.

Battle Plans

You start in Tenochtitlan surrounded by three enemies—the Spanish army to the north, the Spanish navy to the south, and Tlaxcala to the west. The Spanish army, with paladin and Conquistador cavalry, and the Spanish naval fleet pose the greatest immediate danger.

Start construction of war galleys to protect Tenochtitlan's eastern shore. Cycle through idle villagers and assign them to farming, gold mining, and chopping wood. Should you desire additional defenses, mine the stone resource and erect towers around Tenochtitlan's bridge entrances, especially the southwestern bridge, and eastern shoreline.

Produce additional villagers to increase resource production, and build enough houses to support the maximum Aztec population. Produce battering rams (or spend resources to upgrade to capped and siege rams) and three or four trebuchets. The Aztec

military can be found just southwest of the wonder. Organize your troops into infantry, ranged, and siege units.

> **Tip** Key to protecting the Tenochtitlan shoreline against Spanish naval assault are three Elite Turtle Ships (the Korean unique unit) located in the northern corner of the map. Send a war galley to capture the ships, referred to as "gifts from the Gods," for Aztec use (see Figure 5.14). Use villagers to repair any damage to the Elite Turtle Ships, as you can't build any.

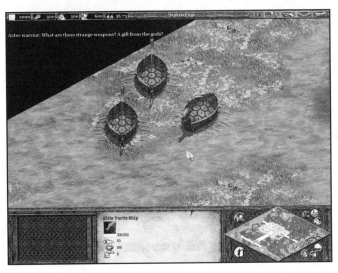

Figure 5.14: The Elite Turtle Ships help protect Tenochtitlan's shoreline.

Build units depending on which civilization you plan to attack first. If you wish to engage the Spanish army to the north, produce pikemen to counter the Spanish paladins and Conquistadors. Should you assault Tlaxcala to the west, produce Jaguar Warriors and crossbowmen.

Though a bridge leads north from Tenochtitlan into the Spanish army camp, it's wiser to attack from the bridge intersection that lies to the west. This intersection leads north to the western portion of the Spanish army base and south into Tlaxcala. Here you'll also discover Tlaxcalan barracks and a gold resource. Clear out the barracks, Tlaxcala villagers, and the mining camp, then send Aztec villagers to begin collecting resources. Protect your new camp with walls and towers.

Tip Skilled players can quickly eliminate the Spanish army by building a battering ram, six petards, and a few infantry for escort (Tlaxcalan eagle scouts are on the prowl). Use the ram to take down the Spanish gate, enter the base with the ram to draw fire from the nearby castle, and destroy the Spanish Army town center with the ram and petards. This can result in the Spanish army resigning just 10 minutes into the mission and makes dealing with the Spanish navy and Tlaxcala much easier.

One of the most challenging aspects of this mission is maintaining a balance between your ground offense against the Spanish army and Tlaxcala and your naval fleet protecting Tenochtitlan's eastern shoreline. Keep villagers near your eastern docks to repair damaged Elite Turtle Ships and war galleys. Look for Spanish navy transports attempting to land on Tenochtitlan. Position towers on the shoreline or eliminate the fragile transports with Turtle Ships and war galleys.

Tip The Spanish ships always begin by attacking your fish traps. Keep a few traps out there and you'll always have ample warning of an impending assault.

The northwestern corner of the map contains a Spanish castle and other structures. Use your trebuchets and battering rams to raze the castle, making sure to protect your siege units with infantry and ranged units. Before advancing northeast into the Spanish army base, move villagers to the gold resource here and begin mining. Protect the resource with towers and walls.

Finish off the Spanish army by heading northeast with your military and siege units. Expect the Spanish to counterattack with paladin and Conquistador cavalry. Use pikemen for their bonuses against cavalry units. Clear out the Spanish army town center and second castle. Once the army resigns, destroy the gate leading across the southern bridge back to Tenochtitlan. Heal your military units with monks and repair battering rams and trebuchets with villagers.

Tlaxcala, positioned along the western side of the map, should be your second target. Reinforce your army with your forward base in the northwest corner. Check your naval units protecting Tenochtitlan's eastern shoreline and make sure that the Elite Turtle Ships are repaired.

Tip An island filled with gold can be found in the northeast corner of the map, just east of the Spanish army shoreline. After forcing the army to resign, build a transport and send villagers northeast to begin mining here. You should be controlling at least three gold mines at this time, providing plenty of resources for expensive unit upgrades and reinforcing your military and navy.

Proceed across the bridges on the western side of the map. The entrance to Tlaxcala contains a town and a castle. Use trebuchets to destroy both structures while remaining out of their defensive fire range. Destroying the Tlaxcala structures triggers Tlaxcalan Jaguar and eagle warriors to attack. Use your infantry, ranged, and cavalry units to repel the attack.

Continue into the Tlaxcalan base and concentrate on military units and structures. You'll find the town center and another castle in the southern portion of the base. Clear out the remaining buildings with your battering rams and siege units.

Gold resources should be plentiful. Eliminating the Spanish army and Tlaxcala frees up additional gold, so mine all remaining resources and purchase any neglected upgrades (see Figure 5.15). Reinforce your military and consider deleting villagers and exchanging them for more infantry or siege units.

Figure 5.15:
Spend time mining the remaining gold after razing the Spanish army and Tlaxcalan towns.

Assaulting the Spanish navy shoreline is quite difficult. There are several docks here, and the navy will continue to produce war galleys and fire ships to counter any naval attack. Secondly, Spanish cannon towers will rip the Aztec vessels apart.

Instead of building an offensive fleet, produce transports, place your military and siege units inside, and escort them to the southeastern tip of the Spanish navy's island. You can't use the bridge south of Tenochtitlan, as it's broken in the middle. Locate the southeastern tip by scouting the Tlaxcalan shoreline to its southern point and heading east. A cannon tower is located here, but just stay along the southern edge of the map and you'll be safe.

Unload your troops and immediately use siege units against the nearby cannon tower. Proceed northwest and use trebuchets to eliminate the cannon towers along the shoreline. The Spanish navy doesn't offer much military resistance, so stay away from the shoreline and the enemy galleons and cannon galleons. Destroy the Spanish navy town center to force it to resign, and the mission and campaign ends in victory.

Designer's Notes

Although most people are aware that Cortéz defeated the Aztecs, many hold the mistaken belief that the outcome of this conflict was inevitable, that the superior technology of the Spanish would prove unbeatable to the Aztecs. Nothing could be further from the truth. Cortéz's siege of Tenochtitlan is remembered because it was brilliantly orchestrated and fought. The Spanish were outnumbered by orders of magnitude, cut off from their homeland, and fighting in terrain with which they were unfamiliar. Had the Spanish not transmitted disease to the Aztecs and had they not made alliances with the Aztecs' many Mesoamerican enemies, the result of the siege of Tenochtitlan would most likely have been a crushing Spanish defeat.

—Greg Street

Battles of the Conquerors

The Conquerors *assembles an exciting set of historical battles, selectable in any order. For the purposes of this walkthrough, we'll present the battles in chronological order. Because you'll assume control of several different civilizations from both the original* The Age of Kings *and* The Conquerors *expansion pack, reference Chapter 7: Civilization Strengths and Weaknesses for important insight into the technology trees and unique units.*

The complete walkthrough for The Conquerors' *Battles of the Conquerors campaign is detailed in this chapter. Over the course of eight missions, you'll take part in the historical battles of Agincourt, Manzikert, and Hastings and control such famous leaders as Henry V, Admiral Yi Sun Shin, and Erik the Red.*

Battles 1: Tours (732)

Initial Objectives

- Prevent the Moslems from destroying any of your three town centers.
- Capture the six trade carts in the Moors' baggage train and bring them to the cathedral in Tours.

Forces

	Their Stance	Your Stance
Berbers	Enemy	Enemy
Moors	Enemy	Enemy

Map Highlights

The city of Tours is in the northern corner of the map, while the army, consisting of knights, the Frankish King Charles Martel, and other Throwing Axemen, begins in the southeast. You'll find a gold and stone mine to the base's northeastern section and a lumber camp outside the gates to the west. Several flocks of sheep are located to the south. In the southwest, you'll find the Berber camp, while the southern corner of the battleground is home to the Moors.

Battle Plans

The mission begins with Berber light cavalry and Moorish knights and camels destroying Frankish farms, mills, and houses. It's impossible to save all the farms and structures. Locate the Frankish army in the southeastern corner, and then organize the military into two groups. Assign the knights to the first group and the Throwing Axemen and Charles Martel, himself a Throwing Axeman, to the second.

Send the Frankish troops up the eastern side of the map. As they move, focus on the three herds of sheep located just south of the Frankish village gates. You're in control of the sheep, so simply select them and move them into the village, next to the town center surrounded by villagers (see Figure 6.1). Next, select the town center and produce four more villagers.

Tip While you move the Frankish army from the southeast corner to the Frankish village in the north, scout the island you'll pass through to locate gold deposits. When you deplete the gold inside your walls, send villagers here to build a new mining camp.

When the sheep arrive, begin harvesting food with your active villagers, then build farms when the sheep are gone. Assign newly created villagers to a second duty, moving some to the lumber camp located west of the city gates and others to the gold and stone mines in the northeastern corner of the map.

Once this task is finished, turn back to your military. Locate the bridge across the central river and head toward the Frankish wall. The Berber and Moorish cavalry units destroying the Frankish farmlands will eventually assault the Frankish village in the northern corner. Move your soldiers inside the village and spread out the axemen along the walls in the western part of the town (throughout this mission, the eastern walls don't come under serious attack).

Figure 6.1:
Obtain the Frankish sheep before they're captured by enemy troops.

Tip After the initial assault, you need to attack the Berber town or the Moors will become too big a threat. If left alone, they can advance to the Imperial Age within 20 minutes. Attack the stables near the far western bridge with all your knights. It's possible to destroy their three stables, three siege workshops, barracks, and town center before they intervene. They won't surrender until you eliminate their last villager, but this effectively takes them out of the picture.

You may need to venture outside with cavalry and Throwing Axemen to eliminate all the raiding parties—just be ready to retreat and have a monk heal injured troops so you don't incur losses. Continue producing villagers and assign them to chopping wood and mining gold and stone.

You're fairly safe inside the city walls. Though the Berbers and Moors will attack with infantry and cavalry, it is quite difficult to penetrate the durable stone walls. Your priority has to be advancing to Castle Age.

As soon as you have enough food and gold, advance to Castle Age. As you're waiting to advance, select the blacksmith and research attack and armor upgrades.

Once you have the stone, build a castle near the city gates, where it will serve as additional defense. Continue to mine stone so you can build a second castle for stronger defense and quicker Throwing Axemen production.

Although Berber and Moorish raiders will likely attack, keep your troops inside city gates and allow your castles, towers, and Throwing Axemen to pummel the attackers from a distance. Keep your troops inside the Frankish base and build food and gold reserves until you can advance to the Imperial Age (see Figure 6.2). Be sure to research resource gathering technologies.

Figure 6.2:
Position your castle and towers near the Frankish walls to hold off attacking Berber and Moorish units.

As you deplete the Frankish resources, send villagers across the bridge to the southeast and mine the gold on the island to the west. Build a castle and walls to protect the villagers from rogue Moorish attackers, or just block off the bridge with walls and a tower (move the miners into the tower when necessary).

Once you've reached the Imperial Age (you should do so within 45 minutes of game time) and possess an impressive stock of resources, prepare for your assault against the Berbers and Moors. Your ultimate objective lies in Poitiers, the Moorish village in the southern corner, where six Moorish trade carts must be captured and escorted back to the Frankish cathedral.

Hit your population limit by creating an army of paladins, pikemen, Elite Throwing Axemen, battering rams, and trebuchets or bombard cannons. If you already

have ample resources, consider deleting some villagers to produce more military units. Include a couple of monks in your army for healing wounded Frankish troops or converting Berber and Moorish units. Continue to gather resources should you need to reinforce your army.

> **Tip** Since you begin the campaign in the Feudal Age, most of the unit upgrades and improvements aren't purchased. It can be quite costly if you attempt to research and upgrade each technology, so choose only the upgrades that will counter the cavalry-heavy army of the Berbers and Moors. Research paladins at the stable, pikemen at the barracks, and Bearded Axe and Elite Throwing Axemen at the castle.

Designer's Notes

Armies of the swift and deadly Moorish cavalry swept across the Pyrenees into southern France in the early eighth century. The Moorish armies captured and looted several European towns by the time they reached Poitiers. There they halted for a time before moving on to take the city of Tours. Eudo, the longtime rival of Frankish King Charles Martel, met his rival's army as it returned from fighting in Germany and warned him of the Moslem advance. As much as an army may sneak, Martel's forces snuck to the south of Tours hoping to catch the train of supplies and loot strung out behind the Moslem line of advance. Fearing for that train, the Moslem general Abd er-Rahman withdrew to near Poitiers where the quicksilver forces of his cavalry met the more ponderous and undisciplined forces of Martel's knights. After twenty years of facing the Moslems, Martel saw victory not in facing cavalry with cavalry, but in presenting a strong line of infantry that effectively blunted the teeth of the swift Moorish cavalry. Abd died in the ensuing battle, and his disheartened forces withdrew across the Pyrenees. Coupled with the Byzantines successfully staving off the siege of Constantinople 14 years prior, the Moslem threat to Christian Europe was ended.

—Karen Sparks

The Berber and Moorish bases shouldn't offer much resistance against your organized army. Attack the Berber town first, then Poitiers moments after—when the Moors have sent reinforcements to Berber. Use your trebuchets, bombard cannons, and

battering rams to raze the Berber and Moorish bases. Protect siege units with your cavalry and infantry. Reinforce your casualties by continuing to produce paladins, pikemen, and Elite Throwing Axemen.

You'll find the Moorish trade carts in the southern section of the Moorish base. Approach the trade carts to capture them, then select the carts and escort them back to the Frankish village. Place them inside the flags just in front of the cathedral and the mission ends in victory.

Battles 2: Vindlandsaga (1000)

Initial Objectives

- ⚜ Erik the Red must survive.
- ⚜ Transport Erik the Red west across the ocean to the New World.

Forces

	Their Stance	Your Stance
British	Enemy	Enemy
Greenland	Enemy	Enemy
Skraelings	Enemy	Enemy

Map Highlights

Erik the Red and the Vikings begin with a small Dark Age village in the southeastern section of the map. The British camp lies to the southwest and can only be reached by transport. This will be necessary to acquire the British gold reserves. Greenland can be found in the northern section of the map. The Skraelings, who occupy the New World, are located in the northwest. A dangerous section of ocean is situated between the southern tip of Greenland and the bottom edge of the map. Viking ships that pass through this stretch of water (identifiable by its dragon icon on the overhead map) are slowly destroyed. To reach the New World in the northwest, you must control and traverse Greenland.

Battle Plans

You start in the southeastern section of the map with Erik the Red, a few Berserks (the Vikings' unique unit), and a small group of villagers. Resources are scarce on this small island. Deer are the only food source besides farms, and there are no gold deposits. In order to acquire gold, you must conquer the British, who are located on a small island just southwest of the Viking village. While the British island is not well defended, be sure to concentrate first on building your economy before making military preparations (see Figure 6.3).

Figure 6.3:
The British island lies west of the Viking camp.

Produce four more villagers and locate the packs of deer positioned north, south, east, and west from the Viking town center. Instead of killing the deer far from the town center and slowly acquiring food, consider constructing a mill near the deer. At only 100 wood, it's not a significant investment; furthermore, when the supply of deer is exhausted, you can plant farms around each mill to increase food production. Also build a lumber camp near a section of dense forest and assign a couple of villagers to chop wood to meet the cost of your mills and future farms. As soon as possible, begin mining the stone in the southeastern corner of the map. You'll need it for a castle.

Scattered wolves can pose problems for your weak villagers. Researching loom at your town center will improve the villagers' fighting skill. At some point, you'll hear the howl of the "king of the wolves." Grab your troops and Erik the Red and scout the outskirts of the Viking village to locate and eliminate Ornlu. Be careful, as he has 400 hit points and an attack of 50!

Tip A sneaky tactic is to build a monastery, get a few monks, and convert the Berserk in the raiding parties. It also makes the raid on the British easier if you send a galley to attack their fishing boats early.

Once you have your economy rolling (farms planted and plenty of villagers chopping wood and mining stone), construct a barracks and advance to the Feudal Age. Don't worry too much about military upgrades; instead, improve resource production

through technologies at the mill and mining/lumber camps. Once in the Feudal Age, construct an archery range and stable far inland, and docks on the western shoreline.

As you near Castle Age advancement, Greenland becomes a significant threat, sending longboats and an occasional transport occupied with a few Berserks and swordsmen to the Viking shores. The longboats have incredible range and can strike inland structures. You likely won't be able to repel the longboat attack until you advance to the Castle Age, recover the British gold, and begin production of war galleys.

Designer's Notes

The Sea of Worms, so named for shipworms, or barnacles, spelled ruin for the wooden hulls of Viking longboats. Once the Vikings landed in the New World, they discovered a wooded and fertile land far different from the harshness of Greenland. To their certain dismay, they discovered the land inhabited by a people they called the Skraelings. These inhabitants were so fierce that they drove the Vikings, a fierce people themselves, from Vinland. By the time of Columbus' voyage, the tales and legends of the Viking exploration of the New World had disappeared.

I had been itching to draw something with terrain when Greg and I got stuck for ideas on how to denote the Sea of Worms. The image of a great lurking dragon ready to rend boats formed in my head, followed by some sketching and some trial and error. Greg Streets' friend Ornlu, mighty king of wolves, makes a return appearance to terrorize the small Viking settlement of Eric the Red, which has just emerged from a hard winter.

—*Karen Sparks*

Advance to the Castle Age as soon as possible (trade stone for gold) and place a castle near your docks to prevent access via the ford. Produce a squad of skirmishers and spearmen (both require only food and wood) to counter raiding parties from Greenland that arrive on transport, or use the monk tactic mentioned above. Improve your defending troops by researching the attack and armor upgrades that only cost food.

About 15–20 spearmen, 15–20 skirmishers, the Berserks, and Erik the Red can overrun the British defending force and town center. Load up your transports along the southern edge of the map and send them southwest along the bottom of the map until you reach the British shoreline. Unload and advance along the southern edge until you encounter military units. Send in the skirmishers and follow with the spearmen when you spot an enemy archery range and archers.

Use your transports to send several villagers to the island and then construct a new town center near the gold (see Figure 6.4). Build a castle on either island (both will be attacked by raiding parties from Greenland). Select your military structures to upgrade attack and armor skills, but conserve enough gold to build a naval fleet.

Figure 6.4:
Build a forward base and docks on the conquered British isle.

Note Destroy the British markets to capture their gold reserves. One market nets 1,100 gold, and the other 600.

Build docks on the western shore of the British island. Upgrade your galleys to war galleys and start construction of 10–12 war galleys to control the shoreline of your two islands. Greenland will continue to send transports from time to time, and it saves aggravation if you can eliminate the transports before they reach the shore. Keep your war galleys together when assaulting Greenland's longboats; they're tough and it's best to save as many war galleys as possible to conserve gold.

To reach the New World, you must travel across Greenland, which lies to the north. The sea west of the British island destroys Viking ships within seconds; if you were able to scout the area, you would notice a serpent icon covering the southern ocean section.

With gold and a castle, begin producing Viking Berserks until you have 20–25 of them. Build a siege workshop and construct three or four battering rams. If you run out of gold, simply use the market to trade for it. Construct enough transports to carry your troops and battering rams over, then unload your army on the eastern side of Greenland.

Advance cautiously west and eliminate the swordsmen and Berserks that approach. Send your battering rams against Greenland's military structures, towers, town center, and castle. Use your Berserks to terminate enemy villagers. Be sure to scout the island and eliminate any villagers building new town centers.

Locate the stone resource in the middle of Greenland. Transport villagers here and begin mining; if you need to reinforce troops, collect this stone and trade it for gold at the market. You can also get gold by leaving Greenland's market intact, building your own market and trade carts, and trading.

Tip There are neutral Berserks located around Greenland. Approach them with your own army and they'll join the Viking cause. Once captured, assign the new Berserks to your infantry group.

When you're ready to head to the New World, build a dock on the northwest shore of Greenland. Manufacture enough transports to carry your army over to the New World. You won't need battering rams any longer, so consider replacing them with troops. If you have plenty of resources, consider deleting villagers and replacing them with troops. Save a handful of villagers, though, as you'll need them to establish a base in the New World.

🛡 **New Objective:** Transport Erik the Red to the New World and establish a colony there.

Establishing a colony (building a town center) is tricky given the large Skraeling population. The Skraelings aren't technologically advanced, but have plenty of troops (see Figure 6.5). As soon as you scout west, expect to encounter Woad Raiders and militia in abundance. Make sure you have at least 20–25 Berserks (improved at the blacksmith if resources allow) before landing on the New World shore. You can also build a castle and lure Skraelings into its arrows.

Once you can, build a town center, and the mission ends in victory.

Figure 6.5:
The Skraeling army appears intimidating, but it mostly contains lowly, easily defeated militia.

Battles 3: Hastings (1066)

Initial Objectives

- William the Conqueror must survive.

- Conquer England by destroying the castle of Harold the Saxon.

Forces

	Their Stance	Your Stance
Harald Hardraade	Enemy	Neutral
Saxon Navy	Enemy	Enemy
Harold the Saxon	Enemy	Enemy

Map Highlights

You start in the southeastern corner of the map. Harold the Saxon's village and castle lie across the river to the northwest. Scattered around the map are Saxon navy camps. Towers and several pikemen block the road leading north from the Frankish village. A small Saxon navy camp can be found west of the Frankish base; you'll find an important gold resource here when you're ready to expand. Two more Saxon navy bases rest on either side of Harold the Saxon's castle. The one to the south should be dealt with to advance against Harold the Saxon, while the one to the north can be ignored. Finally, in the northern corner you'll find Harald Hardaade, a potential ally.

Battle Plans

You begin with a handful of Frankish units (light cavalry, knights, villagers, and William the Conqueror). Start chopping lumber with a few villagers and move the others to the eastern outskirts of your village. Here you'll find plentiful shore fishing, so build a mill and start gathering food. Select your town center and produce more villagers, continuing to produce villagers as you stockpile additional food.

There are two gold deposits you can mine. Mine the gold inside the city first, then move the villagers along the eastern shore to the other patch. As you accumulate lumber, start building houses and military structures. Your base is rather tight, so place the houses to the east and the more important structures inside the heart of it (see Figure 6.6).

Figure 6.6:
Place houses in the forest east of the Frankish base.

 **Optional Objective:** Send transports north to pick up Harald Hardraade's Viking Berserks.

At some point early in the mission, Harald Hardraade, located in the northern corner of the map, offers an alliance—simply use the Diplomacy menu to change your stance from neutral to ally. Once allied, you can see Harald's units and buildings. Harald eventually sends a squad of infantry to attack Harold the Saxon's castle.

Unfortunately, Harald's attack ends in disaster when Harold the Saxon's castle and defenses annihilate the Vikings' small infantry force. As a result, Harald states that while he won't be sending more troops to attack, you're welcome to transport his Viking Berserks to the Frankish base and use them for an assault. Harald's Viking Berserks are well protected inside his base, so leave them there until you're ready to assault Harold the Saxon. Do, however, send over a transport and you'll get 1,000 gold.

Your first target should be the Saxon navy base southwest of the Frankish castle. It's likely that the Saxon swordsmen, pikemen, and battering rams located there will attack the Frankish village. If you've enclosed the town in walls, your towers and Throwing Axemen can eliminate the force without much trouble. If not, you need to be prepared with more than your default units. Select your military structures and produce a mixture of infantry and cavalry units. Don't hesitate to produce these units now, as unit upgrades will be applied in the future.

Assemble a mixed group of infantry and cavalry, and add some battering rams. You should hit the population limit. Advance along the road toward the Saxon navy base to the southwest. Follow the road north of the mountain plateau, and cross the bridge that leads into the Saxon navy village.

Expect light resistance if you were previously attacked by the Saxons; if not, you'll encounter infantry and pikemen. Use your ranged units to weaken the Saxon infantry and finish them off with your cavalry and infantry group. Send in the battering rams to level the Saxon towers, town center, and military structures (see Figure 6.7).

> **Tip** The Saxon navy outpost to the southwest of the Frankish castle is located just to the west of a gold deposit. Towers and pikemen protect the gold. Send your infantry and battering rams to clear the area, then move villagers over to begin mining.

Your next target should be the Saxon navy base that lies across the river northwest of the base you just conquered. This Saxon base can be found just southeast of Harold the Saxon's castle. Harold's troops will come to assist in this battle, so you'll need a sizable force in order to take and hold the position. The first order of business, however, is to produce a naval fleet to protect your transports and wrestle the shoreline from Saxon navy control.

Build a few docks along the western shoreline of the Frankish island. Research appropriate upgrades for your naval vessels and produce around 10–12 galleons. Send them along the river toward the west. Here you'll encounter a Saxon dock and several vessels, including fire ships and war galleys. Engage the fire ships first, then finish off the war galleys. Stay clear of the tower protecting the docks. Eliminate any ships produced by the Saxon dock and then target the structure itself. This is made even more effective if you transport troops to the Isle of Wight and destroy Chatham with ground forces.

If you haven't already, it's time to acquire Harald Hardraade's Berserks. Send a transport to the southern edge of Harald's island. Board the Viking Berserks and carry them over to Normandy.

Figure 6.7:
Level the Saxon navy base southwest of the Frankish village to gain access to additional gold.

Designer's Notes

By the time Edward the Confessor died early in 1066, the proper succession to the throne of England was muddled. Harold the Saxon held the throne by right of actually sitting on it. The King of Norway, Harald Hardraade, wanted land in England, not the crown, but when rebuffed by Harold the Saxon, he sought the crown itself. William, Duke of Normandy, once named Edward's successor, claimed his right to the throne. Confusing matters further, Harold the Saxon had pledged to forfeit the crown to William after being shipwrecked off the coast of Normandy and finding himself somewhat at the mercy of the young duke.

We kept adding enemies to this scenario. In earlier versions, the Saxons were content to wait in England while the Norman player built up an army of vast size by exploiting every resource available in France. We added a Saxon navy, and later some Saxon interlopers, to keep the player on his or her toes while building their forces.

—*Karen Sparks*

Produce enough transports to ferry your entire military over to the Isle of Wight. You should have little trouble razing the Saxon navy base. Expect enemy reinforcements to arrive from the northwest, however, as Harold the Saxon will send troops. Include a monk in your party to heal wounded between combat (see Figure 6.8). Destroy the Saxon navy base, especially military structures, so the town no longer poses a threat and you can begin your assault on Harold the Saxon's castle.

Figure 6.8:
Monks are invaluable, both to heal wounded troops and convert Harold the Saxon's forces.

Annihilating Harold the Saxon's castle requires siege units (battering rams and bombard cannons work best) and the patience to protect those siege units from constant enemy attacks. Position your infantry and ranged units in front of the siege weapons and intercept any enemy troops headed for them. Destroy the gate and walls enclosing the castle. The mission ends in victory once the castle is destroyed.

Battles 4: Manzikert (1071)

Initial Objectives

- Receive tributes from the Themes of Galatia by capturing their town center.
- Receive tributes from the Themes of Pisidia by capturing their town center.
- Receive tributes from the Themes of Cappadocia by capturing their town center.
- Defeat the Byzantine army.

Forces

	Their Stance	Your Stance
Cappadocia	Enemy	Enemy
Pisidia	Enemy	Enemy
Galatia	Enemy	Enemy
Byzantine Army	Enemy	Enemy
Persians	Enemy	Enemy

Map Highlights

You start in the Turkish village in the southern corner of the map. The nearest city, Cappadocia, is located just north of the village. Pisidia is located north of Cappadocia and in the center of the map. You'll find Galatia just above Pisidia. This Saracen town is in the northwest corner of the map. The well-protected Byzantine army base is on a plateau in the east.

Battle Plans

The Turks lack villagers, so in order to gather resources, you must guide your army into several cities and capture their town centers. Once you're in control of each city, its villagers periodically pay tribute in the form of valuable wood, food, and gold, which you can use to reinforce your military.

You begin the mission with swordsmen, light cavalry, camels, and cavalry archers. Organize your military into two groups, placing the infantry and melee cavalry into one and the cavalry archers into the second (see Figure 6.9).

You have a limited amount of resources at your disposal. The first city to assault, Cappadocia, lies just north of the Turkish base. It's protected by several towers, which could pose problems for your ground attack. Use available resources to produce two or three battering rams. Use your remaining resources to research bonuses to attack or armor strengths, and some hand cannoneers are also useful.

Once you've prepared your assault group, head northwest from the Turkish base and you'll encounter Byzantine Cataphracts (anti-infantry cavalry units). Weaken them with your cavalry archers and finish them off with your cavalry (preferably camels). This event triggers the launching of an assault group from the Byzantine army in the east. A group of Byzantine Cataphracts, swordsmen, pikemen, and battering rams accompanied by monks advances from its eastern base through the map's center and down the western side to the Turkish base.

> **Tip** Garrison infantry troops inside the battering rams to speed them up. You'll encounter multiple towers at once when assaulting Cappadocia, so it's important that the battering rams move as quickly as possible to minimize damage.

Before you advance into Cappadocia, deal with the Byzantine attack, which you'll encounter on the western side of the map if you maintain your position above the Turkish base. With the Byzantine attack thwarted, proceed east into Cappadocia, using your battering rams with their garrisoned units against the gates. Once you get a unit to the town center, you capture the town, so don't destroy any towers on your way in.

By capturing Cappadocia, you gain a university, stable, and blacksmith in addition to the structures at your home base. The villagers, mostly located in the southeastern portion of the town, continue their work. You'll receive periodic tributes of wood, food, and gold resources, which you might want to use for upgrading to heavy camels. When you receive the first tribute, produce additional infantry units and leave them in Cappadocia to protect your new city from Byzantine raiding parties.

Figure 6.9:
Prepare your military by separating melee and ranged units into two groups.

Note When you capture Pisidia, you gain towers, an archery range, barracks, stable, and a siege workshop in addition to the tribute. It's also a great forward base to use in reinforcing your military, as the Turkish base you started from is too distant to help in your struggle with the Byzantine army.

Exit Cappadocia to the west and advance along the path to the north. You'll encounter the town of Pisidia next. Assemble your troops and head up the ramp into the settlement. Approach and capture the town center, just as you did in Cappadocia. Once it has been seized, you'll begin receiving a tribute from Pisidia. The added resources should allow you to create additional infantry, hand cannoneers, cavalry, and cavalry archers, and to research any military technologies and unit improvements (see Figure 6.10).

Figure 6.10:
Tributes from Pisidia
and Cappadocia offer
resources and
structures.

♦ **Optional Objective:** Destroy the four Persian towers so that your allies can mine their gold.

Once you've captured Pisidia, proceed to the Saracen town in the northwest corner of the battleground. If you can destroy the towers surrounding the Persian gold, you will receive additional tributes from Pisidia's citizens.

Assemble your battering rams (build more at your siege workshop in Pisidia if necessary) and eliminate the towers. One Persian tower will be unreachable by ram, so construct a few mangonels and use them to eliminate it. Once all towers are destroyed, the objective is completed and you'll receive additional gold tributes. Continue to reinforce your military with each tribute received. Maximize your population with infantry, cavalry, cavalry archers, and four to five battering rams. Spend additional resources on improving and upgrading your units at their respective military structures; make sure you upgrade to siege rams.

Return to Pisidia and exit via the ramp to the northwest. Galatia lies to the north. It's well defended with two castles flanking the main gate, so keep your military units at a distance and advance your battering rams with their garrisoned units. The castles will attack the battering rams when you assault the main gate, but if you have at least four of them doing the pounding, you should easily break your way in before suffering losses.

Once the gate is down, race to the town center to capture Galatia. You'll take damage from the castle and towers, but you should have enough resources to replace any casualties. When you capture Galatia, you gain all three Galatian castles.

The Galatian castle can produce trebuchets, perfect for an assault against the Byzantine army's plateau. Build four to six trebuchets, reinforce any military casualties, and advance slowly toward the eastern corner of the map. You'll encounter a Byzantine castle and small camp first. Unpack your trebuchets and use the siege weapon to raze the Byzantine castle (see Figure 6.11). Intercept any Byzantine troops as they emerge to disrupt your siege—hand cannoneers are very effective.

Designer's Notes

Treachery, treachery, and more treachery. Emperor Romanus's lieutenant, Andronicus Ducas, conspired with Empress Eudocia to become Byzantine Emperor. Under his orders, the screening element of the Byzantine army did not report seeing and skirmishing with the light cavalry and cavalry archers of the Seljuk Turks as they advanced. His forces did not turn to fight but kept retreating as the surprised Byzantine army recovered from a Seljuk ambush and turned to face their foe. The Seljuks were able, with light cavalry, cavalry archers, and harrying ambush tactics, to annihilate the Byzantine army in the east. The catastrophic loss at Manzikert all but sealed the doom of the Byzantine Empire. It never again fielded the armies it had in the past, and the Seljuk Turks continued to advance.

—Karen Sparks

Figure 6.11:
A group of trebuchets can lay waste to the Byzantine base in a matter of minutes.

Continue to the east, destroying the Byzantine military structures, castles, and town center first. Send your infantry against the Byzantine villagers and cavaliers, hand cannoneers, and champions to protect the trebuchets as you advance through the base. Once you've destroyed the Byzantine town center and marketplace (or eliminated all villagers), the mission ends in victory.

Battles 5: Agincourt (1415)

Initial Objective

⬥ King Henry V must survive.

Forces

	Their Stance	Your Stance
French Knights	Enemy	Enemy
Voyeni	Enemy	Enemy
Amiens	Enemy	Enemy
Frevent	Enemy	Enemy
Harfleur	Enemy	Enemy

Map Highlights

The English army starts in the southern corner just outside the walls surrounding Harfleur. Your eventual goal, the Frankish knights and village, lies to the north. Just east of your starting location is the town of Voyeni. Amiens can be found just south of Voyeni along the southeastern edge of the map. Just north of Voyeni is Frevent. Follow the road north from Frevent to reach the French knight base and the transport that will take King Henry V back to English soil.

Battle Plans

Harfleur knights storm out the city gates and attack your swordsmen and cavalry units as soon as the mission begins. Immediately select all your troops, assign them to stand ground, and retreat.

Select your swordsmen and cavalry and immediately move them back toward your Longbowmen. Attack the Harfleur knights emerging from the city gate with your infantry and knights while Longbowmen finish them off. You can also use the two monks at your disposal to convert Harfleur knights.

⬥ **New Objective:** King Henry V must return home to England.

Once you've eliminated the Harfleur counterattack, proceed north, and heal wounded troops. You may encounter swordsmen, archers, and spearmen from Amiens and Voyeni entering from the north and east. You shouldn't have trouble defeating them with Longbowmen (see Figure 6.12).

Your eventual goal is the docks along the northern river. A transport there will take Henry V back to England, but to reach the docks you must first travel through the dangerous French knight base.

Figure 6.12: Concentrate the firepower of the English Longbowmen on enemy military troops.

> **Tip** You also begin the mission with two battering rams for use against enemy structures. Garrison infantry troops inside the rams to increase their speed and damage to buildings. Your small reserve of gold and wood can be used to repair damaged rams, but first you'll need the services of a villager. Convert one with a monk if repairs are necessary.

Advance north from the Harfleur gates to the town of Voyeni to the east. Scout the outskirts of Voyeni to discover villagers gathering resources. Use your monks to convert a villager, then use him to repair damage to your battering ram. As you won't be able to gather additional wood or gold, you can no longer repair the battering rams once your stores run out.

♥ **Optional Objective:** Destroy the university in Voyeni to recover and learn from the great texts stored there.

When you enter Voyeni, you're presented with an optional objective—to level the town's university and gain technology. Proceed east into Voyeni, making sure to avoid the Voyeni castle to the south.

The Voyeni university is located just southeast of the mill and planted farms. Protect your battering rams with your Longbowmen, then send in the battering rams with their garrisoned units to raze the school. Once it's destroyed, you receive "Greek fire," which supplies devastating flame arrows to your Longbowmen.

Though you could proceed north from Voyeni through Frevent and eventually to the French knight base, it's wiser to investigate the town of Amiens, located to the south. Here you can complete another optional objective to further improve your units and eliminate a dangerous adversary.

🛡 **Optional Objective:** Destroy the blacksmith in Amiens to recover armor and weapons.

There's an entrance to Amiens located southeast of Harfleur, but it's protected by towers and blocked by stone. Avoid it and head to the northern entrance east of Voyeni. To reach it, you must advance east through Voyeni and deal with the castle, just south of the university you just destroyed.

To safely destroy the castle, keep your Longbowmen, infantry, and cavalry units at a distance and send in your battering rams with their garrisoned units. Once you're inflicting damage to the castle, move in your melee and ranged units to assist. Keep monks busy healing wounded troops. Raze the castle and continue out of Voyeni to the east.

> **Note** Destroying the Amiens' blacksmith nets you improved military armor and boosts cavalry and infantry attack. (+1/+2 armor, +2 attack.) Though it's not vital to complete the mission, you'll face a tough battle against the French knights at the end of the mission. Any unit improvements will help you survive.

Head southwest and locate the entrance to Amiens. Use battering rams to open the city gates and destroy the guard towers, then send in a scout to locate the blacksmith, just above the horse pen. Avoid approaching the Amiens military structures and keep your Longbowmen active eliminating any enemy swordsmen or archers that approach. Raze the Amiens' blacksmith with your battering rams. Exit the town once the structure is destroyed.

Proceed north around Voyeni and into the small town of Fervent. You aren't offered any optional objectives inside the settlement, but you're told you can safely rest wounded troops. Use your monks to heal wounded troops, then head north along the road. You'll approach an area of muddy grasslands separating the northern and southern sections of road. The French knights await you just north of the mud.

Send a scout to lure the French knights to your formation of Longbowmen. As the knights (and one paladin) get close, send in your own cavalry and swordsmen. Continue to pound the enemy cavalry with your Longbowmen and attempt conversions with your monks (see Figure 6.13).

Figure 6.13:
The French knights are intimidating. Keep your Longbowmen back and weaken them before sending in your own cavalry.

Stay put once you've eliminated the knights and spend time healing wounded troops. The French will periodically send additional knights, so keep your Longbowmen in formation and terminate them as they arrive.

After you're healed, proceed north into the French base, avoiding the towers and castle. You can use the battering rams to eliminate the towers, but you're likely to sustain damage as multiple towers target you at the same time. You're told to free the trebuchet on the eastern side of the French base—do so, then use it against the towers.

Designer's Notes

Agincourt was an unexpected victory for Henry V. After defeating the French, Henry V did not press his victory, but rather returned to England. Had he stayed and fought, winning more decisive victories, would the words of a young peasant girl 14 years later have been enough to rally the beleaguered French to victory, or would Henry have already claimed the French throne? Agincourt and Poitiers are largely remembered for the triumph of British longbows over French knights. Of course, the knights were massively outnumbered and had to trudge up a muddy hill to meet the British archers. If anything, Agincourt is known today because it was an upset that marked a shift in power—much like the English defeat of the Spanish Armada and the Roman defeat of the Carthaginians during the Punic Wars.

—Greg Street

Follow the path through the base to the western side. Use battering rams and your melee units to destroy the French structures blocking the path to the docks. Approach the docks and gain use of the transport.

🛡 **New Objective:** Henry V must set foot on English soil.

Place King Henry V (and other military units if you desire) into the transport and hug the northern edge of the map to avoid nearby enemy towers. Head southwest until you spot the small strip of land and gate revealed on the overhead map. Unload the transport and move Henry through the gate to complete the mission.

Battles 6: Lepanto (1571)

Initial Objective

🛡 Complete and then defend your wonder from the Turkish navy for 200 years.

Forces

	Their Stance	Your Stance
Turks	Enemy	Enemy
Greek Village	Neutral	Neutral

Map Highlights

The Spanish base is located along the northern edge of the map. A potential ally, the Greek village, can be found in the northwest. To the south you'll find the enemy Turks. Three islands filled with gold and stone resources are scattered throughout the body of water separating the Spanish and Turkish shores. One island lies to the east and is protected by Turkish towers, another island can be found to the west and is protected by Greek walls and towers, while a final island lies to the south and is also protected by Turkish towers.

Battle Plans

The majority of the Spanish villagers start around the wonder-in-progress you must protect. However, finishing the wonder should be secondary to producing your naval and military force. Assign a couple of villagers to work on the wonder and the others to chop trees.

The Spanish base is divided into two main sections. The eastern half includes the farms and houses, and the western half features the military structures, wonder, and docks. Pan to the eastern section and use the town center here to produce additional villagers. Assign those villagers to the farms that surround the town center.

Select a Spanish dock and upgrade your war galleys to galleons. Use other docks and begin producing additional naval vessels. Assemble your war galleys, fire ships, and cannon galleons and steer them slightly north of their starting position. Position them off the shoreline, between the western and eastern sections of the Spanish base, and spread them out on patrol (see Figure 6.14).

Figure 6.14:
Scout the body of water between the Spanish and Turkish bases to spot Turkish transports.

Tip Gold is scarce as the mission begins. As neither Spanish village contains a gold resource, you must use the market to trade wood or food for gold. Concentrate on defending the Spanish shore from Turkish naval attack, but find time to transport miners to the gold-rich islands south of both Spanish villages.

Prepare to intercept Turkish transports, which begin about 10 minutes into the mission and are filled with 20 Elite Janissaries and bombard cannons. It's imperative that you eliminate the transports before they reach land, as you want to hold on to your troops as long as possible.

The Turkish navy closely follows the transports—prepare to deal with galleons, elite cannon galleons, and fast fire ships. Once you've defeated the transports, concentrate your firepower on the fire ships. Locate the heavy demolition ships near the Spanish docks and use them against Turkish naval formations. Weakening the Turkish navy with your demolition ships is key to surviving the tough initial battle.

Designer's Notes

Don Juan of Austria, a Spaniard, led the Christian forces at the Battle of Lepanto. The Turks were fighting losing battles on almost every front of their empire, but it was here where they lost thousands of irreplaceable veteran composite archers in a ferocious sea battle. I kidded with Sandy Petersen while discussing the "Battles of the Conquerors" campaign histories that all of them had some element of treachery involved. Truly, many did. Lepanto stands out because the Venetians and Spanish, rightfully mistrustful of one another and each expecting betrayal, were not betrayed. They were likely more shocked by this than by their victory over the larger Turkish force.

And larger it is—in this scenario, the Turks start out with 16 packed transports! That comprises 320 units alone, without even considering their fleet. I was originally worried that all of the units would make the scenario an unplayable slide show, but units in a transport have little impact on scenario performance. Not all of these transports will come into play on easier difficulties, but harder settings make it a real nail-biter to see if the Spanish forces can hang on.

—Karen Sparks

Send damaged Spanish vessels back to the shore and order a villager to repair them. Select the Spanish university and research chemistry to improve the galleon missile attack.

Keep Spanish naval units scattered and on patrol off the shoreline near the center of the map. Defeat any approaching Turkish navy units, but pay special attention to any transports that the Turks periodically send to the western and eastern Spanish shores, as you lack ground support to handle the Janissaries they carry. Use naval vessels to intercept the transports until you stockpile enough gold and other resources to produce a military strong enough to hold off the Turkish ground assaults.

Once you've produced a strong Spanish naval presence, scout the island south of your town center and farmlands. Use nearby Spanish cannon galleons for the attack. Send villagers over and begin mining gold. Protect the island from Turkish naval reprisals, but don't neglect any approaching transports.

◆ **Optional Objective:** Give the Greeks a tribute of 800 gold so they will ally with you.

Once you control the eastern island, investigate the western island just south of the Spanish docks. The Greeks control it and have enclosed the gold and stone mines with walls and towers. Send units from the western Spanish village to the Greek village in the northwest and initiate contact.

The Greeks offer an alliance if you pay them a tribute of 800 gold. If you don't have enough gold, trade for it. Once allied, the Greeks will assist in protecting your western Spanish village (don't expect much help, though), allow you to mine the gold on the southern island and in their northwestern village, and periodically give you 400 gold and 300 wood. Send transports of villagers over to the Greek island and start mining gold.

With a sizable navy and consistent gold coming in, begin producing ground forces to help defend the Spanish wonder from attack. Upgrade your units at their respective military structures and use the barracks to research attack and armor bonuses. Produce a mixed force of infantry, ranged, and cavalry units, and use the Spanish castle to produce Conquistadors (research Elite Conquistadors as soon as you have the resources). Use a siege workshop and build scorpions and mangonels to further defend against a Turkish onslaught.

> **Tip** The Turkish transports emerge from a cove on the southeastern section of the map. Position the Spanish fleet around the cove and intercept enemy transports as soon as they emerge. Continue to reinforce your fleet by producing galleons at the Spanish docks.

The Turks will send transports to the western and eastern town approaches; it's important to use your navy to scout well and either intercept the transports or at least know the Turkish transports' destinations. Though you may feel the eastern base isn't worth defending (since the wonder is located to the west), protecting your farms and houses is very important. If you lose your homes, you can't produce more units and must spend time and wood rebuilding the Spanish houses.

With an adequate Spanish navy and ground military assembled, assign more villagers to the wonder. Once it's constructed, you must defend it for 200 game years (see Figure 6.15).

Expect the Turkish transport attacks to intensify at this point. If one happens to reach the Spanish shore, position your navy close by so the galleons can assist in defending the town. Mine (or trade for) stone and build towers and walls around the wonder as a last line of defense.

The mission concludes in victory once you have defended the Spanish wonder for the full 200 years.

Figure 6.15:
Once the Spanish villagers finish the wonder, you must keep it intact for 200 game years.

Battles 7: Kyoto (1582)

Initial Objective

⬥ Rescue your lord, Nobunaga, from Kyoto.

Forces

	Their Stance	Your Stance
Osaka	Enemy	Enemy
Kyoto	Enemy	Enemy
Nobunaga	Ally	Ally
Hyogo	Enemy	Enemy

Map Highlights

Kyoto is along the northeastern side of the map. In the southwestern corner of the battlefield, Nobunaga's player-allied transports deliver a small military and villager force to nearby Osaka. Hyogo, the nearest enemy village, can be found north of Osaka (in the northwest corner of the battleground).

Battle Plans

When the mission begins, you can see Lord Nobunaga in his Kyoto prison (check the overhead map). There are four Samurai (the Japanese unique unit) with Lord Nobunaga, but all are wounded and don't survive the attack, which comes almost immediately.

⬥ **New Objective:** Establish a base from which to attack Kyoto.

The first transport supplies cavaliers, Samurai, and hand cannoneers. Assign the cavaliers and Samurai to the first attack group and place the hand cannoneers in the second. Head northeast and approach the walls surrounding Osaka. Direct your units to attack the wall, and a transport promptly delivers petards to do the job for you. All you have to do then is walk through the gap they create. Proceed north first to capture four bombard cannons, assigning them to a third group.

Designer's Notes

I had originally designed this scenario as a rescue mission that goes afoul. The player, as Hideyoshi, must hurry to rescue Nobunaga, who is being held hostage in Kyoto. Midway through the scenario, Nobunaga is executed, and then the player exacts revenge on the traitors in Kyoto. It all worked fine until Microsoft Japan notified us that samurai never took prisoners. It was much more prestigious to deliver an enemy's head to one's lord, so there was no concept of hostage taking or ransom in feudal Japan. Oops. We hastily reworked the beginning of the scenario so that Nobunaga could fall in battle (though most Japanese schoolchildren could probably tell you that he actually took his own life).

—*Greg Street*

Tip Monitor your new bombard cannons carefully. Though you want to knock out the Osaka buildings, you shouldn't destroy the walls surrounding your new base.

Approach the Osaka stone wall to the east and use the bombard cannons to open a section of it. Send your troops through and capture the town center (or shoot it once with the bombard cannon). Another Nobunaga transport now arrives at the shore delivering villagers. Assemble the villagers and escort them into your new base (see Figure 6.16). Select the town center and create more villagers for planting farms, chopping lumber, and mining gold.

Figure 6.16:
Receive villagers from the Nobunaga transport and start construction of a town center inside the Osaka walls.

New Objective: Destroy all three of Kyoto's castles to punish it for the murder of Lord Nobunaga.

Concentrate on the growth of your economy. Produce additional villagers to mine the gold west of your town center. Locate the stone resource to the east and mine it to produce protective towers, gates, and a castle. Build military structures—barracks, archery range, stable, and siege workshop—as soon as possible. Also build a blacksmith and begin researching attack and armor improvements.

Though you aren't in immediate danger, you should start producing troops to prepare for an assault on Kyoto. Kyoto possesses all the relics on the map, and it won't be long (20–25 minutes into the game) before its monks transfer them to the Kyoto monastery. Once they do, you have 300 game years to break its control over the relics or the mission ends in failure.

Produce a mixture of infantry, cavalry, and ranged units. Use available resources to upgrade each particular unit at its respective military structure. Select the siege workshop and produce three to five battering rams for use against the Kyoto walls and towers protecting the relic monastery. You must work quickly once Kyoto captures all the relics. If you're in a crunch, build and use a market to trade for specific resources, or concentrate a majority of villagers on particular resources to keep your most needed reserves increasing.

Send a villager to the shoreline north of Osaka. Build a dock here and produce enough transports to carry your military and battering rams to the Kyoto shore. Once in the water, head northwest to Kyoto. Unload the troops and scout ahead. Search the outskirts of the Kyoto base to locate towers positioned just behind a stone wall. Though the towers are imposing, it's a safer point of entry than trying to head through the well-guarded front entrance.

Use your battering rams and bombard cannons to demolish a section of the city's stone wall. Usher your military units and battering rams inside and find the monastery to the north. Move quickly to avoid fire from the towers; destroy the nearest with your battering rams if you're suffering too much damage.

Order all troops to level the monastery and terminate the nearby monks. Once the monastery is destroyed, Kyoto's control over the relic ceases, as does the countdown to your defeat (see Figure 6.17). Move your troops out of Kyoto, as it's unlikely you can mount an effective assault just yet. Instead, return to your own base and continue to bolster your economy and research unit improvements.

Figure 6.17: Destroy the Kyoto monastery to gain control of the relics.

Tip Send five monks when you assault Kyoto's monastery to recover the relics. Use them to grab the relics and take them back to your own monastery. This gives you a gold bonus and ensures that Kyoto can't regain relic control.

Before you mount an assault against Kyoto's castles, deal with the town of Hyogo, located northwest of Osaka. Plentiful gold resources needed for expensive trebuchets, unit upgrades, and technology improvements can be found here.

Heal your wounded troops and repair damaged battering rams and bombard cannons. Reinforce your military with additional infantry, cavalry, and ranged units. Proceed northwest from Osaka to the outskirts of the Hyogo base. Protect your siege weapons with your melee and ranged

units, and intercept any attackers that emerge from Hyogo. Destroy military structures, castles, and town centers first, then attack the villagers and civilian structures.

Once you've leveled Hyogo, you should migrate your villagers to start a new forward base. Kyoto sends naval vessels, including galleons and cannon galleons, into the river south of Osaka, so it's likely that your structures will come under attack. A couple of war galleys and fire ships should repel the attacks. If you prefer to play it safe, move your base into the former Hyogo. Mine the gold there and construct a new town center, castle, and military structures.

Max out your population with infantry, Elite Samurai, cavalry, arbalests, trebuchets, battering rams, and bombard cannons. Produce four to six trebuchets for best results, even though you must protect the expensive siege units from Kyoto's counterattack of pikemen, Samurai, scorpions, and trebuchets. Consider taking villagers along to repair siege units.

Build docks on the eastern shore and produce enough transports to carry your sizable military to the Kyoto base. You should also produce a few war galleys to protect your transports from attack, as you need to make sure the transports reach the Kyoto shore.

Move your troops through the section of wall demolished on the previous attack. Use siege weapons to eliminate the houses and civilian structures located on the northern end of Kyoto. Advance southwest through the base, keeping an eye out for Samurai and scorpions. Intercept the Kyoto Samurai with your own and keep your units in a spread formation to counter the scorpion attack. Send speedy cavalry units to dispatch the Kyoto scorpions.

As you near the Kyoto castles, expect to encounter trebuchets. Target the siege weapons with your own, but also send cavalry units to engage them at close range. Raze the Kyoto castle perched on a plateau and continue your advancement southeast, demolishing military structures as you move (see Figure 6.18).

Leveling Kyoto shouldn't pose much trouble if you keep your siege weapons repaired and defended. Destroying the three castles satisfies all mission requirements, but you should also demolish military structures, including siege workshops, to prevent Kyoto reinforcements from entering the battle.

Figure 6.18:
Use trebuchets to level the Kyoto castles and exact vengeance for the murder of Lord Nobunaga.

Battles 8: Noryang Point (1598)

Initial Objectives

🛡 Prevent the Japanese from destroying the Korean wonder (optional).

🛡 Defend Korea from the Japanese.

Forces

	Their Stance	Your Stance
Japanese Navy	Enemy	Enemy
Chinese	Ally	Ally
Admiral Yi Sun Shin	Ally	Ally
Japanese Raiders	Enemy	Enemy

Map Highlights

The Koreans occupy the middle section of the map and you'll find the Japanese navy across the south. The Japanese Raiders are in the northeast, on the same island as the Koreans. Admiral Yi Sun Shin is located just north of the Koreans, behind a barrier of mountains and forests; you must risk slipping a transport past the Japanese Raiders to reach Admiral Yi's land. A small Chinese base can be found on an island west of the Korean stronghold.

153

Battle Plans

A hectic start makes defending the Korean wonder difficult. The wonder is located in the northeastern section of the Korean city, while the Korean navy, a mixture of war galleys, cannon galleys, and fire ships, starts to the southwest. The wonder will be under attack from Japanese galleons, elite cannon galleons, and fast fire ships almost immediately. Select the Korean fleet and assign the ships to your first attack group, then steer it toward the Japanese attackers.

It's very difficult to save the Korean wonder; insufficient defensive towers and the overpowering Japanese elite cannon galleons usually spell doom for the structure. Saving it isn't critical to mission success, however, so don't worry if the wonder falls to Japanese naval attack. Remember, though, that you can order castles to fire at specific ships.

Keep the Korean naval fleet together as you approach the Japanese ships. Eliminate the Japanese fast fire ships first, as they are particularly dangerous. If the wonder is destroyed, the Japanese fleet begins to move south along the shore to the Korean docks. Concentrate the Korean fleet's fire on a specific Japanese ship until it's sunk, then keep moving from ship to ship until the attackers are destroyed (see Figure 6.19).

Figure 6.19: Demolish the Japanese fleet before it assaults the Korean docks and structures.

Japanese ships will enter from the south and assault the Korean docks. Return your fleet to the docks and eliminate the Japanese ships. Once you've researched galleons, start producing the ships at each of the docks. Keep wood gathering high. Assembling a large naval fleet can be costly, but assigning 15 or more villagers to chopping wood should provide enough resources to keep production moving.

Other methods to improve your ship production and abilities include additional villagers on wood; researching the two-handed saw at the lumber camp to increase wood gathering speed; researching to improve galleon missile strength; researching bodkin arrow and bracer to boost range and attack strength; and positioning a villager next to each dock to repair damaged vessels.

> **Tip** It takes a few moments for your ships to intercept the Japanese fleet. Take the time to upgrade your war galleys to galleons and assign villagers to farming, gold mining, and chopping lumber. Concentrate on producing more galleons to defend the Korean shore and worry about assembling ground troops later.

Keep the Korean shoreline scouted to pinpoint the location of Japanese ships and transports. Position galleons throughout the ocean separating the Korean and Japanese shores to maintain line-of-sight awareness of enemy fleet movements. If you spot Japanese ships, move your fleet to intercept.

Once you've manufactured a large Korean navy (15–20 ships), you should concentrate on defending against a ground attack by Japanese Raiders that will come from the northeast section of the map. Send villagers to repair the walls and towers located northeast of the Korean base (where, unless you got lucky early on, your wonder used to be). Mine additional stone (located near the Korean gold mine) and build additional towers northwest of your base. Research ballistics and bombard towers to further bolster defenses.

New Objective: Find Admiral Yi and learn of his secret weapon.

At some point you will be notified about Admiral Yi, who reportedly possesses a secret weapon that might prove useful for the Koreans. Though you could scout north of the Korean base, you won't be able to reach Admiral Yi's camp, as forest and mountain cliffs block the route.

In order to reach Admiral Yi, you must commandeer a transport located in the Japanese Raider base, positioned northeast of the Korean camp. You should already be preparing for a ground attack, so select your military structures and begin upgrading units. Start producing infantry, ranged, and cavalry units if you haven't already done so, and use the blacksmith to research attack and armor bonuses. Construct a siege workshop and produce battering rams (or research capped rams) to compliment your cannon galleon's attack against the Japanese Raider towers and structures.

Designer's Notes

Hideyoshi, who was the good guy in the previous scenario, was so successful in unifying Japan that he then set about conquering Japan's neighbors, with Korea first in line. Fortunately for the Koreans, their naval technology was a step ahead of the Japanese. Admiral Yi built only something like six Turtle Ships, yet they were more than capable of routing the entire Japanese navy. The challenge in making this scenario was denying the player the ability to build Turtle Ships until he or she has found Admiral Yi. We did this by denying the player the ability to build castles. Once Admiral Yi's castles are found, a section of forest mysteriously vanishes, giving the War Wagons a shortcut back to the Korean town. We also used vanishing terrain to prevent the player from finding Yi's Turtle Ships by sea—a wall of rocks goes away after Yi is located.

—Greg Street

Tip Acquiring Admiral Yi's "secret weapon" provides three Korean castles in his base, in addition to the weapon itself, the Korean unique War Wagon unit. Build two transports immediately. Soon, the Chinese make a gift of about 20 units.

The Japanese Raiders will send a mixed force to assault the Korean base. Your towers should hold them off as you move your own military to intercept them. Knock out the Japanese battering rams before they can destroy your towers and structures, then continue into the northeast section of the map. Remember to protect your battering rams from Japanese infantry and cavalry units as you move the siege units against the enemy's towers and structures.

Once you've cleared out the Japanese presence, locate the transport in the small waterway west of the destroyed base. Place a unit inside and move across to Admiral Yi's shore. Unload the transport and navigate the unit into his base. Move it along the northern edge of the map and locate three Elite Turtle Ships that you'll gain once you get close enough. Select the ships and move them west out of Admiral Yi's territory, pausing to assign them to your naval fleet group. Note that Admiral Yi's flagship has twice the hit points, 50 percent stronger attack, and greater range, but weaker armor than the two other Turtle Ships

New Objective: Use Turtle Ships to defeat the Japanese navy.

Elite Turtle Ships are extremely powerful and key to holding off Japanese attacks. It's important to keep them intact, so return damaged ones to the Korean shore and assign villagers to perform repairs.

There's no shortage of gold on the Korean island. Once you've depleted the initial deposit, you'll find additional resources just north of the Korean base, along the western shore, and in the northeastern corner beyond the former Japanese Raider stronghold.

Use your stone supply to build towers and bombard towers along the Korean shore and near the town center. If Japanese transports slip by, your towers should eliminate the Samurai and other attackers who will be unloaded.

With enough resources pouring in, research all unit upgrades and technology bonuses to attack and armor strength. Produce Elite War Wagons, and consider researching the Korean unique technology, Shinkichon, if you plan to implement mangonels and onagers into your assault (see Figure 6.20).

Figure 6.20:
Build the Korean unique unit, the War Wagon, in preparation for your ground assault against the Japanese docks.

New Objective: Destroy all of the Japanese docks to end their threat to Korea.

You'll find most of the docks along the Japanese shore, although a few that lie on the western side of the Japanese island are inland and protected by towers and structures.

Move the majority of your naval fleet to the eastern edge of the map and locate the Japanese shore to the south. Send a transport filled with bombard cannons and battering rams with your fleet. Unload the transport on the eastern side of the Japanese

island and use these siege weapons against the bombard towers that protect the docks. Position your fleet near the shore to protect your siege weapons from infantry counter-attack.

Tip Scout the sea west of the Korean island to discover the Chinese outpost. The Chinese donate 10 bombard cannons and 10 elite Chu Ko Nu (fast-firing crossbowmen) to the Korean cause. Send over a transport to obtain the Chinese units.

Continue west, eliminating Japanese towers, structures, and docks. Usher over more ground troops—a mixture of infantry, ranged, and cavalry units—to the eastern Japanese shore. Use siege weapons to annihilate enemy military structures and towers while keeping your naval ships assaulting docks and protecting your ground troops. The mission ends in victory once all Japanese docks are destroyed.

Civilization Strengths and Weaknesses

The Conquerors expansion pack adds five civilizations to The Age of Kings' thirteen. Each features specific economic and military bonuses, unique units and technologies, and a shared team bonus for multiplayer games. Exploiting your civilization's strengths and your opponent civilization's weaknesses is key to consistent success.

In this chapter, we examine each civilization's strengths and weaknesses, including tips on how to play as, against, and alongside each. Changes to Age of Kings' original civilizations, and the resulting strategic implications, are also explored. Finally, we conclude each section with detailed strategy suggestions from expert player Out4Blood. These step-by-step strategies will require slight tweaking given the variation of map types, playing styles, and starting game conditions, but they are an excellent starting point as you begin your multiplayer mastery of this deep-strategy game.

Civilizations in The Conquerors

This section describes the five new civilizations—Aztec, Hun, Korean, Mayan, and Spanish—in *The Conquerors* and examines each civilization's attributes, unique unit and technology, team bonus, and missing technologies.

Note The resource-gathering strategies detailed in Chapter 1 offer techniques to maximize villager efficiency. This chapter includes suggestions on improving that efficiency by exploiting civilization bonuses.

Aztecs

Civilization Attributes
- Start with eagle warrior, not scout cavalry.
- Villagers carry +5 more.
- All military units are created 15% faster.
- Monks +5 HP for each monastery technology researched.

Unique Unit
- **Jaguar Warrior and Elite Jaguar Warrior:** This heavily armored fighter has an attack bonus versus other infantry.

Unique Technology
- **Garland Wars:** +4 infantry attack; +6 attack bonus versus cavalry.

Team Bonus
- Relics generate +33% gold.

Missing Technologies
Building: Masonry, Architecture, Hoardings, Keep, Bombard Tower. **Economy:** Two-Man Saw, Guilds. **Infantry:** Harberdier. **Missile/Siege:** Cavalry Archer, Heavy Cavalry Archer, Hand Cannoneer, Heavy Scorpion, Bombard Cannon, Ring Archer Armor, Thumb Ring, Parthian Tactics. **Cavalry:** All units and upgrades. **Ship:** Galleon, Demolition Ship, Cannon Galleon, Elite Cannon Galleon.

Playing As

The Aztecs' resource-gathering bonus—villagers carry five more resource units—allows speedy advancement through the ages. It's an important advantage, because the Aztecs lack cavalry and gunpowder units that can dominate the late stages of a game.

Use the Aztec resource bonuses to reach the Feudal and Castle Ages quickly and research two important military upgrades, Elite Jaguar Warrior and Garland Wars (which turns infantry units into powerhouses and includes an important anti-cavalry bonus).

The Aztecs' unique unit, the Jaguar Warrior, is a powerful fighter with bonuses against enemy infantry. Expect your opponent to eschew infantry to negate this bonus and instead concentrate on ranged and cavalry units. Counter by producing pikemen for use against enemy cavalry and researching squires to increase infantry speed for use against enemy ranged units.

The Aztecs (and Mayans) start with an eagle warrior instead of scout cavalry. The speedy eagle warrior is roughly equivalent to a man-at-arms and features slight bonuses against cavalry, ranged, and siege units. Use them to scout terrain, particularly early in the game. Have them intercept enemy ranged and siege units while you engage infantry and cavalry with Jaguar Warriors and pikemen, respectively.

The hit-point bonus to monks enables the Aztecs to pull off monk-heavy offensives. Each technology researched at the monastery increases a monk's maximum hit points by five. Research fervor (+15% monk speed), illumination (+50% monk rejuvenation speed), block printing (+3 conversion range), and sanctity (+50% monk hit points) for a powerful conversion force with 65 hit points each. You'll need heavy resources of gold in order to afford the technologies and monks.

Playing Against

Avoid amassing large amounts of infantry or face the consequences against the superior Aztec Jaguar Warriors. Concentrate on cavalry, ranged units, and anti-infantry siege weapons such as the scorpion and mangonel. Spend resources saved from infantry and its upgrades on improving your cavalry and ranged units. Pikemen and halberdiers are also not needed against the cavalryless Aztecs.

Countering the Aztecs' resource-gathering bonus will require flawless execution of your own gathering skills. Scout your opponent's resource-gathering points as early as possible and plan for a Feudal Age infantry rush to disrupt and eliminate villagers. Build outposts and palisade walls around important resource points, particularly gold resources, to remain aware of Aztec expansion.

Playing With (Team Games)

The Aztecs' relic bonus—coupled with *The Conquerors* increased relic gold bonus—provides quite the incentive to control a map's relics. Because of the Aztecs lack of cavalry and impressive naval units, carefully select the ally civilization and avoid stable, cavalry, and naval bonuses. For instance, the team-farm bonus (+45 food) of the Chinese nicely complements the Aztecs' gathering speed.

Offset Aztec weaknesses with a powerful cavalry-based (Franks, Byzantines, Persians) or ranged-based civilization (Britons or Chinese). Allow the Aztecs to concentrate on infantry and its bonuses while the ally pours resources into its cavalry or ranged strength.

Out4Blood's
Aztec Feudal Attack

Because of the lack of stable units, you'll need to make use of your economic advantages to advance quickly. Build near the enemy so you can launch early strikes on his economy. If you attack from your own town, your slow units will have difficulty reaching the enemy before solid defenses have been built. We recommend getting to the Feudal Age rapidly and launching an early assault with your faster training warriors. Because your villagers carry more, they'll be more efficient gatherers, which helps you advance to the next age faster. You'll be about one minute slower than a Chinese player doing a FLUSH (FeudaL rUSH), assuming you make the same number of villagers, but your military and economic advantages may help you carry the day.

The strategy is to attack early and deny the enemy wood, so your assault can't be countered.

- Concentrate on fast-food sources like sheep, turkey, or boars.
- Chop only enough wood to make a lumber camp just before clicking the button to advance to the Feudal Age.
- Research the Feudal Age early, with around 22–23 villagers, to reach Feudal Age around 10:30–11:00.
- Switch your economy to mostly wood and gold; save your berries for later.
- In the Feudal Age, attack with archers and a couple of towers to deprive the enemy of resources, especially wood; make new villagers and send them to gather berries.
- Continue to attack, and use your scout to find the enemy's secondary lumber camps.

Villager/Time	Action	Notes
1–3	Build 2 houses, then move to food ASAP	Scout in concentric circles to find sheep, berries, 2 boars, wood, gold, and stone
4–10	Sheep and berries	If needed, force villagers to deposit food in order to keep a constant flow of villagers
		Research loom
11	Lure boar #1	Bring boar to town center
12	Build house; then move to wood	
13	Food	
14	Lure boar #2	Bring it to your villagers at the mill, or to your town center, if closer

continued

Villager/Time	Action	Notes
15–16	Food	
17	Build house; gather wood	
18–22	Wood, build lumber camp at forest	
8:20–9:00	Click the Feudal upgrade	Time will be 8:20 or so if you're doing well, though anything short of 9:00 is okay
	Send 2 villagers to build near enemy; send 14 villagers to wood; send 6 to mine gold	Scout the enemy town looking for lumber camp plus gold and stone; identify wood and likely places your foe will run to for more once you attack; when you have enough wood, build a barracks near the enemy
10:30–11:00		Reach Feudal Age
	Build an archery range near the enemy; begin training archers; build a tower near enemy resources, then a second archery range	
23–29	Berries	
	Once berries are gone, hunt deer or make farms	
	Switch 4–8 villagers from wood/gold to stone	You'll need to get stone to make more towers

Continue to train archers at your forward base and give them stand-ground orders, so they don't attack the enemy town center. Scout for new resource locations and keep your foe from gathering wood. If your opponent doesn't collect wood or stone, he can't defend against your attack. If he builds a tower for defense, move your archers under its minimum range and then use the stand-ground order.

Try to encircle the enemy base with archers and/or towers to cut off access to straggler trees and prevent farming. You should be in good shape if you've cut off the wood supply. If your opponent manages to reach the Castle Age, build some spearmen to protect your town and archers.

Huns

Civilization Attributes

- Start –100 wood but don't need houses.
- Cavalry archers cost –25% Castle Age, –30% Imperial Age.
- Trebuchets +30% accuracy.

Unique Unit

🛡 **Tarkan and Elite Tarkan:** A cavalry unit with an attack bonus against buildings. The Tarkan is also strong versus archers, cavalry archers, siege units, and monks. It carries the same shortcomings as other cavalry, being weak against pikemen, knights, and camels.

Unique Technology

🛡 **Atheism:** +100 years wonder/relic victory time; −50% spies/treason cost.

Team Bonus

🛡 Stable creates units 20% faster.

Missing Technologies

Building: House, Fortified Wall, Guard Tower, Keep, Bombard Tower, Architecture, Hoardings, Herbal Medicine. **Economy:** Stone Shaft Mining, Crop Rotation. **Monk:** Redemption, Block Printing, Theocracy. **Infantry:** Eagle Warrior, Elite Eagle Warrior, Champion, Plate Mail Armor. **Missile/Siege:** Arbalest, Hand Cannoneer, Heavy Scorpion, Onager, Siege Onager, Bombard Cannon, Ring Archer Armor, Heated Shot, Siege Engineers. **Cavalry:** Camel, Heavy Camel. **Ship:** Fast Fire Ship, Elite Cannon Galleon, Shipwright.

Playing As

The nomadic Huns don't need houses to support military and civilian units. Eliminating houses saves wood and villager micromanagement. These savings can quickly get you to Castle Age, as you can divert more attention to scouting, hunting, and farming.

The wood savings from no housing can be used for fishing boats, enabling a large boat boom. With both fishing boats and villagers working steadily, the Huns can quickly gather a huge amount of food, permitting late Feudal and early Castle Age attacks.

You must make use of terrain features, such as forests and rivers, to create choke points to protect your base. The Huns lack a fortified wall, guard tower, keep, and bombard tower, which could pose defensive problems late in the game. Use stone walls and gates, and carefully position towers and the Hun castle to offset these defensive shortcomings. Also, play to the Huns' history. Be nomadic and seek to quickly control as much of the map as possible. It's important to remain aggressive with this strong hit-and-run civilization.

Given the fast-producing stables and cheap cavalry archers, cavalry plays an important role in the Hun offensive. Tarkans are great for assaulting resource outposts, forward bases, and main towns. Use them to target buildings while your cavalry, cavalry archers, and infantry eliminate your foe's military. Don't neglect cavalry archers in the Castle and Imperial Ages. The combination of cheaper cavalry archers and higher lumber reserves (saved from housing construction) makes the ranged horseback unit an inviting complement to a strong cavalry offensive. Be sure to research cavalry- and cavalry archer-related technologies, such as bloodlines, husbandry, and Parthian tactics.

Playing Against

Exploit the Huns' defensive weaknesses with consistent military pressure and slow down their advance to the Castle Age and their production of inexpensive cavalry archers. Use skirmishers and elite skirmishers to counter the Hun cavalry archer force, and produce pikemen, halberdiers, and camels to counter Hun cavalry.

Position your structures behind defensive walls and towers to negate the Tarkan bonus against buildings. Research murder holes (towers can attack units against the tower) so Tarkans can't eliminate towers without resistance. The Huns lack mangonels, scorpions, and bombard cannons, so don't hesitate when sending in your military.

Playing With (Team Games)

Combine the Huns' fast stable production with cavalry-based civilizations or the Goths' rapid barracks production to produce raiding parties that can overwhelm an unprepared foe. Offset the Huns' lack of gunpowder and siege units to help protect their powerful cavalry and cavalry archers from attack by elite skirmishers and pikemen.

Allow an ally to assist with defensive towers, a Hun weakness. Support a strong allied infantry or cavalry force with Hunnic cavalry archers and Tarkan cavalry.

Out4Blood's
Hun Boat Boom

The Huns will be a favorite civilization to play simply because you no longer have to make those pesky houses all the time. This not only saves time and aggravation, but it also gives them a significant speed advantage in getting to the Castle Age. The Hun player saves wood (from not needing houses), and the villager saves time (from not having to build them). You can also do a quick rush to the Feudal Age and strike with archers, similar to the Chinese FLUSH strategy detailed later in this chapter. Another strategy for the Huns is to rush to the Castle Age and attack with the cheap (and much-improved) cavalry archers. Cavalry archers make excellent raiders now that their speed, fire rate, and creation time have been boosted.

Finally, the Huns make an excellent boat-booming civilization, since the more villagers you make, the more wood you're saving in housing costs. A boat boom is powerful because the dock is the only place, aside from the town center, where you can build resource-gathering units in the Dark and Feudal Ages. This enables you to build a huge economy as the added food income from the fishing boats begins to pile up. This strategy works especially well if you're allied with a Viking player, who receives cheaper docks. You have many excellent strategic choices, but let's try a boat boom.

The strategy is to exploit the housing advantage to quickly save wood for boats and build up a dominant economy:

 Minimize the number of villagers gathering food and place the rest on wood collection throughout the Dark and Feudal Ages.

continued

- Build a dock as early as possible.
- Continue to make as many fishing boats as possible, building a second dock as soon as you're able.
- Achieve a Castle time under 17:00 with around 43—48 villagers (including boats).
- Have a surplus of resources to devote to attacking the enemy.

Villager/Time	Action	Notes
1–3	Chop wood at the start until a scout finds sheep	Collect at least 30 wood
1–7	Sheep/turkeys—avoid building a mill immediately to save on wood	Scout in concentric circles to find sheep, berries, two boars, wood, gold, and stone; you may need to force the villagers to drop off food in order to keep a constant flow of villagers
8	Build a lumber camp; gather wood	Once you've thoroughly scouted wood, look for the water so you can build a dock near large quantities of fish
9–12	Wood; research loom	
13	Lure boar #1	
14	Build a dock	Start building a dock around the 4—5 minute mark; assign fishing boats to deep-sea fishing far offshore, as they provide food at nearly twice the rate that the smaller fish locations do
15	Lure boar #2	Once your villagers run out of sheep/turkeys and boars, move to berries
16–24	Wood	Berries are slower to gather, and you'll want some extra villagers to help take out boars; you should have around 17 villagers on wood and seven on food; build a second dock with your original dock builder when you've collected enough wood
25–30	Build a mining camp; mine gold	Begin mining gold at this point, but keep pumping out the fishing boats; you should have 28–30 villagers and 12–15 fishing boats from at least two docks—growing any larger than this will leave you vulnerable to an early attack
11:00–11:30	Click the Feudal Age upgrade	Begin scouting out enemy locations to prime yourself for an attack; once you have around 15 or so fishing boats, it's a good idea to stop making them, as they're hard to defend in the Castle Age and you'll be needing the wood elsewhere
13:10–13:40	Train 2 more villagers; have 2 villagers build a market and 2 more build a blacksmith	Reach Feudal Age
		As your land-based food sources run out, place your villagers on a second source of wood nearby

continued

Villager/Time	Action	Notes
14:10–14:40	Click the Castle Age upgrade; immediately send 2–3 villagers to the enemy in preparation for building military buildings near his base	Also, depending on the terrain, the time at which your enemy castled, and your resources, you may want to consider walling in your town. This makes it more difficult to attack you. You might want to shift some of your economy to stone to enable you to build more walls or later, a castle
16:50–17:20		Reach Castle Age

Quickly build up a raiding force of cavalry archers, or use a large force of knights, rams (or petards and Tarkans when you build a castle), and priests to attack the enemy base.

The Huns have faster stables for making knights, but they also have cheaper cavalry archers, a viable choice for early attacks. Keep the pressure on your opponent and wall in your town to prevent counterattacks. Put most of your villagers on wood (50%), gold (30%), and stone (20%). Your boats will continue to bring in food. If the enemy attacks your fishing fleet, you'll need to make farms to supply food.

Koreans

Civilization Attributes

- Villagers +2 line of sight.
- Stone miners work +20% faster.
- Tower upgrades free (bombard tower requires chemistry).
- Towers range +1 Castle Age, +1 Imperial Age (for +2 total)

Unique Units

- **War Wagon and Elite War Wagon:** A well-armored cavalry range unit with excellent range and damage potential to infantry and archers. The War Wagon is weak against cavalry, skirmishers, and pikemen.
- **Turtle Ship and Elite Turtle Ship:** An expensive but powerful naval unit suitable for destroying enemy vessels at close range (though it's weak against fire ships). An Elite Turtle Ship carries no additional damage potential, but 33% more hit points and better armor. It can be built at a dock once the Korean castle has been constructed.

Unique Technology

- **Shinkichon:** +2 mangonel, onager range.

Team Bonus

- Mangonels and onagers possess +1 range.

167

Missing Technologies

Building: Hoardings. **Economy:** Crop Rotation, Sappers. **Monk:** Redemption, Atonement, Heresy, Illumination. **Infantry:** Eagle Warrior, Elite Eagle Warrior, Blast Furnace. **Missile/Siege:** Siege Ram, Heavy Scorpion, Parthian Tactics. **Cavalry:** Paladin, Camel, Heavy Camel, Bloodlines, Plate Barding Armor. **Ship:** Demolition Ship, Heavy Demolition Ship, Elite Cannon Galleon.

Playing As

With bonuses to stone mining, watchtower range, and free upgrades to guard tower and keep (saving heaps of food and stone), the Koreans can excel defensively; however, it's equally effective to put these bonuses to offensive use. If you're left alone to mine stone, you should have a castle up before your opponent or be able to pin your opponent in with garrisoned towers. Koreans possess a solid military, though don't excel in one particular area. The lack of bloodlines and Parthian tactics hurts cavalry and cavalry archers while no blast furnace keeps infantry from maximum damage.

Mangonels are an important part of the Korean attack force. Enhance the siege weapon by researching Shinkichon at the Korean castle and improve mangonel range by approximately 28%, surpassing both onager and siege onagers. Korea also has access to gunpowder units; implement bombard cannons and hand cannoneers to help support the otherwise nondescript Korean military.

The Korean civilization features two unique units, both requiring a castle for production. The War Wagon and Elite War Wagon (built at the castle) are excellent supports for infantry and cavalry units. Use the War Wagon to weaken enemy infantry while using pikemen and halberdiers against opposing cavalry. Protect war wagons from archers with skirmishers and towers. Improve war wagons with all archer and missile-weapon improvements.

The Turtle Ship and Elite Turtle Ship, the second Korean unique unit, is produced at docks. The Turtle Ship serves as a close-range cannon galleon, but with a greater damage potential and armor rating than even the elite cannon galleon. Turtle Ships are an expensive investment, but can annihilate galleons and cannon galleons when supported by friendly galleons and fire ships. Protect the costly investments well by repairing Turtle Ships with shoreline villagers.

Playing Against

Scout the Korean base early and attack villagers at stone deposits with infantry and archers to disrupt the Korean stone supply and halt a potential tower rush. The Koreans can't produce camels or heavy camels, leaving them vulnerable to cavalry attack. If the Korean player fails to produce pikemen or halberdiers, accelerate cavalry production and lay waste to the Korean war wagon, mangonel, infantry, and ranged attack.

On water maps, protect yourself against Korean Turtle Ships by producing fire and fast-fire ships to counter the attack. Turtle Ships are extremely expensive; if your Korean opponent is massing a large naval fleet, it's likely at the expense of a ground military. Force your opponent to overproduce the navy while you produce units (include battering rams and their upgrades to use against towers) for a ground assault.

Playing With (Team Games)

The Celts offer a compounding team bonus—siege workshops produce units 20% faster—allowing for quick-producing, longer-range mangonels. The Celts benefit greatly as well. Siege weapons fire 20% faster as part of the Celt civilization attributes; the longer mangonel range offered by the Korean team bonus presents a powerful combination.

Use the Koreans' superior towers and stone mining to help defend ally resource outposts and forward bases. For water maps, concentrate on Turtle Ships and allow the ally to construct supporting galleon, cannon galleon, and fire ships.

Out4Blood's Korean Castle Rush

The Koreans are a slow civilization to develop, and their bonuses do not take effect until the Castle Age. Despite the tower bonuses and stone mining advantages, resist the urge to make a lot of towers. The Koreans will be a hard civilization to play on games starting in the Dark Age, but once you get them into the Castle and Imperial Ages, they'll be tough to beat. We recommend getting to the Castle Age quickly, as your tower bonuses will take effect and you can begin to push back the enemy.

The strategy is to reach the Castle Age as quickly as possible and wall in your town to enable you to reach the Imperial Age:

- Concentrate on the fast-food sources: sheep/turkey and boars.

- Chop wood for farms.

- Lay around 5–6 farms as early in the Dark Age as possible.

- Wall in your town to prevent raids.

- Send early villagers to the enemy base and build a stable near its town; as you reach the Castle Age, raid with knights to keep the enemy focused on defense.

- Work on reaching the Imperial Age, where your units will be superior to the other civilizations.

Villager/Time	Action	Notes
1–3	Build 2 houses, then move to sheep	Scout in concentric circles to find sheep, berries, two boars, wood, gold, and stone
4–7	Sheep and berries	If needed, force villagers to deposit food in order to keep a constant flow of villagers
8	Build mill; berries	

continued

Villager/Time	Action	Notes
9–10	Wood	
11	Build house; wood	
12	Wood; research loom	
13	Lure boar #1	
14	Food	
15	Lure boar #2	
16–21	Wood	When boars are gone, move boar eaters to berries and wood
22	Farm	
23	Wood	
24–28	Farm	
10:30–11:00	Click the Feudal Age upgrade	Send 3–4 villagers to gold so you'll have enough to advance to Castle Age
12:40–13:10		Reach Feudal Age
	Train 2 more villagers if you have enough food; have 2 villagers build a market and 2 others build a blacksmith	
13:40–14:10	Click the Castle Age upgrade	
	Build a tower or two to defend your key resource locations	Have 2–3 villagers mine stone, so you can build a couple of towers before the Castle Age
16:20–16:50		Reach Castle Age

Continue to build your economy and wall in your town. Korean bonuses are primarily defensive in nature and you'll have an advantage if you can make it to the Imperial Age. Defend against rams and archers with your superior mangonels. Guard against cavalry attacks with pikemen. Build your forces and get to Imperial Age as quickly as you can.

Mayans

Civilization Attributes
- Start with eagle warrior, not Scout Cavalry.
- +1 Villager, −50 food.
- Resources last 20% longer.
- Archery Range units cost −10% Feudal Age, −20% Castle Age, −30% Imperial Age.

Unique Unit
- **Plumed Archer and Elite Plumed Archer:** A fast archer akin to a crossbowman given its armor and damage potential.

Unique Technology
 **El Dorado:** +40 eagle warrior hit points

Team Bonus
Walls cost –50%.

Missing Technologies
Building: Bombard Tower. **Economy:** Gold Shaft Mining. **Monk:** Redemption, Illumination. **Infantry:** Champion. **Missile/Siege:** Hand Cannoneer, Cavalry Archer, Heavy Cavalry Archer, Parthian Tactics, Siege Engineers. **Cavalry:** Scout Cavalry, Light Cavalry, Hussar, Knight, Cavalier, Paladin, Camel, Heavy Camel, Husbandry, Bloodlines, Scale Barding Armor, Chain Barding Armor, Plate Barding Armor. **Ship:** Cannon Galleon, Elite Cannon Galleon.

Playing As
The Mayan technology tree is nearly equivalent to that of the Aztecs—both are without cavalry and cavalry archers, and neither can advance to gunpowder units. The extra starting villager provides a slight advantage in the important first 30 seconds of producing villagers, building houses, and gathering resources. The Mayans excel at reaching Feudal Age quickly, and the bonus to resources ensures more reserves come Castle Age.

Without cavalry, it's important to exploit the potential of the Mayan eagle warrior, which is even more powerful than its Aztec cousin. The eagle warrior is fast and has slight bonuses against archers, cavalry, and siege units. Research the Mayan unique technology, El Dorado, to turn the eagle warrior into a tough fighting machine.

The archery range features significant cost reductions, depending on the current age, so use the quick, technology-enhanced eagle warriors (research all infantry improvements) to protect the bulk of the Mayan force—archers and Plumed Archers, the Mayan unique unit. Don't neglect researching thumb ring, which increases the fire rate and improves the accuracy of archer units.

Mayan villagers can extract 20% more material from resource points, so scout for as many resource areas as possible (including shore fishing and berries). Seek out additional gold deposits and protect them with the Mayans' 50% cheaper walls.

Playing Against
Though the Mayan archer force isn't as powerful as the British Longbowmen, it's important to produce skirmishers early and upgrade to elite skirmishers in the Castle Age to protect against the expected large archer assault. Research improvements to piercing armor as well as squires (to increase infantry speed) and bloodlines (to increase cavalry hit points) to improve infantry and cavalry effectiveness against archers. Use resources you would have spent on pikemen or halberdiers to improve cavalry, infantry, and siege units.

It will cost the Mayans significant resources to enhance eagle warriors and Plumed Archers, and to prepare a crossbowman or an arbalest attack group. Guard gold and other long-distance resources from the Mayans and force them to choose a heavy eagle warrior or Plumed Archer group. Maintain a scout on the Mayans' military units and counter their chosen route. Should you encounter El Dorado-enhanced elite eagle warriors, use improved infantry and monks to terminate or convert them.

Playing With (Team Games)

The Mayans' cheap walls team bonus will assist defense-minded civilizations even further. The Koreans, with their bonuses to stone mining and impressive towers (and free tower upgrades) should protect the map's resource points and allow the Mayans to gather to utilize its civilization bonus. A strong cavalry-based civilization like the Franks offsets the Mayans' primary shortcoming and can help protect the eagle warrior and ranged unit army.

Out4Blood's
Mayan Feudal Attack

The Mayans have a slight economic bonus in that their resources last 20% longer. Coupled with cheaper archery-range units, the Mayans make an excellent Feudal Age attacker. It's important to try to get an early offensive advantage with the Mayans, though, since you lack the shock effect of a good knight rush.

The strategy is to attack early and deny the enemy wood, so he cannot counter your assault:

- Concentrate your villagers on fast-food sources, namely sheep, turkey, and boars.

- Chop only enough wood to make a lumber camp just before hitting the Feudal Age upgrade.

- Research the Feudal Age early with around 22–23 villagers, reaching the Feudal Age around 10:30–11:00.

- Save your berries for later and switch your economy to mostly wood and gold.

- In the Feudal Age, attack with archers and a couple of towers to deprive your opponent of resources, especially wood. Make new villagers and assign them to berries.

- Continue to attack and use your scout to find the enemy's secondary lumber camps.

Villager/Time	Action	Notes
1–3	Build 2 houses, then move to sheep ASAP	Scout in concentric circles to find sheep, berries, 2 boars, wood, gold, and stone
4–9	Sheep and berries	If needed, force villagers to deposit food in order to keep a constant flow of villagers
10–11	Wood	Research loom

continued

Villager/Time	Action	Notes
12	Build house; wood	
13	Lure boar #1	Send boar to the town center
14–15	Food	
16	Lure boar #2	Send second boar to your villagers at the mill, or to the town center if closer
17	Build house; food	
18–22	Food	
8:20–9:00	Click the Feudal Age upgrade	Time should be around 8:20 or so if you are doing well, but anything short of 9:00 is okay
	Send 2 villagers to enemy; send 14 villagers to wood; send 6 to mine gold; build a barracks near the enemy or in your town for defense once you have enough wood	Scout out the enemy town looking for lumber camp and gold and stone piles—most important is to identify his lumber camp and likely places he'll run to for more wood once you attack
10:30–11:00		Reach the Feudal Age
	Build two archery ranges near the enemy; begin training archers; build a tower near enemy resources	
23–29	Berries	
	Hunt or farm once the berries are gone	
	Switch 4–8 villagers from wood/ gold to a stone mine	You'll need stone to make towers

Continue to train archers at your forward base. Scout for new resource locations and keep your foe from gathering wood. If your opponent doesn't collect wood or stone, he can't defend against your attack. If he builds a tower for defense, move your archers under its minimum range and then use the stand-ground order.

Try to encircle the enemy base with archers and/or towers to cut off access to straggler trees and prevent farming. You should be in good shape if you've cut off the wood supply. If your opponent manages to reach the Castle Age, build some spearmen to protect your town and archers.

Spanish

Civilization Attributes

- Builders work 30% faster (except on wonders).
- Blacksmith upgrades don't cost gold.
- Cannon galleons benefit from ballistics (fire faster, more accurately).

Unique Units

- **Conquistador and Elite Conquistador:** The equivalent of a mounted hand cannoneer, the Conquistador is strong versus swordsmen, monks, Teutonic Knights, and war elephants. It's more effective at close range, as its cannon weapon is inaccurate at longer distances. The Conquistador is weak against cavalry, camels, and pikemen.

- **Missionary:** The second Spanish unique unit is essentially a mounted monk. The Missionary's advantage is its increased speed. The Missionary can't carry relics, though, and possesses a smaller line of sight and conversion range (approximately 25% smaller than the monk).

Unique Technology

- **Supremacy:** Villager combat skills increased.

Team Bonus

- Trade cart and trade cog return +33% gold.

Missing Technologies

Building: Treadmill Crane. **Economy:** Gold Shaft Mining, Crop Rotation. **Infantry:** Eagle Warrior, Elite Eagle Warrior. **Missile/Siege:** Crossbowman, Arbalest, Heavy Scorpion, Siege Onager, Heated Shot, Siege Engineers, Parthian Tactics. **Cavalry:** Camel, Heavy Camel.

Playing As

Spanish blacksmith upgrades don't require gold, which should allow you to research all blacksmith improvements (they'll cost only food) and save a startling 1,745 gold to use for units or other Castle Age and Imperial Age technologies (unfortunately this is offset by the Spaniards lack of gold-shaft mining). You'll be able to enhance your cavalry and infantry much sooner than an opponent. Exploit this advantage and send raiding parties to disrupt villagers at resource points.

The Spanish feature poor ranged unit upgrades and can't produce crossbowmen or arbalests. You could produce cavalry archers and heavy cavalry archers, but they wouldn't be able to benefit from Parthian tactics.

Instead, the Spanish rely mostly on gunpowder units to support infantry and cavalry. Reach Castle Age and produce Conquistadors, the Spanish unique mounted hand cannoneer that features all the bonuses and limitations of a cavalry unit. Protect the Conquistador from other cavalry, camels, and pikemen. Research bloodlines to boost Conquistador hit points and husbandry to increase the unit's speed.

Conquistadors function similarly to hand cannoneers, though hand cannoneers can inflict greater damage and feature a slightly longer range. Position Conquistadors close to the battle for optimum results, as the Conquistadors' cannons aren't accurate, and you'll waste their potential if you keep them at long range.

The Spanish, with a full slate of naval units and upgrades, excel on water maps. Support the superior Spanish cannon galleon fleet with galleons and fire ships.

Playing Against

Controlling the sea will prove extremely difficult against the Spanish, particularly if not controlled by Imperial Age. The Spanish feature no naval cost bonuses, so only civilizations with either naval cost bonuses or unit enhancements could compete. Keep the Spanish from producing a cannon galleon force.

The Spanish lack impressive foot-ranged units. Produce and enhance your own to counter Spanish short-range Conquistadors, as well as their solid infantry force. Use pikemen, halberdiers, camels, or heavy camels against the Spanish supporting cavalry.

Playing With (Team Games)

The Spanish team bonus to trade carts and trade cogs (both return +33% gold) encourages market trading. Be sure to research cartography and then caravan to increase the speed of carts and cogs and further enhance the team bonus. Help support early Spanish raids. A civilization with archer or archery-range bonuses can offset a Spanish weakness. The Turks, with their team bonus to gunpowder units (train 20% faster), enhance the Spanish Conquistador force.

Out4Blood's
Spanish Castle Rush

The Spanish receive almost no economic bonuses, and their military bonuses are most effective only in the Imperial Age. Improved trading makes them good allies, but they'll be at a disadvantage until the later stages of the game. To survive as the Spanish, you'll need to get to the Castle (and Imperial) Age quickly.

The strategy is to reach the Castle Age as quickly as possible and wall in your town to enable you to reach the Imperial Age:

- Concentrate on the fast-food sources: sheep/turkeys and boars.

- Chop wood for farms.

- Lay 5–6 farms in the Dark Age as early as possible.

- Wall in your town to prevent raids.

- Send early villagers to the enemy base and build a stable near his town; as you reach the Castle Age, raid with knights to keep the enemy focused on defense.

- Work on reaching the Imperial Age, where your units will be superior to the other civilizations.

- Trade with your allies early to take advantage of your economic bonuses.

continued

175

Villager/Time	Action	Notes
1–3	Build 2 houses, then move to food ASAP	Scout in concentric circles to find sheep, berries, 2 boars, wood, gold, and stone
4–7	Sheep and berries	If needed, force villagers to deposit food in order to keep a constant flow of villagers
8	Build mill; berries	
9–10	Wood	
11	Build house; wood	
12	Wood; research loom	
13	Lure boar #1	
14	Food	
15	Lure boar #2	
16–21	Wood	When boars are gone, shift boar eaters to berries and wood
22	Farm	
23	Wood	
24–28	Farm	
10:30–11:00	Click the Feudal Age upgrade	Send 3–4 villagers to gold so you'll have enough to advance to Castle Age
12:40–13:10		Reach Feudal Age
	Train 2 more villagers; have 2 villagers build a market and 2 villagers build a blacksmith	
13:40–14:10	Click the Castle Age upgrade	Have 2–3 villagers mine stone, so you can build a castle and wall in your town
16:20–16:50		Reach Castle Age

You won't really be very strong until you can reach the Imperial Age and begin taking advantage of your bonuses. Make sure to concentrate on advancing as much as possible. If you are playing in a team game, begin trading early. Your trade bonus will be very powerful and bring in a lot of gold. This will give you an economic advantage if you can defend your trade routes.

Civilizations from The Age of Kings

All 13 civilizations from *The Age of Kings* have been given new technologies and units in *The Conquerors*. Some civilizations have been significantly altered through changes to attributes or team bonuses, while others feature enhancements to particular units.

In this section, you'll find comprehensive techniques for the civilizations from the original game, including how to take advantage of economic and military bonuses and how to adjust to *The Conquerors'* changes to units, attributes, and team bonuses.

Note For more on *The Conquerors'* global technologies and units, see Chapter 8: New Technologies and Units.

Britons

Civilization Attributes

- Town centers cost −50% wood in Castle Age.
- Foot archers +1 range Castle Age, +1 range Imperial Age (for +2 total).
- Shepherds work 25% faster.

The Conquerors Changes

- Town centers cost 50% less wood, but only after Castle Age.

Unique Unit

- **Longbowman:** An archer with weak armor but a deadly long-range attack. It's extremely effective in large numbers, but must be supported with cavalry or infantry.

Unique Technology

- **Yeoman:** +1 to archer range, +2 to tower attack. Use it to further boost the powerful Longbowman and forward towers.

Team Bonus

- Archery ranges create units 20% faster.

Playing As

With fast archery ranges, range bonuses, and Longbowmen, the Britons clearly specialize in ranged units. The Britons' shepherd bonus can accelerate the civilization into the Castle Age, where you can build a castle and start Longbowmen production. Produce archers and especially Longbowmen in numbers and protect them with pikemen and cavalry.

The Britons' cheap town centers can serve as forward bases, towers, and resource centers, though the 100 stone cost and slower build time makes this tactic less appealing than in the original *The Age of Kings*. To support heavy expansion, place villagers on stone mining as you near the Castle Age.

If you're attempting an early Castle Age offensive, place a town center within range of your enemy's gold- or lumber-resource area. Produce and garrison villagers inside the town center. Place a siege workshop behind the town center (so enemy units must charge past the town center to engage the workshop), and make battering rams to prepare a building assault. Support your battering rams with cavalry and archers or Longbowmen.

Playing Against

Scout well to keep an eye on Briton expansion, especially on the outskirts of your main base, resource centers, and houses. Intercept forward builders with infantry or scout cavalry. Place stone walls around key resource areas to keep Briton town centers away. Concentrate on generating a large economy and demolish the expansions with battering rams.

With so many ranged bonuses, expect plenty of Briton archers, crossbowmen, arbalests, and Longbowmen. Counter archers with elite skirmishers and upgraded cavalry (research piercing armor improvements). If the Britons counter with pikemen, use upgraded infantry. Onagers also prove effective against the arrow-firing hordes; be sure to protect your siege units with ample ground soldiers. Don't use archers, as it's impossible to compete with the Britons' range and bonuses.

Playing With (Team Games)

The Britons' Longbowmen become even more powerful when combined with civilizations that feature powerful infantry (Goths, Vikings), cavalry (Franks, Huns), or gunpowder units (Turks, Spanish). Use Longbowmen to support your teammate's force and vice-versa. Fast-producing archery ranges can enable crippling Feudal Age archer rushes.

Out4Blood's
Briton Feudal Attack

The Britons were one of the most powerful civilizations in *The Age of Kings*, primarily due to their cheap town centers. Now that the town center has been toned down significantly, the Britons must rely on their economy and speed to keep pace with other civilizations. We recommend an early Feudal Age attack, as the short-lived shepherd bonus and the faster archer training bonus make the Britons a hard civilization to counter in this period. Get to the Feudal Age rapidly and launch an assault with your archers. Once you progress to the Castle Age, your archers will become more powerful, although you'll need to protect them from large groups of infantry or knights.

continued

The strategy is to attack early and deny the enemy wood, so he cannot counter your assault:

- Concentrate your villagers on fast-food sources: sheep/turkeys and boars.

- Chop only enough wood to make a lumber camp just before hitting the Feudal Age upgrade.

- Research the Feudal Age early, with around 22–23 villagers, to reach the era around 10:30–11:00.

- Switch your economy to mostly wood and gold, and save your berries for later.

- In the Feudal Age, attack with archers and a couple of towers to deprive your opponent of resources, especially wood. Make new villagers and send them to berries.

- Continue to attack and use your scout to find the enemy's secondary lumber camps.

Villager/Time	Task	Notes
1–3	Build 2 houses, then move to food ASAP	Scout in concentric circles to find sheep, berries, 2 boars, wood, gold, and stone
4–10	Sheep and berries	If needed, force villagers to deposit food in order to keep a constant flow of villagers; research loom
11	Lure boar #1	Bring boar to your town center
12	Build house; wood	
13	Food	
14	Lure boar #2	Bring boar to your villagers at the mill, or to your town center if closer
15 – 16	Food	
17	Build house; wood	
18–22	Wood, build lumber camp at forest	
8:20–9:00	Click the Feudal Age upgrade	Time will be 8:20 or so if you are doing well, but anything short of 9:00 is okay
	Send 2 villagers to build near enemy; send 14 villagers to wood; send 6 to mine gold	Scout enemy town looking for lumber camp, gold, and stone—most important is to find lumber camp and likely places he'll go for more wood; when you have enough wood, build a barrack near the enemy
10:30–11:00		Reach Feudal Age
	Build an archery range near the enemy; begin training archers; build a tower near enemy resources, then a second archery range	
23–29	Berries	
	Once berries are done, hunt deer or farm	
	Switch 4—8 villagers from wood/gold to stone	You'll need stone for towers

continued

Continue to train archers at your forward base and give them stand-ground orders so they don't attack the enemy town center. Scout for new resource locations and keep your foe from gathering wood. If your opponent doesn't collect wood or stone, he can't defend against your attack. If he builds a tower for defense, move your archers under its minimum range and then use the stand-ground order.

Try to encircle the enemy base with archers and/or towers to cut off access to straggler trees and prevent farming. You should be in good shape if you've cut off the wood supply. If your opponent manages to reach the Castle Age, build some spearmen to protect your town and archers.

Byzantines

Civilization Attributes

- Buildings +10% hit points Dark Age, +20% Feudal Age, +30% Castle Age, +40% Imperial Age.
- Camels, skirmishers, pikemen, halberdiers cost −25%.
- Fire ships +20% attack.
- Advance to Imperial Age costs −33%.

The Conquerors Changes

- Monks heal 50% faster (changed from three times the normal speed in *The Age of Kings*).

Unique Unit

- **Cataphract:** A heavily armored cavalry unit with bonuses against enemy infantry. Counter it with pikemen and halberdiers.

Unique Technology

- **Logistica:** Adds trample damage to the Cataphract.

Team Bonus

- Monks +50% heal speed.

Playing As

With a robust technology tree, the Byzantines can excel at almost any strategy. On water maps, they benefit from full naval technology and increased fire ship power. On the ground, they have use of full infantry, archer, cavalry, and cavalry archer technology trees. However, the Byzantines lack important upgrades, such as blast furnace, bloodlines and Parthian tactics. In Imperial Age battles, the Byzantines aren't as formidable as a civilization with full upgrades available.

Regardless, the Byzantines' technological shortcomings are offset by excellent counter-unit bonuses. Byzantine camels, skirmishers, pikemen, and halberdiers cost 25% less and make inexpensive support for your primary attacking force. If you're

facing an archer-heavy civilization, concentrate on cavalry and skirmishers. Should you engage a cavalry-heavy civilization, produce pikemen, halberdiers, camels, and ranged units.

The Byzantines have no resource-gathering bonuses, but cheap counter-units should provide enough defenses to hold off early rushes. Keep your opponent's military scouted and build the appropriate counter units. Resources saved from cheap Imperial Age advancement—combined with inexpensive counter units—should enable an early Imperial Age assault.

Playing Against

You'll need to be just as versatile as the Byzantines in order to survive their inexpensive units. Use civilizations with resource bonuses to advance to the Feudal and Castle Ages quickly, and begin your battles there to slow Byzantium's advance to the Imperial Age.

Use pikemen and halberdiers against Byzantine Cataphracts. Although the Byzantines possess bombard cannon, they have no access to the heavy scorpion, siege onager, and siege engineer technology.

Playing With (Team Games)

Faster healing Byzantine monks can help any teammate. Allow the Byzantine player to supply inexpensive counter-units and powerful Cataphracts. Use your own strengths and feed off the Byzantines' well-rounded technology tree and inexpensive counter-units.

Out4Blood's
Byzantine Castle Rush

While the Byzantines have no economic bonuses whatsoever, they are still a solid civilization. Because you have cheap counter-units, defense will be easier, but you can also expect your opponent to plan on attacking with infantry forces instead of cavalry.

One strategy is to build a forward base near the enemy and begin harassment with cheap skirmishers and spearmen. This will allow you to advance to the Castle Age relatively safely. Because of their low cost, you can build a horde of effective units. Combine this strategy with a jump to the Castle Age to keep your civilization relatively safe.

The strategy is to reach the Castle Age as quickly as possible and attack as you upgrade your cheap counter-units:

- Concentrate on fast food sources: sheep/turkeys and boars.

- Chop wood for farms and plant 5–6 as early as possible in the Dark Age.

- Send villagers to the enemy base early and build barracks and an archery range near his town. As you upgrade to Castle Age, attack with spearmen, skirmishers, and archers.

- Wall in your base and achieve a Castle time under 17:00.

continued

Villager/Time	Task	Notes
1–3	Build 2 houses, then move to food ASAP	Scout in concentric circles to find sheep, berries, 2 boars, wood, gold, and stone
4–7	Sheep and berries	If needed, force villagers to deposit food in order to keep a constant flow of villagers
8	Build mill; berries	
9–10	Wood	
11	Build house; wood	
12	Wood	Research loom
13	Lure boar #1	Bring boar to town center
14	Food	
15	Lure boar #2	Bring boar to mill or town center
16–21	Wood	
22	Farm	
23	Wood	
24–28	Farm	Begin scouting enemy locations to attack
10:30–11:00	Click the Feudal Age upgrade; send 2 villagers to build barracks near	Move 3–4 villagers to gold so you'll have enough to research Castle Age opponent's base
12:40–13:10		Reach Feudal Age
	Train 2 more villagers	
	Have 2 villagers build archery range near enemy and 2 villagers build blacksmith in your town	These four villagers will quickly construct two Feudal Age buildings so that you may advance. Wall in your base to defend against pesky Knight raids
13:40–14:10	Click the Castle Age upgrade	
	Build a few spearmen and skirmishers to attack the enemy's wood production	Use your forward builders to build a tower near enemy resources; keep your economy on wood and food and build a large force of troops
16:20–16:50		Reach Castle Age

Continue to train pikemen, skirmishers, and archers. Scout for new resource locations and keep the enemy from getting wood. If your opponent does not get wood or stone, he cannot defend against your attack. Try to encircle his base with skirmishers, archers, and/or towers so that he cannot farm or chop straggler trees. Follow up with knights to kill his villagers and priests to heal your troops. Once you have enough resources, build rams to demolish his town center and buildings.

Celts

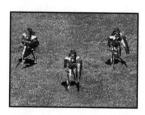

Civilization Attributes

- Infantry moves 15% faster.
- Lumberjacks work 15% faster.
- Siege weapons fire 20% faster.
- Sheep cannot be converted if in a Celt unit's line of sight.

The Conquerors Changes

- Woad Raiders are created faster and have piercing armor.

Unique Unit

- **Woad Raider:** An exceptionally fast infantry unit excellent at disrupting enemy ranged and siege units.

Unique Technology

- **Furor Celtica:** +50% hit points to units produced at the siege workshop.

Team Bonus

- Siege workshops 20% faster.

Playing As

The Celts lumberjack bonus means you shouldn't hesitate to start farming in the late Dark Age, once your other food sources are exhausted. Research lumber camp bonuses to further increase wood gathering and prepare to exploit a Celt advantage: siege units. Use garrisoned battering rams against enemy buildings, and scorpions and mangonels against troops. Woad Raiders provide excellent support for Celt siege attacks. If your opponent counters with cavalry, include pikemen or halberdiers in your infantry group. The Celts' ranged units are weak, lacking arbalest, thumb ring, Parthian tactics, bracer, and ring archer armor. Counter ranged units with Woad Raiders or upgraded scorpions or onagers.

Playing Against

Archers supported by cavalry can effectively counter the expected Celt Woad Raiders, infantry, and siege units. Keep archers in a spread formation to avoid massive damage from siege weapons. Attempt to flank the Celts' siege units with cavalry.

Playing With (Team Games)

The Celts can support with infantry and better siege units, though all teammates will benefit from their fast-producing siege workshops. Use the Celts quick infantry to harass enemy resource centers. Support their infantry, Woad Raiders, and siege weaponry with high-powered ranged or gunpowder civilizations. Combine the Celts' infantry bonus with the Goths' fast-producing barracks and the Celts' siege workshop bonus with the Koreans' improved mangonel and onager range.

Out4Blood's
Celt Boat Boom

The Celts are a good civilization for aggressive players. Their faster infantry means you can actually kill enemy villagers, rather than just chase them around the map. A good strategy for the Celts on water is to build docks early and use the lumberjack bonus to create a large fishing fleet that will give you a powerful economic advantage:

- Minimize the number of villagers gathering food and place the rest on wood throughout the Dark and Feudal Ages.

- Build a dock as early as possible.

- Continue to make as many fishing boats as possible, and construct a second dock when able.

- Achieve a Castle Age time under 17:00 with around 43—48 villagers (including boats).

- Have a surplus of resources to devote to attacking the enemy.

Villager/Time	Action	Notes
1–3	Build 2 houses, then sheep/turkeys—avoid building a mill immediately to save on wood	Scout in concentric circles to find sheep, berries, 2 boars, wood, gold, and stone
4–7	Sheep/turkeys	If needed, force villagers to deposit food in order to keep a constant flow of villagers
8	Build lumber camp; wood	Once you have thoroughly scouted wood, look for the water so you can build a dock near large quantities of fish
9–12	Wood	Research loom
13	Lure boar #1	
14	Build dock, houses	The goal is to start building a dock around the 4–5 minute mark. Use the dock builder to make additional houses, and don't forget to make houses more often since the docks will quickly boost your population; assign fishing boats to deep-sea fishing far offshore since they provide food nearly twice as fast as smaller locations
15	Lure boar #2	Once villagers run out of sheep/turkeys, hunt boar, then switch to berries
16–24	Wood	You should have around 16 villagers on wood, 7 on food, and 1 building houses; when you collect enough wood, build a second dock with your original house/dock builder

continued

Villager/Time	Action	Notes
25–30	Build a mining camp; mine gold	Begin mining gold at this point, but keep pumping out the fishing boats; by now you should have 28–30 villagers and 12–15 fishing boats from at least two docks; growing larger than this will make you vulnerable to an early attack
11:00–11:30	Click the Feudal Age upgrade	Begin scouting the enemy; once you have around 15 fishing boats, stop making them—they're hard to defend in the Castle Age, and you'll need the wood elsewhere
13:10–13:40		Reach the Feudal Age
	Train 2 more villagers	As your land-based food sources run out, place your villagers on a second source of wood.
	Have 2 villagers build a market while 2 villagers build a blacksmith	Don't make too many fishing boats. They are hard to defend in Castle Age and you'll need the wood to make military buildings
14:10–14:40	Click the Castle Age upgrade	
	Immediately send 2–3 villagers near the enemy base to build barracks, stable	Depending on the terrain, your resources, and the time at which your enemy Castles, you may want to consider walling in your town. You might want to shift some of your economy to stone to enable you to build more walls or a castle
16:50–17:20		Reach Castle Age; you should have a population of at least 45–50 by now

Use your resource advantage to quickly build up a large force of knights, rams, and monks to attack the enemy base. Back home you can build a couple of new town centers, then use the extra food you've collected to train large numbers of villagers.

At this point, you decide whether to devote resources to defending your large fleet of fishing boats or to concentrate on farming for food. In comparing fishing to farming, it's interesting to note that fishing becomes less productive as the game progresses and farming becomes more productive. If you decide to guard your fishing fleet, you'll need to keep a lot of villagers gathering wood and use that wood to make warships. If you decide to farm, you can devote just a few resources to a small fleet to prevent harassment, or neglect your fishing altogether.

Chinese

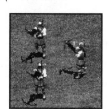

Civilization Attributes

- Start +3 villagers, but –150 food, –50 wood.
- Technologies cost –10% Feudal Age, –15% Castle Age, -20% Imperial Age.
- Town centers support 10 population.
- Demolition ships +50% hit points.

The Conquerors Changes

🛡 Start with −50 wood.

Unique Unit

🛡 **Chu Ko Nu:** An excellent crossbowman that lacks the range of the Britons' Longbowmen, but can fire multiple arrows simultaneously. The Chu Ko Nu is strong against infantry, monks, and cavalry archers and weak against cavalry and skirmishers.

Unique Technology

🛡 **Rocketry:** +2 Chu Ko Nu pierce attack, +4 scorpion pierce attack.

Team Bonus

🛡 Farms +45 food.

Playing As

The Chinese six-villager start propels them into the Castle Age and confirms the civilization as the best rushing civilization in *The Age of Kings*. Losing 50 wood at the start of a scenario in *The Conquerors* (a change from the original game) means you should assign villagers to wood as soon as you have enough food production to maintain a continuous stream of new villagers.

Superlative Castle Age times are possible with the Chinese (averaging around 16 minutes with 29 Dark Age villagers and lots of practice), giving them an advantage in early Castle Age attacks. Chinese infantry and range units excel. Though they have no inherent bonuses, both feature complete unit upgrades and technologies (including thumb ring), and blacksmith enhancements. The lack of paladins, hussars, and bloodlines hinders Chinese cavalry, so use pikemen, halberdiers, camels, and heavy camels to counter enemy paladins. Support your infantry and garrisoned battering rams with archers and Chu Ko Nu.

Playing Against

It's difficult to keep up with the Chinese race to Castle Age unless you're extremely efficient with Dark Age villagers. Scout a Chinese opponent well to gauge military activity, so you can prepare for a possible early Castle Age attack. The Chinese lack gunpowder units and fully upgraded siege technology, so counter the expected infantry and archer units with scorpions, heavy scorpions, onagers, elite skirmishers, and hand cannoneers.

Playing With (Team Games)

The Chinese +3 villager bonus provides a head start to Feudal and Castle Ages, and an economic-friendly teammate could enable even faster advancement. The Teutons and Franks benefit greatly from the Chinese team bonus (farms contain +45 food). On water maps, the Vikings' cheap docks can help the Chinese build fishing boats. Support the superior Viking infantry and Berserks with Chinese ranged units and Chu Ko Nu.

Out4Blood's
Chinese Fast Feudal Rush

The Chinese are extremely powerful, having the best economic bonus in the game: extra villagers. They are very good on both land and water maps, and they are the civilization of choice for executing the FLUSH (FeudaL rUSH), a devastating early Feudal attack that is popular among online players.

This strategy works best on Arabian maps because you need to be able to get into your opponent's base early. The goal is to deprive the enemy of wood, which is relatively scarce in Arabia. Furthermore, it's difficult to wall a determined FLUSHer in Arabia, while other maps have smaller choke points that can be cut off early in the game. This strategy will be even more popular in the expansion pack since the primary defense to the FLUSH—"castling" quickly and building town centers—has been seriously weakened.

The strategy is to attack early and deny the enemy:

- Concentrate your villagers on fast-food sources: sheep/turkeys and boars.

- Chop only enough wood to make a lumber camp just before clicking the Feudal Age upgrade.

- Research the Feudal Age when you've reached around 22–23 villagers, and advance around 9:30–10:00.

- Switch your economy to mostly wood and gold, saving your berries for later.

- In the Feudal Age, attack with archers and a couple of towers to deprive the enemy of resources, especially wood; assign new villagers to berries.

- Continue to attack and use your scout to find secondary enemy lumber camps.

Villager/Time	Action	Notes
1–6	Build 2 houses, then move to food ASAP	Scout in concentric circles to find sheep, berries, 2 boars, wood, gold, and stone
7	Food (if you had sheep immediately, send this villager to build a mill and harvest berries)	Research loom; build a house with the next villager that drops off food
8–9	Food	You may need to force the villagers to drop off food in order to keep a constant flow of villagers; make sure you have villagers on both sheep and berries
10	Wood	You now need to chop some wood to make the next house, since you have ~50 wood at the start
11	Lure boar #1	Bring boar to the town center
12	Build a house, then lure boar #2	Bring boar to the mill
13–15	Food	
16–22	Wood	

continued

Villager/Time	Action	Notes
	Click the Feudal Age upgrade	Time should be around 7:20 or so if you're doing well, but anything short of 8:20 is good
	Send 2–3 villagers to build near enemy; send 15 villagers to wood; send 5 to gold	Once you have enough wood, build a barracks between your wood and gold pile; scout the enemy for lumber camp, gold, and stone—most important is to find lumber camps and likely places he'll run to for more once you attack
9:30–10:30		Reach Feudal Age
	Build an archery range near the enemy; begin training archers; build a tower near enemy resources	
23–29	Berries	Farm when berries are gone
	Switch 4–8 villagers from wood/gold to stone	You'll need stone for towers

Continue to train archers, scout for new resource locations, and prevent the enemy from obtaining wood. If your opponent does not collect wood or stone, defending against your attack is impossible. Encircle the enemy base with archers and/or towers to stop farming and wood collection. If your foe manages to castle, build some spearmen to protect your town and archers.

Franks

Civilization Attributes

- Castles cost −25%.
- Knights +20% hit points.
- Farm upgrades are free (requires mill).

Unique Unit

- **Throwing Axeman:** A strong infantry unit with a ranged attack. Effective against infantry and archers but weak against cavalry, siege units, and skirmishers.

Unique Technology

- **Bearded Axe:** +1 Throwing Axeman range.

Team Bonus

- Knights +2 line of sight.

Playing As

The Franks' knight bonuses ensure a cavalry-heavy army. Don't be complacent and produce massive single-unit armies, though. Support your knights (+20% hit points and +2 line of sight) with champions, crossbowmen, hand cannoneers, and Throwing

Goths

Civilization Attributes

- Infantry cost −10% Feudal Age, −15% Castle Age, −25% Imperial Age.
- Infantry +1 attack versus buildings.
- Villagers +5 attack versus wild boar; hunters carry +15 meat.
- +10 population over the limit in Imperial Age.

The Conquerors Changes

- Hunters now carry +15 meat.

Unique Unit

- **Huskarl:** *The Conquerors* boosts the Huskarl attack bonus against archers and adds additional piercing armor. Coupled with the Goths' two unique technologies—Anarchy and Perfusion—the Huskarl is quickly produced and versatile as both an archer counter and building razer.

Unique Technologies

- **Anarchy:** Allows the Goth unique unit Huskarl to be produced at a Goth barracks.
- **Perfusion:** Barracks units created 50% faster.

Team Bonus

- Barracks units created 20% faster.

Playing As

Although the Goths lack a significant number of technologies, inexpensive infantry enables early and consistent attacks against unprotected enemy resource points and villagers. Multiple barracks (as many as you can afford) are essential to keep the Goth infantry production flowing. Though not a significant resource bonus, the Goths' hunting bonuses means you aren't required to research loom before hunting.

The Goth unique unit, the Huskarl, serves well to protect infantry from archer attack. Include pikemen and halberdiers for protection against cavalry, and skirmishers to counter range units. Spread infantry units apart should your opponent use scorpions and mangonels, and keep light cavalry and hussars handy to eliminate enemy siege weapons.

In Imperial Age battles, research the Goths' unique technologies, Anarchy and Perfusion, to produce Huskarls on the front line without need of additional castles (allowing you to transfer stone miners to food or gold to keep infantry production high). Support the infantry with battering rams or trebuchets for walls and garrisoned town centers.

Playing Against

Siege weapons (scorpions, heavy scorpions, mangonels, onagers) can annihilate Goth infantry. Defend against flanking cavalry with pikemen. If the Goth player rushes early, however, you may not have the Castle Age benefit of siege weaponry. Concentrate on ranged units early to protect villagers from raiding attacks and exploit the Goths' lack of walls.

A mix of upgraded cavalry, ranged, and siege weaponry can hold off the Goth infantry assault. Thoroughly scout the perimeter of your base to spot forward builders and barracks-preparing infantry. Keep the Goths from gold mines and force them to produce wood-based units, limiting their civilization advantage.

Playing With (Team Games)

The Koreans and their bonus to stone mining and towers can help defend the Goths' base while they use cheap infantry to harass opponent resource collection. Protect Gothic infantry hordes from archers and cavalry units with elite skirmishers, camels, and halberdiers. Complement the infantry with fast-producing archers (Britons) or cavalry (Huns).

Out4Blood's
Goth Castle Rush

The Goths were the weakest of the original 13 civilizations, and the designers have not done much to change this in the expansion pack. However, if you play aggressively, the Goths can be a viable civilization to play. We recommend a castle rush followed up with a massive infantry and ram attack on the enemy town. Your cheap, fast-producing infantry can give you a significant advantage if you attack early enough.

The strategy is to reach the Castle Age as quickly as possible and swarm the enemy with cheap, fast-building infantry:

- Concentrate on the fast-food sources: sheep/turkeys and boars.

- Chop wood for farms and plant 5–6 as early in the Dark Age as possible.

- Send villagers to the enemy base and build barracks near its town early; as you upgrade to Castle Age, attack with infantry, supported by skirmishers or archers.

- Concentrate your economy on food and gold to keep producing large quantities of infantry.

- Follow up with siege weapons to demolish his town.

- Wall in your base and achieve a Castle time under 17:00.

continued

Villager/Time	Action	Notes
1–3	Build 2 houses, then to food ASAP	Scout in concentric circles to find sheep, berries, 2 boars, wood, gold, and stone
4–7	Sheep and berries	If needed, force villagers to deposit food in order to keep a constant flow of villagers
8	Build mill; berries	
9–10	Wood	
11	Build house; wood	
12	Wood	
	Research loom	
13	Lure boar #1	Bring to town center
14	Food	
15	Lure boar #2	Bring to mill or town center
16–21	Wood	Build a house with 1 villager
22	Farm	
23	Wood	
24–28	Farm	Begin scouting enemy
10:30–11:00	Click the Feudal Age upgrade; build a barracks near enemy base with 2 villagers; send 4 villagers to mine gold	
12:40–13:10		Reach Feudal Age
	Train 2 more villagers if you have enough food	
	Have 2 villagers build an archery range near the enemy while 2 othersbuild a blacksmith in your town;build another barracks near enemy	
13:40–14:10	Click the Castle Age upgrade	
	Begin training men-at-arms and upgrade them with extra attack and armor	Build a tower to increase the pressure on enemy defenses; keep your economy on food and gold to build a large infantry force
16:20–16:50		Reach the Castle Age

Keep making large numbers of infantry so the enemy cannot recover from your attack. If the enemy retreats to the town center, attack resource locations. Build a siege workshop and attack with rams to take out the town center. Make skirmishers to protect against archers and cavalry archers. You'll want to keep your economy well balanced with wood, food, and gold so you can make buildings, siege weapons, and infantry.

Japanese

Civilization Attributes

- Fishing ships 2X hit points; +2 piercing armor; work rate +5% Dark Age, +10% Feudal Age, +15% Castle Age, +20% Imperial Age.
- Mill, lumber camp, and mining camp cost −50%.
- Infantry attack 10% faster in Feudal Age, 15% faster in Castle Age, 25% faster Imperial Age.

The Conquerors Changes

- Samurai move faster and have an even greater attack bonus versus other unique units.

Unique Unit

- **Samurai:** A fast infantry unit with attack bonuses against other civilizations' unique units.

Unique Technology

- **Kataparuto:** Trebuchets fire, pack, and unpack faster.

Team Bonus

- Galleys +50% line of sight.

Playing As

Japanese excel on water maps. The fishing boat bonus can generate a significant amount of food over the ages, especially if your opponent doesn't attempt to disrupt gathering or you're able to control the sea with Japanese galleys. Cheaper mills, lumber camps, and mining camps provide additional Dark Age wood. Use this extra wood to build an early dock. Use villagers otherwise assigned to lumberjacks to hunt boar and advance to Castle Age quickly.

The Japanese possess nearly complete naval technology (lacking only heavy demolition ships), making them extremely formidable on the seas, particularly if you can protect the fast-working fishing boats. Produce cannon galleons and bombard the enemy shores.

Feudal and Castle Age attacks are a specialty of the Japanese. A weak Imperial Age economy (gold or stone-shaft mining are not available in Castle Age) means it will be difficult competing with a heavily producing opponent. Utilize the Japanese fast-attacking infantry and support them with ranged units that boast full technology, including thumb rings and arbalests.

Don't use Samurai in place of standard swordsmen or champions. Samurai include specific bonuses against other civilizations' unique units. Use ranged units and your infantry to battle enemy ground troops and assist with Samurai only if your enemy hasn't begun producing unique units. Keep your infantry and Samurai in separate attack groups so you can assign targets independently.

Playing Against

On water maps, be ready to assign more lumberjacks to guarantee a steady influx of wood—you'll need a naval fleet to control the seas and keep the Japanese economy from booming thanks to their fishing boats. The Vikings' cheap docks and warship bonuses can cause serious problems against Japanese players planning to gather large amounts of seafood.

Prepare for late Feudal and Castle Age ground attacks. If you can limit the size of the Japanese fishing and naval fleets, you should be able to survive ground attacks and develop a greater economy in the Imperial Age. Protect your unique units from the Samurai with enhanced archers and cavalry and use skirmishers against Japanese archer support.

Playing With (Team Games)

The Vikings' cheaper docks can help the Japanese crank out fishing boats and gain a significant advantage by the Castle and Imperial Ages. Fast-working Gothic barracks can assist the Japanese-improved infantry. The excellent Japanese infantry and archers benefit from a complementing cavalry or siege-based civilization. Use the Japanese resource bonuses to advance to Feudal Age quickly and coordinate early rush attacks.

Out4Blood's
Japanese Boat Boom

The Japanese make an excellent seafaring civilization and, like the Celts, are prime candidates for building up a large fishing fleet. The better Japanese fishing ships collect fish faster, while their cheaper mills and camps allow the player to save wood for an early dock.

Finally, the powerful Japanese infantry are arguably the best in the game. Unfortunately, they have a weak Imperial Age economy, so you'll need to get to the Castle Age quickly and finish off your opponent. In this example, we'll make use of the cheaper Japanese mill and lumber camps to do a boat boom, similar to the Vikings and Persians.

The strategy is to use the cheap lumber camp and mill bonuses to quickly build up a dominating economy:

- Minimize the number of villagers you place on food and keep the rest on wood throughout the Dark and Feudal Ages.

- Build a dock as early as possible.

- Continue to build as many fishing boats as possible, building a second dock as soon as you're able.

- Achieve a Castle Age time under 17:00 with around 43–48 villagers (including boats).

- Have a surplus of resources to devote to attacking the enemy.

continued

Villager/Time	Action	Notes
1–3	Build 2 houses, then move to sheep/turkeys—avoid building a mill immmediately to save on wood	Scout in concentric circles to find sheep, berries, 2 boars, wood, gold, and stone
4–7	Sheep	If needed, force villagers to deposit food in order to keep a constant flow of villagers
8	Build lumber camp; wood	Once you've thoroughly scouted wood resources, look for the water so you can build a dock near large quantities of fish
9–12	Wood; research loom	
13	Lure boar #1	Bring boar to town center
14	Build a dock	Start building a dock around the 4—5 minute mark; assign fishing boats to deep-sea fishing far offshore, as they provide food at nearly twice the rate that the smaller fish locations do; use dock builder to make more houses
15	Lure boar #2	Once your villagers run out of sheep/turkeys, hunt boars, then switch to berries
16–24	Wood	You should have around 16 villagers on wood, 7 on food, and 1 building houses. When you get enough wood, build a second dock with your original house/dock builder
25–30	Build a mining camp; gold	Begin mining gold at this point, but keep pumping out the fishing boats; you should have 28–30 villagers and 12–15 fishing boats from at least two docks; be careful not to grow further as you'll become more vulnerable to enemy attack
11:00–11:30	Click the Feudal Age upgrade	Begin scouting enemy; once you have around 15 fishing boats, stop making them—they're hard to defend in the Castle Age and you'll be needing the wood
13:10–13:40		Reach Feudal Age
	Train 2 more villagers	As your land-based food sources run out, place villagers on a second source of wood nearby
	Have 2 villagers build a market while 2 others build a blacksmith	
14:10–14:40	Click the Castle Age upgrade	
	Send 2–3 villagers to the enemy in preparation for building military structures	Depending on the terrain, the time at which your enemy castled, and your resources, consider walling in your town; shift villagers to stone so you can build walls and a castle
16:50–17:20		Reach Castle Age
	Use your resource advantage to build up a large force of knights, rams, and priests to attack the enemy base	Build a couple of new town centers, then use the extra food you've collected to train large numbers of villagers

continued

Use your resource advantage to quickly build up a large force of infantry, knights, rams, and monks to attack the enemy base. Back home you can build a couple of new town centers, then use the extra food you've collected to train large numbers of villagers.

At this point you need to choose whether to devote resources to defending your large fleet of fishing boats or to concentrate on farming for food. In comparing fishing to farming, it's interesting to note that fishing becomes less productive as the game progresses while farming becomes more productive. If you decide to guard your fishing fleet, you'll need to keep a lot of villagers gathering wood and use that wood to make warships. If you decide to farm, you can devote just a few resources to a small fleet to prevent harassment, or neglect your fishing altogether.

Mongols

Civilization Attributes

- Cavalry archers fire 20% faster.
- Light cavalry, hussar +30% hit points.
- Hunters work 50% faster.

Unique Unit

- **Mangudai:** A fast cavalry archer with an attack bonus against siege units. The Mangudai is strong against infantry and monks but weak against light cavalry, foot archers, and skirmishers.

Unique Technology

- **Drill:** Increases the movement speed of siege workshop units by 50%.

Team Bonus

- Scout cavalry, light cavalry, hussar +2 line of sight.

Playing As

The Conquerors' improvement to cavalry archers boosts the Mongols' Castle Age offensive capabilities. Mongol bonuses can propel the civilization into the Castle Age, where they possess their attacking advantages. Use the enhanced scout cavalry to locate sheep and boar quickly so you can take advantage of the hunting bonus to gather a significant amount of food quickly and rapidly move through the ages.

Send the enhanced scout cavalry to map out your opponent's base, particularly areas suitable for forward builders in a potential late Feudal or early Castle Age attack. Use the Mongols' improved light cavalry to harass villagers and slow down opponent resource gathering.

Mangudai are solid ranged units, but are rather expensive compared to other unique units and other Mongol choices. Mangudai alone won't overcome a mixed foe,

so support them with cavalry, pikemen, camels, infantry, and foot archers. Research thumb ring and Parthian tactics (improves cavalry archer armor, particularly to enemy ranged units) if you're concentrating on ranged units. The Mongols are weaker in Imperial Age, lacking gunpowder units and top-tier blacksmith armor upgrades to infantry, cavalry, and archers.

Playing Against

Expect your base to be scouted early. Wall off resource areas and produce a few spearmen to counter Mongol light-cavalry harassment. Be sure to research archer upgrades before infantry and cavalry upgrades to improve skirmishers and elite skirmishers—important units against the expected Mongol cavalry archers and Mangudai. Outlast the Feudal and early Castle Age assaults by playing defensively or by applying pressure with a forward town center or castle.

Mongols possess a full-siege technology tree (minus bombard cannons), including the university's siege engineers upgrade. Prepare for the Mongols to combine onagers and heavy scorpions with Mangudai. Use camels or heavy camels, if available, or flank the siege weaponry with light cavalry.

Playing With (Team Games)

The Huns' fast-working stable can help the Mongols mass a large cavalry archer force. Every civilization gains from the Mongols' improved scout cavalry line of sight, which can be used to locate resources quickly.

Out4Blood's
Mongol Cavalry Archer Rush

The Mongols are a fun civilization to play. The hunting bonus, better cavalry archers, and tough light cavalry all take finesse to manage well. Good Mongol players are hard to counter because they can always back up the above with a strong infantry attack. Cavalry archers were seriously weak in *The Age of Kings*, but they are much improved in *The Conquerors* expansion pack. This gives Mongol players around the globe new hope for building an empire.

On maps where hunting is plentiful, you'll be able to mount a lightning-fast attack. On maps where hunting is limited, you'll have trouble making the most of your civilization's advantages. We recommend you play as the Mongols on maps with lots of hunting grounds, such as Scandinavia, and we outline the strategy for such below. On these maps, the FLUSH is almost mandatory, although a quick Castle Age jump is a good option, too. The strategy is to use your superior economic bonus to achieve an early Castle Age, then dominate with superior troops:

- Concentrate your villagers on fast-food sources, namely boars and deer.

- Research the Feudal Age with around 25–27 villagers, reaching it around 11:30–12:00.

continued

- Have enough wood to immediately erect two Feudal Age buildings. Click the upgrade to Castle Age around 12:00–12:30.
- Reach the Castle Age at around 14:40–15:10 and begin attacking with light cavalry, cavalry archers, or knights.

Villager/Time	Action	Notes
1–3	Build 2 houses, then move to food ASAP	Scout in concentric circles to find sheep, berries, 2 boars, wood, gold, and stone
4–8	Sheep and berries	If needed, force villagers to deposit food in order to keep a constant flow of villagers
		Research loom
9	Lure boar #1	Bring boar to your town center
10	Food (boar)	
11	Build house; wood	
12	Lure boar #2	Bring boar to town center or mill
13–14	Food (boar)	
15	Build mill at the next deer/boar site	
16	Sheep	Send 7–8 boar eaters to next site, the rest on wood
17	Build house; wood	
18–23	Wood; build lumber camp as soon as you have 100 wood; build another house	
24–25	Gold	
9:20–9:50	Click the Feudal Age upgrade	Time should be around 9:20 or so if you are doing well, but anything short of 10:00 is okay
	Keep chopping wood and hunting animals; move sheep villagers to gold mining; you should have 7–8 hunting, 10 or so chopping wood, and 6–7 mining gold	Scout out the enemy town looking for lumber camps and gold and stone piles
11:30–12:00		Reach Feudal Age
	Build a market and blacksmith; make two more villagers from your town center if you have enough food; have one or more of them begin walling in your base to prevent counterattacks	
12:00–12:30	Click the Castle Age upgrade	Time should be around 12:00 if you're doing well, but anything short of 12:30 is okay

continued

Villager/Time	Action	Notes
	Send 2 of your hunters to forward build; the rest of the hunters should go on wood at a second lumber camp in case you are attacked early; build a barracks in your town; build 2 archery ranges near enemy	You should have two forward builders, 6—7 villagers mining gold, and 16—17 on wood
14:40—15:10		Reach Castle Age
	Train cavalry archers and raid the enemy; build a siege workshop and create mangonels and rams to follow up the attack on the enemy town	Use cavalry archers to kill villagers, infantry, and pikemen, and mangonels to take out any skirmishers; rams are handy to help destroy town centers and other buildings

Continue to train archers and give them stand ground orders so they don't attack the enemy town center. Scout around to locate new resource locations, and keep the enemy from getting wood. Keep the pressure on once you reach the Castle Age, but don't neglect your economy; you'll want to use that extra wood to lay down farms. Take the time to wall in your base early so enemies can't counterattack while you're assaulting them.

Persians

Civilization Attributes

- Start with +50 wood, +50 food.
- Town centers and docks 2X hit points; work rate +10% Feudal Age, +15% Castle Age, +20% Imperial Age.

Unique Unit

- **War Elephant:** A lumbering pachyderm with very high hit points, trample damage (causing damage to multiple units at once), and heavy armor. War Elephants are effective against cavalry, swordsmen, foot archers, and buildings, and weak against monks, pikemen, and retreating cavalry archers.

Unique Technology

- **Mahouts:** Increases War Elephant speed by 30%.

Team Bonus

- Knights +2 attack versus archers.

Playing As

Bonus starting food and wood makes Persia one of the top rushing civilizations and allows it to reach the Feudal and Castle Ages quickly. The extra food should ensure constant villager production, while the bonus wood supports an early dock and fishing boats on water maps.

Fast-working docks are more important than the fast-producing town center (which affects villager production, technology research, and age advancement, not gathering rates). Enhanced docks help the Persians (with full naval units and all technologies besides shipwright) mass a large naval fleet and produce late Dark Age fishing boats. Feudal Age attacks are certainly an option, as the food and wood bonus means you're likely more advanced than your opponent.

Double hit points turn the Persian town center into a small castle. Garrisoned Persian town centers can take a while to destroy, even with battering rams. Use the extra time wisely and usher in supporting cavalry and infantry forces. Having these durable town centers means you're unlikely to be rushed in the Feudal Age.

War Elephants are extremely powerful units, particularly against infantry and cavalry. They're also good building crushers, but they cost bushels of food. Should you choose to use War Elephants, protect them from monks (particularly theocracy-upgraded ones), ranged units, pikemen, and halberdiers. Combine them with garrisoned battering rams for a fierce, structure-razing force. Elephants, cavalry, and hand cannoneers make a powerful, but expensive, Imperial Age combination.

Playing Against

The Persians are weak in ranged (no arbalest, no bracer technology), infantry (no two-handed swordsman, no champion), and monk (lack five of 10 technologies) units. If the Persian opponent fails to prepare for monks, a force of pikemen, infantry, skirmishers, and monks could spell doom for an elephant, cavalry, and hand cannoneer force. While converting elephants is often much easier than defeating them, keep plenty of pikemen and halberdiers around to combat the Persian beasts.

Remain aware of potential Persian Feudal and early Castle Age attacks, particularly if the Persian player reaches the Feudal Age quickly. Garrisoned Persian town centers are extremely tough to defeat; protect your resources (gold mine, lumber area) well and don't let an opponent plant a town center near your camp.

Playing With (Team Games)

Persian economic bonuses ensure quick Feudal and Castle Age times. The extra wood, combined with a Viking teammate, enables early fishing boats on water maps—nearly essential to supporting War Elephant food requirements. The Persian knight bonus can help cavalry-based civilizations, but the Persians already possess good cavalry and are weak with ranged and infantry units. Complement cavalry with a ranged or infantry-based race.

Out4Blood's
Persian Boat Boom

The Persians are a strong civilization in both random map games and in deathmatches. Their initial wood bonus makes them a threat to build a large fishing-based economy, but watch out! They have very weak infantry units, so they can lose a game in the Imperial Age unless you can maintain the food surplus long enough to make your cavalry-based army large enough to crush the enemy.

Persians also have one of the fastest early Feudal Age attacks because they start off with more food and wood than other civilizations. Unless you're successful in killing off your opponent early, however, much of the Persian army will eventually consist of food-intensive units, meaning you'll need a very strong economy to pump out all the food you will need.

So, for our simple strategy, you'll take advantage of the Persian starting bonus and devote it to a spectacular boat boom. Also use your starting economic bonus to quickly build up a dominant economy:

- Minimize the number of villagers working on food and place most on wood gathering throughout the Dark and Feudal Ages.

- Build a dock as early as possible.

- Continue to build as many fishing boats as possible, and make a second dock when able.

- Achieve a Castle Age time under 17:00.

- Have a surplus of resources to devote to attacking the enemy.

Villager/Time	Action	Notes
1–3	Build 2 houses, then to sheep/turkeys—avoid building a mill immediately to save on wood	Move your scout in concentric circles to find sheep, 2 boars, deer, and berries; scout out wood for a lumber camp
4–6	Sheep, berries	If needed, force villagers to deposit food in order to keep a constant flow of villagers
7	Wood	Once wood has been thoroughly scouted, look for water so you can build a dock near large quantities of fish
8	Build lumber camp; wood	
Villager/Time	Action	Notes
9	Build a dock	Build a dock around the 4–5 minute mark; use the dock builder to build additional houses—don't forget that you'll need to make houses more often because the docks will quickly boost your population

continued

Villager/Time	Action	Notes
10–15	Wood	As your fishing boats come out, you'll need to assign them to deep-sea fishing far from shore, which provides food at nearly twice the rate of other fish locations
16	Build mill; berries	Once sheep/turkeys run out, use berries or boars as a new food resource
17–18	Food	
19–24	Wood	You should have around 15 villagers chopping wood, 8 gathering food, and 1 building houses; when you get enough wood, build a second dock with your original house/dock builder
25–30	Build mining camp; gold	Keep pumping out the fishing boats; you should have 28–30 villagers and 12–15 fishing boats from at least 2 docks
11:00–11:30	Click the Feudal Age upgrade	Begin scouting enemy; once you have around 15 fishing boats, stop making them as they can be hard to defend in the Castle Age and you'll require the wood in other areas
13:10–13:40	Reach the Feudal Age	
	Train 2 more villagers; use 2 villagers to build a market while 2 others build a blacksmith	As your land-based food sources run out, place your villagers on a second source of wood nearby
14:10–14:40	Click the Castle upgrade	
	Immediately send 2–3 villagers to the enemy and prepare to build military buildings near its base	Depending on the terrain, the time at which your enemy castled, and your resources, consider walling in your town. You might also want to shift some of your economy to stone for walls and a castle
16:50–17:20	Reach Castle Age	
	Use your resource advantages to build a large force of knights, rams, and priests to attack the enemy base	Build a couple of new town centers back home, then use the extra food you've collected to train large numbers of villagers

At this point, you need to choose between devoting resources to defending your large fleet of fishing boats or concentrating on farming for food. As fishing becomes less productive as the game progresses and farming becomes more productive, you might well decide to abandon the waves. Switching to farms also means that you won't have to build warships to protect your fishing fleet.

Regardless of what method you select, the Persian army will require a lot of food, so be sure to devote yourself to one tactic or the other. You'll also need plenty of food to build your unique unit: the War Elephant.

Saracens

Civilization Attributes

- Market trade costs only 5%.
- Transport ships 2X hit points, 2X carry capacity.
- Galleys attack 20% faster.
- Cavalry archers +3 attack versus buildings.

Unique Unit

- **Mameluke:** A mounted camel with a ranged attack. The Mameluke is strong against infantry, monks, and cavalry units but weak against archers and siege weapons.

Unique Technology

- **Zealotry:** Increases camel and Mameluke hit points by 30%.

Team Bonus

- Foot archers +1 attack versus buildings.

Playing As

The Saracens lack economic bonuses, which means achieving a fast Feudal or Castle Age time requires near flawless Dark Age villager performance. Prepare to defend yourself against a Feudal Age rush if you're playing a civilization with early economic bonuses (Chinese, Japanese, Persians, Britons).

The Saracen market bonus can help shave seconds from Castle Age advancement. Build a market as soon as you reach the Feudal Age and trade available stone for food or wood (to produce other required Feudal Age buildings and/or advance to Castle Age).

Exploit water maps with the Saracen galley bonus. However, other water civilizations—the Japanese and their fast-working fishing boats, and the Vikings with their cheaper docks and warships—could pose problems if left to boom. The Saracen attack bonus encourages early naval aggression.

Very weak in cavalry (lacking cavalier and paladin), the Saracens boast full archery range and barracks units (minus the new halberdier). Should your opponent concentrate on cavalry, counter with pikemen, camels, and heavy camels. The Saracen unique unit, the Mameluke, is also effective against cavalry but requires support. Research Zealotry in the Imperial Age to help counter cavalry with Mamelukes. Use ranged units in your attack group (research thumb ring) to protect Mamelukes from pikemen and infantry. Deploy skirmishers should your opponent utilize archers. Mangonels, onagers, and bombard cannons are also effective.

Playing Against

Reach Feudal Age quickly and harass Saracen resource areas with archers and spearmen. Maintain early Castle Age pressure with forward builders. Construct a town center plus a barracks, archery range, or stable, depending on your civilization's strength.

Use cavalry in Castle Age attacks and early Imperial Age assaults; cavalry will prove less effective in late Imperial Age battles against Zealotry-enhanced Saracen camels and Mamelukes. Pikemen are less effective against camels in *The Conquerors*, but selecting a civilization with halberdiers should help against expected Saracen camels and heavy camels.

Playing With (Team Games)

The Saracens will shine once you reach Imperial Age and improve camels and Mamelukes with Zealotry. A cavalry-based civilization can support the civilization's weakness, though it's better to complement Saracen forces with powerful siege or ranged-based weaponry.

Out4Blood's
Saracen Monk Rush

As castle times get faster and faster, you begin bumping into the limit of how fast you can be and still have sufficient resources to attack your enemy. Castling too fast, however, leaves you weak and unable to develop sufficient military to take advantage of your speed. It makes sense that there is some optimal time for castling that allows speed but also sufficient economy. That optimal time is around 15:30–16:00 or so.

Most players will opt to perform a more standard start, but the Saracens don't get much in the way of economic bonuses besides the market, and they don't have any military bonuses in the Feudal Age. However, when using the Saracens (and to some extent the Turks and Chinese), there is another strategy that relies on hitting your opponent very hard, very early. The Saracen Monk Rush (SMUSH) relies on an early castle time of around 13:30–14:00 and employs monks to launch a surprise attack on the enemy. While risky and difficult to execute, it can be very effective if your opponent isn't ready for it.

The strategy is to reach the Castle Age extremely early and to attack enemies with Castle Age troops while they're still in the Feudal Age:

- Research the Feudal Age early with only 19 villagers.

- Using the market, boost the Saracens' early economy by trading your initial stone for wood and food, improving your Castle time significantly. This is why you use Saracens for this strategy — their market-trading rates are better.

- Mine stone almost exclusively, then trade it away for gold, which you can be used to buy extra wood for building castles.

continued

🛡 Use monks, who have virtually no counter this early in the game. Deploying them en masse will allow you to focus most of your economy on gold.

Villager/Time	Action	Notes
1	Build house, then mill; berries	Scout in concentric circles to find sheep, berries, and 2 boars, then wood, gold, and stone
2–3	Build house; sheep	
4–6	Sheep	Assign as many villagers per sheep as possible
7	Berries	
8–9	Sheep	Move your next sheep closer to the villagers so they can start on the next one immediately
10	Gather berries	
11	Build house; berries	
12–14	Chop wood (stragglers)	
15	Lure boar #1	You don't have a loom, so be very careful; use 10 villagers to eat boar
16–17	Berries	
18	Lure boar #2	You don't have a loom, so be very careful; use 10 villagers to eat boar
	Have two wood-choppers build a lumber camp	
19	Chop wood at lumber camp	Scout enemy
7:30–8:00	Click the Feudal Age upgrade	
	Send 3 boar eaters to wood, the rest to sheep	
9:40–10:10		Reach Feudal Age
	Immediately begin building a market	Use one villager (berries) if possible, unless you have enough food
	Move sheep villagers to wood production	
	Trade 200 stone for gold, then buy 100 food and 100 wood	
	Build blacksmith	
11:00–11:30	Click on the Castle Age upgrade	Note that you have researched nothing
	Move 2 villagers to near enemy base	Use your scout to escort these future forward builders
12:30 or so	Begin mining stone with 9 villagers	You should now have 2 forward villagers, 2 on berries, 9 mining stone, and 6 chopping wood
	Build 2 houses	
	Sell stone at market and buy just enough wood to build 2 monasteries (350 wood)	
13:40–14:10		Reach Castle Age

continued

Villager/Time	Action	Notes
	Immediately build 2 monasteries	Be sure to keep your forward villagers safe
	Train 2 monks	
	Train villagers as your food supply allows	
	Begin converting enemy villagers	
	Train 2 more monks	
	As berries run out, use wood to make two farms	
	When the selling price of stone drops below 100, move all miners to the gold pile	
	Research fervor and sanctity	This increases monk speed and hit points
	Research redemption as swiftly as possible	
	Use new peons that you converted to mine stone in the enemy town	
	Build a siege workshop to finish off the enemy town center	

Other civilizations are possible choices for this strategy, but the tactics would have to be modified to account for poorer market-trading performance. For example, the Chinese should be able to get to the Castle Age very early, and they could also make only monks. It is important to have both sanctity and redemption, however. In team games, having a Byzantine ally makes this strategy even better. Your monk army is nearly invincible, since the Byzantine team bonus is 50% faster healing.

Beware the most effective counter: light cavalry and attacks on your defenseless base. Just a few archers can devastate your base if done early enough in the scenario. It is especially important in team games that your ally also rushes the other opponent to prevent aid from coming and hurting you.

Teutons

Civilization Attributes

- Monks heal from 2X as far.
- Towers garrison 2X units, fire 2X normal garrison arrows.
- Murder holes free.
- Farms cost −33%.
- Town center +2 attack, +5 line of sight.

The Conquerors Changes

🛡 Town centers have +5 line of sight instead of +5 range, which tones down the offensive capabilities of the Teutons' town centers.

Unique Unit

🛡 **Teutonic Knight:** Slow but heavily armored infantry unit with a powerful attack. Teutonic Knights are strong against cavalry and buildings, and weak against archers, towers, and siege weapons.

Unique Technology

🛡 **Crenellations:** +3 castle attack range. Improves the attack of castles, towers, and town centers by allowing garrisoned infantry to fire arrows as if they were villagers.

Team Bonus

🛡 Units are more resistant to conversion.

Playing As

The Conquerors' adjustments to all town centers significantly reduces the main source of Teutonic power—the town center rush. The Teutons must now rely on economic and military strength instead of sheer town center power. Their farm bonus enables late Dark Age farming without assigning many villagers to chopping wood, increasing food production nicely if you don't neglect hunting.

    Hoarding stone resources is effective once you reach the Castle Age. The Teuton tower bonus offers significant advantages. Build bases and towers near enemy resource areas, making sure to garrison twice as many units into each tower for significant damage. Advance the towers into the enemy base and intercept any battering rams or siege weaponry with Teutonic Knights or cavalry.

    The Teutons' unique technology, Crenellations, improves castle attack range, but you'll need tons of stone to support multiple castles, towers, and town centers. Scout the enemy base and locate perimeter stone mines, then place forward bases near these mines and control the resource. With so many durable (and powerful) structures, your opponent must produce expensive siege weaponry to counter. Prepare knights (the Teutons lack light cavalry and hussars) to intercept siege weaponry.

Playing Against

Castles, towers, town centers, and Teutonic Knights are the heart and soul of a Teutonic assault. The Teutons are weak in ranged units, lacking arbalests, thumb rings, and bracers. They are also weak in inexpensive cavalry, light cavalry, hussars, camels, and husbandry. Monks and archers are effective against the slow-moving Teutonic Knights. Cavalry units can crush them, however, so support the archers with upgraded infantry.

Stopping the Teutonic push requires controlling stone resources, including those that lie along the outskirts of your base. Build palisade walls to protect resource gatherers and scout other resource areas to spot and intercept Teutonic forward builders.

Playing With (Team Games)

Have teammates tribute excess stone to support powerful Teutonic towers and castles. The Koreans can assist the Teutons in this fashion with 20% faster stone miners and their own decent towers (free upgrades and longer watchtower range). Support Teutonic Knights with superior archers and siege weaponry.

Out4Blood's
Teutonic Knight Rush

The Teutons are a good choice if you like to play a passive style where you let the enemy attack first. They have some of the best defenses and it is hard to attack them until the Castle Age. This well-rounded civilization has economic and defensive advantages in the early ages, with cheaper farms and formidable town centers, and has an excellent military in the later stages of the game, with paladins, Teutonic Knights, and good siege weapons. Additionally, the Teutons are one of the easiest civilizations to play since it's easy for new players to take advantage of their farm bonus.

The strategy involves exploiting the cheap farm bonus to save on resources needed to get to the Castle Age, resulting in a quicker time and an early attack on the enemy:

- Concentrate on the fast food sources: sheep/turkeys and boars.

- Chop wood for farms.

- Lay around 10–12 farms as early as possible in the Dark Age.

- Achieve a Castle Age time under 16:00.

- Launch an early knight rush on the enemy.

Villager/Time	Action	Notes
1–3	Build 2 houses, then move to food ASAP	Scout in concentric circles to find sheep, berries, 2 boars, wood, gold, and stone
4–7	Sheep and berries	If needed, force villagers to deposit food in order to keep a constant flow of villagers
8	Build mill; berries	
9–10	Wood	
11	Build house; wood	
12	Wood	
	Research loom	
13	Lure boar #1	
14	Food	

continued

209

Villager/Time	Action	Notes
15	Lure boar #2	As your boar eaters finish, send them to berries and to build around 10 farms
16–21	Wood	
22–26	Farm	
10:00–10:30	Click the Feudal Age upgrade	Send 3–4 villagers to mine gold so you'll have enough to advance to Castle Age
12:10–12:40		Reach the Feudal Age
	Train two more villagers if you have enough food; use 2 villagers to build a market, and 2 others to build a blacksmith	
13:10–13:40	Click Castle Age upgrade	
	Send 2–3 villagers to the enemy town and get ready to build a stable; build a barracks in your town for defense	
15:50–16:20		Reach Castle Age
	Quickly make a few knights and raid the enemy town, focusing on the lumber camp; follow up by building a siege workshop and some rams; use priests to heal your knights	

Keep raiding with knights so the enemy can't recover from your attack. If the enemy retreats to the town center, attack resource locations such as wood, stone, and gold. Make a siege workshop and attack with rams to take out the opposing base.

Try to get a feel for the battle. If you're winning, keep making more knights and press your advantage. If you aren't doing much to hurt the enemy, stop your attack and concentrate on building your economy at home. The threat of attack will keep him busy as you further develop your economic base.

Turks

Civilization Attributes

- Gunpowder units +25% hit points, researching gunpowder technologies costs −50%.
- Gold miners work 15% faster.
- Chemistry free.
- Light cavalry, hussar upgrade free.

The Conquerors Changes

- Hussar upgrade is now free. Gunpowder units have +25% hit points, changed from +50%.

Unique Unit

- **Janissary:** An improved hand cannoneer with longer range and no minimum range. The Janissary is inaccurate from a distance, but extremely powerful in groups at close range.

Unique Technology

- **Artillery:** +2 range for bombard towers, bombard cannons, cannon galleons.

Team Bonus

- Gunpowder units train 20% faster.

Playing As

The Turks feature no early economy bonuses and don't start to excel until the Castle and Imperial Ages, when gunpowder units become available. Mine gold heavily once you reach the Castle Age and take advantage of the Turks' faster miners. Maintaining the Turk Imperial Age force requires a lot of gold. Be prepared to scout other resource areas and start mining early.

Exploit the Turks' free light cavalry upgrade and harass enemy resource points in the early Castle Age. Build stables and a town center just outside an enemy base and send light cavalry to pester enemy lumberjacks and gold miners. If your opponent begins countering with pikemen, pull back and prepare some Janissaries.

The Turks excel with gunpowder units. Both hand cannoneers and Janissaries have been improved in *The Conquerors*. Hand cannoneers feature increased anti-infantry attack and carry no upgrade cost, except chemistry, which is already free for the Turks. Janissaries and Elite Janissaries possess increased attack strength. Both work to the Turks' advantage, but you must control gold deposits to fund the expensive Imperial Age attack.

The Turks lack the siege engineer university upgrade, but make up for it with their unique technology, Artillery, which boosts bombard and cannon technologies with +2 range. Turk bombard cannons are lethal, but expensive and require protection.

Playing Against

Don't allow the Turks to roam around the map sweeping up gold mines with their +15% faster miners and mining camp technologies. Keep gold away and starve the Turks' Imperial Age economy. The Turks lack several important military upgrades, including arbalests, elite skirmishers, paladins, pikemen, and halberdiers.

Cavalry, supported with elite skirmishers, could prove effective if the Turk player fails to counter with camels. The skirmishers are helpful against hand cannoneers and Janissaries.

Playing With (Team Games)

The Turks rely heavily on gunpowder, which makes them a good ally for the Spanish, who rely on the hand cannoneer and Conquistador to support cavalry and infantry (the Spanish lack crossbowmen and arbalests). Gunpowder units cost loads of gold, so concentrate on controlling as many gold mines as possible and allow the Turks' fast-working miners to sweep them up. Use market trade (another benefit of the Spanish) to gain additional gold reserve.

Out4Blood's Turk Light Cavalry Rush

The Turks are a powerhouse civilization in the Imperial Age with cheap gunpowder technologies and faster-training gunpowder units. They're no chumps when it comes to quick-strike attacks either. The free light-cavalry upgrade means you can attack with a devastating force immediately upon reaching the Castle Age. We recommend a quick jump to the Castle Age, followed by a light-cavalry rush. Then take advantage of the powerful Janissaries to give yourself time to build up to the Imperial Age.

The strategy is to exploit the free light cavalry upgrade to hit your opponent with a large force of light cavalry immediately upon reaching the Castle Age:

- Concentrate on the fast-food sources: sheep/turkeys and boars.

- Make 26–28 villagers.

- In the Feudal Age, train 3–4 scout cavalries.

- Move all scout cavalry into position and attack just as you are reaching the Castle Age.

- Achieve a Castle time under 16:30.

- Attack his key resources areas with your newly upgraded light cavalry.

Villager/Time	Action	Notes
1–3	Build 2 houses, then move to food ASAP	Scout in concentric circles to find sheep, berries, 2 boars, wood, gold, and stone
4–7	Sheep and berries	If needed, force villagers to deposit food in order to keep a constant flow of villagers
8	Build mill; berries	
9–10	Wood	
11	Build house; wood	
12	Wood; research loom	
13	Lure boar #1	
14	Food	
15	Lure boar #2	

continued

Villager/Time	Action	Notes
16–21	Wood	Shift your boar eaters to berries and wood
22	Farms	
23	Wood	
24–28	Farms	
10:30–11:00	Click the Feudal Age upgrade	Assign 3–4 villagers to gold so you'll have enough when ready to research the Castle Age upgrade
	Build a barracks in your town; send 2 forward builders to the enemy	
12:40–13:10		Reach Feudal Age
	Train 2 more villagers; have 2 villagers build a blacksmith; build a stable near the enemy with your forward villagers	
13:40–14:10	Click on the Castle Age upgrade	
	Train 3–4 scout cavalry during the upgrade and position them near the enemy town	Keep a lot of food gatherers busy as you'll need food to make scout cavalry
16:20–16:50		Reach Castle Age
	Attack immediately with light cavalry, hitting your opponent's wood, stone, and gold	

Continue to harass the enemy with your light cavalry, avoiding pikemen and the town center. Meanwhile, wall in your town and build a castle so you can produce Janissaries. Once you get a mass of Janissaries and a large infantry force, you should able to finish the enemy off if your light cavalry did its job.

Vikings

Civilization Attributes

♦ Warships cost −20%.

♦ Infantry +10% hit points Feudal Age, +15% Castle Age, +20% Imperial Age.

♦ Wheelbarrow, handcart free.

The Conquerors Changes

♦ Docks cost −25%, not −33%.

Unique Unit

- **Berserk:** An infantry unit that heals itself over time. The Berserk is effective against cavalry and buildings and weak against archers and siege weapons. *The Conquerors* gives the Berserk piercing armor.
- **Longboat:** A fast-firing, multiple-shot naval vessel.

Unique Technology

- **Berserkergang:** Improves Berserks' regeneration rate.

Team Bonus

- Docks cost −25%.

Playing As

Though the Vikings receive no bonus to fishing-ship cost, the cheaper docks allow them to start fishing sooner. A common Viking Dark Age gathering group could consist of over two dozen villagers and a dozen fishing boats. If they're left alone, they will soon gather a large supply of food that will propel them into the Castle Age with enough wood to produce additional town centers and military structures.

Concentrate on infantry to exploit the Vikings' hit point bonuses. Berserks and pikemen serve to protect against enemy cavalry (Vikings can't produce camels or halberdiers), counters that could prove more difficult in late Imperial Age battles against heavily upgraded paladins or civilizations with specific cavalry bonuses.

The Vikings' own cavalry units aren't particularly tough, lacking bloodlines, husbandry, hussars, and paladins. Use elite skirmishers against enemy archers and hand cannoneers, and position arbalests (research thumb ring) to protect Viking infantry. The superior Viking infantry is vulnerable to mangonels and scorpions, so beware of siege attacks.

The Vikings' cheaper warship bonus goes a long way on water maps and can outlast Persia's fast-working docks. Concentrate naval fire on enemy fire ships first and use Longboats to support galleons and cannon galleons. Control the sea and rivers with multiple docks and gather plentiful food there.

Playing Against

Protect your mangonels and scorpions when faced with Viking infantry hordes. Upgrade your cavalry to paladin (and research attack, armor, and bloodlines technologies) and tear through Viking infantry if not guarded by pikemen and Berserks. Support your cavalry with upgraded ranged units to counter pikemen and Berserks, and use the cavalry specifically against the Viking swordsmen and champions. Gunpowder units can prove effective against the infantry-heavy civilization.

Countering a Viking naval fleet will be tough, but you can exploit their lack of fire ships with your own. If you eschew naval units, be prepared to face cannon galleon bombardment. Position your town centers and other valuable structures far from shorelines.

Playing With (Team Games)

Vikings, with their cheap dock team bonus and inexpensive warships, make exceptional teammates on water-based maps. The cut-rate docks help civilizations build fishing boats sooner, gaining more food, and allowing villagers otherwise assigned to food production to work on gathering lumber. The exceptional Viking infantry can also be boosted with the Goths' barracks bonus on land maps.

Out4Blood's
Viking Boat Boom

The Vikings are one of the most versatile random-map civilizations. They are strong on land maps with their wheelbarrow and handcart bonuses, and they are excellent on water maps with their cheaper docks, cheaper warships, and the Longboat. Finally, in the Imperial Age, their champions are the bane of non-Viking opponents. Only the Japanese have champions that can compete with the Vikings.

In this example, we'll make use of the Vikings' cheaper docks to do a boat boom, similar to the one we did with the Persians. The strategy is to use the cheap dock bonus to quickly build up a dominant economy:

🛡 Minimize the number of villagers producing food and place most on wood throughout the Dark and Feudal Ages.

🛡 Build a dock as early as possible.

🛡 Continue to build as many fishing boats as possible, constructing a second dock as soon as you're able.

🛡 Achieve a Castle Age time under 17:00 with around 43—48 villagers (including boats).

🛡 Have a surplus of resources to devote to attacking the enemy.

Villager/Time	Action	Notes
1—3	Build 2 houses, then to food ASAP	Scout in concentric circles to find sheep, berries, 2 boars, wood, gold, and stone
4—7	Sheep and berries	If needed, force villagers to deposit food in order to keep a constant flow of villagers
8	Sheep	Once you have thoroughly scouted wood, look for the water so you can build a dock near large quantities of fish
9	Build lumber camp; wood	
10—13	Wood	
14	Build dock	Start building a dock around the 4—5 minute mark, then use the dock builder to erect additional houses that will be needed when the docks start to increase your population; assign your fishing boats to deep-sea fishing far offshore to take advantage of the better fishing available there

continued

Villager/Time	Action	Notes
	Research loom	
15	Lure boar #1	When boar #1 only has about 100 food left, send one of the hunters out to lure boar #2
16–17	Wood	
18–24		
	Wood	You should have around 16 villagers on wood, 7 on food, and 1 building houses; when you get enough wood, build a second dock with your original house/dock builder
25–30	Build a mining camp; gold	Begin mining gold, but keep building fishing boats as well; by now you should have 28–30 villagers and 12–15 fishing boats from at least two docks
11:00–11:30	Click the Feudal Age upgrade	Scout enemy; once you have around 15 fishing boats, stop making them, as they're hard to defend in the Castle Age and the wood will be needed for other construction
13:10–13:40		Reach Feudal Age
	Train 2 more villagers	When your land-based food sources run out, place your villagers on a second source of wood nearby
	Use 2 villagers to build a market while 2 others build a blacksmith	
14:10–14:40	Click the Castle Age upgrade	
	Immediately send 2–3 villagers toward the enemy in preparation for building military buildings there	Consider improving your defenses by walling in your town; also think about shifting some of your economy to stone to enable you to build more walls or, later, a castle
16:50–17:20		Reach Castle Age
	Use your resource advantage to quickly build up a large force of knights, rams, and priests to attack the enemy base	Build a couple of new town centers at home, then use the extra food you've collected to train large numbers of villagers

At this point, you need to choose whether to devote resources to defending your large fleet of fishing boats or to concentrate on farming for food. As fishing becomes less productive as the game progresses and farming becomes more productive, switching over to agrarian food production is a good idea. If you decide to guard your fishing fleet, you'll need to keep a lot of villagers gathering wood and then use that wood to make warships. If you decide to farm, you can devote a few resources to a small fleet to prevent harassment, or ignore fishing altogether.

New Technologies and Units

T he new technologies and units in The Conquerors create a wide array of choices for the player. The variables may seem daunting at first, but this chapter will help you learn to make the most of these new offerings. We'll look at the benefits (and restrictions) of the new items and offer tactical advice on how to best use them.

New Technologies

In the sections below, you'll learn about the new technologies offered in *The Conquerors*. They fall into two classes: general technologies available to many or all, and unique technologies available to only specific civilizations. Read on to learn the cost and benefits of the new technologies.

General Technologies

The technologies that follow are available to most civilizations in the game. Availability is based on both the historical natures of the civilizations and play-balance concerns. Very rarely will a player's economy facilitate the research of all game technologies, so choose those that best support the strengths of your civilization and the goals of your strategy.

Bloodlines

Bloodlines is an important and inexpensive technology for players relying on cavalry. The increase in hit points makes the workhorse knight unit even more attractive, and the heavy cavalry archer is transformed into a deadly and resilient unit for Castle and Imperial Age offensives.

Available to:	Chinese, Goths, Huns, Mongols, Persians, Saracens, Spanish, Teutons, Turks
Researched at:	Stable
Age Available:	Feudal
Cost:	150 food and 100 gold
Effect(s):	Increases the hit points (+20) for all cavalry units
Prerequisite(s):	None

Caravan

The trade system in *The Age of Kings* was often too cumbersome to be bothered with, but this technology makes trading a great source of additional income. Setting up an aggressive trade route and investing in caravan will allow you to stockpile much-needed gold for the Imperial Age.

Available to:	All civilizations
Researched at:	Market
Age Available:	Castle
Cost:	200 food and 200 gold
Effect(s):	Trade carts move at double speed, increasing the speed of trade (and gold income)
Prerequisite(s):	Cartography

Herbal Medicine

The herbal medicine technology makes garrisoning units a viable means to bring a fighting force back to health. By rotating your forward troops with defending ones, you can maximize the longevity of your fighting units in a fast and cost-effective manner.

Available to:	All civilizations except Teutons and Vikings
Researched at:	Monastery
Age Available:	Castle
Cost:	350 gold
Effect(s):	Units garrisoned within buildings will heal at four times the normal rate
Prerequisite(s):	None

Heresy

Heresy is an expensive technology (consider how many units you can train for 1,000 gold) and is only useful if you face a foe who relies on monks to a great extent. While the computer player will use monks for conversion, it won't do so in force, and it's fairly easy to kill the monks on the field of battle. Some human opponents are wont to use mass conversions as a way to bolster their armies—if this is the case, heresy will shut that practice down in a hurry.

Available to:	Aztecs, Britons, Byzantines, Celts, Franks, Huns, Mayans, Mongols, Saracens, Spanish, Teutons, Turks, Vikings
Researched at:	Monastery
Age Available:	Castle
Cost:	1,000 gold
Effect(s):	Units converted by enemy monks or Missionaries die rather than become converted
Prerequisite(s):	None

Parthian Tactics

Mounted archers of Parthia developed a technique of accurate shooting while in retreat that was so devastating they often feigned falling back while actually delivering a powerful offensive. This cost-effective technology makes late-game mounted archers survive even longer in combat. If you're playing one of the civilizations that can combine this technology with bloodlines, you can develop a truly devastating force.

Available to:	Huns, Japanese, Mongols, Persians, Saracens, Teutons, Turks
Researched at:	Archery range
Age Available:	Imperial
Cost:	200 food and 250 gold
Effect(s):	Cavalry archer's normal armor is +1 and piercing armor is +2
Prerequisite(s):	None

Theocracy

This is a very expensive technology that is only worthwhile if you plan to use monks in "pack attacks" to convert opposing forces. If that's your style, theocracy will allow the conversion process to move from subject to subject with much more rapidity. To make this cost-effective, convert at least a dozen units to your cause.

Available to:	Aztecs, Byzantines, Chinese, Franks, Goths, Japanese, Koreans, Mayans, Persians, Saracens, Spanish, Teutons, Turks, Vikings
Researched at:	Monastery
Age Available:	Imperial
Cost:	400 food and 800 gold
Effect(s):	When a group of monks (or Missionaries) converts an enemy unit, only one of the monks must rest before attempting another conversion
Prerequisite(s):	None

Thumb Ring

A thumb ring hooks into the gut drawstring of the bow, allowing an archer to draw the string back to his ear. This extra torque allows greater range, and the ring itself lets an archer quickly pull back the gut and fire faster. This technology is a bargain. For a relatively low investment, archers can become significantly more daunting in the open field and can strike more rapidly and accurately during Castle Age harassment raids.

Available to:	Byzantines, Chinese, Huns, Japanese, Koreans, Mayans, Mongols, Persians, Saracens, Spanish, Turks, Vikings
Researched at:	Archery range
Age Available:	Castle
Cost:	300 food and 250 wood
Effect(s):	Archers fire faster and with 100% accuracy
Prerequisite(s):	None

Unique Technologies

All of the civilizations in *The Conquerors* have unique technologies that they can research. As a general rule, these technologies improve the performance of the civilization's unique units. All are researched in the Castle Age, and with one exception (noted below), they are all Imperial Age technologies.

Aztec: Garland Wars

This technology is a great and powerful boost to the Imperial Age Aztec army. Since the Aztecs can't have mounted units, they will have a far larger proportion of infantry units, so the effect of this technology is readily felt. The primarily wood-based cost makes this very economical, as most building will be finished by this point.

Cost:	450 food and 750 wood
Effect(s):	+4 attack for all infantry units

Britons: Yeoman

The British longbow was a technological leap in battlefield weaponry, and as the longbow grew into widespread use, elite archers called "yeomen" evolved from the ranks. This technology offers both offensive and defensive punch. The bonus tower attack makes towers a potent defensive tool to protect towns, while the range bonus makes standard archers, as well as Longbowmen, able to strike from a slightly longer range, affording great hit-and-run guerrilla attacks.

Cost:	750 wood and 450 gold
Effect(s):	+1 range for foot archers; +2 attack for towers

Byzantines: Logistica

Logistica is only worth the considerable investment if you make heavy use of the Byzantine unique units. Properly employed, however, this technology allows you to

develop a powerful mounted force that can rush opponents and damage them with both arrows and hooves. Trample damage works best when charging a tightly clustered force of enemy troops. By grouping two or three strike teams of Cataphracts or Elite Cataphracts, you can create a powerful attack. Have one force-charge and trample while the other attacks from long range, then loop the trampling force around and use it for a ranged attack while you charge in with the other force. Add in some healing monks, and you have quite an offensive going.

Cost:	1,000 food and 600 wood
Effect(s):	Cataphracts cause trample damage

Celts: Furor Celtica

"Celtic Fury" was the term given to the emotional bursts of aggressiveness often seen in Celtic forces. This technology attempts to represent the Celtic Fury by only increasing the hit points of siege units by 50 percent. Use Furor Celtica to bolster the strength of scorpion units, which are devastating against infantry. With the boost in hit points, a force of scorpions (which still must be guarded) can deliver a deadly first strike.

Cost:	750 food and 450 gold
Effect(s):	+50% hit points to all siege workshop units

Chinese: Rocketry

Modern gunpowder evolved from Chinese experiments with controlled explosives. While they never mastered an accurate delivery system, primitive Chinese military rockets could wreak havoc on closely packed enemies. Rocketry signifies advancements in Chinese military fireworks, and increases the piercing attack of both the Chu Ko Nu and the scorpion.

Cost:	750 wood and 750 gold
Effect(s):	+2 piercing attack for Chu Ko Nu; +4 piercing attack for scorpions

Franks: Bearded Axe

This technology represents the evolution to the Bearded Axe (which elongated the lower portion of the blade for a more boomerang type of throwing action) and models the increased range of the new blade design. It transforms Throwing Axemen into powerful guerilla warfare and first-strike units.

Cost:	400 food and 400 gold
Effect(s):	+1 range for Throwing Axemen

Goths: Anarchy

Anarchy reflects the Goth's ability to train elite troops almost anywhere. This inexpensive technology allows Goth players to create unique units right on the front lines of battle, or wherever they can quickly build a cheap barracks. It's a great investment.

Cost:	450 food and 250 gold
Effect(s):	Huskarls can be trained at the barracks

Note: This unique technology is available in the Castle Age.

Goths: Perfusion

Perfusion further reinforces that the nomadic Goths could rapidly marshal infantry units. With both it and Anarchy in place, the barracks becomes a potent tool for the Goths, since they can be constructed quickly and cheaply anywhere. From there, all infantry, elite infantry, and unique units can be churned out.

Cost:	400 wood and 600 gold
Effect(s):	Barracks units are created 50% faster

Note: This is the second unique Goth technology, available in the Imperial Age.

Huns: Atheism

This technology represents the practical aspects of the Huns' atheistic beliefs by increasing the victory conditions for wonders and relics for all players in the game. It's a valuable technology when enemies are attempting such a victory.

Cost:	500 food and 500 gold
Effect(s):	Relic and wonder countdown timers are +100 years; researching spies/treason costs 50% less

Japanese: Kataparuto

Kataparuto reflects the Imperial Age efficiency with which Japanese forces could unleash and deliver attacks using their siege weapons. With this technology researched, trebuchets become a more lethal weapon with their increased rate of fire. Faster unpacking also means less waiting when you move your siege weapons into position. It's a must-have before entering into massive Imperial Age confrontations.

Cost:	750 wood and 400 gold
Effect(s):	Trebuchets unpack and fire faster

Koreans: Shinkichon

While the Chinese were responsible for gunpowder, it is believed that the Koreans were the first to use gunpowder-powered rockets in a military capacity. This technology reflects the development of Shinkichon rocketry as it applies to siege weapons. The increased range of siege weapons reflects the greater distance that could be attained by using rockets over physical catapults. This allows the player to marshal catapult units and keep out of harm's way as enemy troops or structures are pummeled.

Cost:	800 wood and 500 gold
Effect(s):	+2 range for magonels, onagers, and siege onagers

Mayans: El Dorado

El Dorado represents the increased combat effectiveness of the eagle warriors when they were "backed into a corner" by the Conquistadors. The increase in hit points allows them to dive into a toe-to-toe melee battle with a significant advantage. Mayan players can use this to mount a devastating attack, especially if eagle warriors can be cycled into a building for healing between battles.

Cost:	750 food and 450 gold
Effect(s):	+40 hit points to eagle warriors

Mongols: Drill

The Drill technology simulates the Mongol level of skill and practice. While most armies would have unskilled soldiers manning siege weapons, the Mongols practiced to achieve great efficiency in the control of their tools of war. Faster siege units means that the units can be brought into battle (and pulled back out of harm's way) with great effectiveness.

Cost:	500 wood and 450 gold
Effect(s):	Siege workshop units move 50% faster

Persians: Mahouts

The Persian War Elephant was a fearsome beast that could sustain more damage than anything else on the battlefield. This technology transforms the elephant into a deadly weapon of war. With the 30 percent increase in speed, they can strike more quickly and can actually retreat effectively should the opposing player offer too much resistance.

Cost:	300 food and 300 gold
Effect(s):	War Elephants move 30% faster

Saracens: Zealotry

Saracen warriors were renowned for their devotion and their absolute belief in the God that was guiding their conquests. This deep belief acted as a force multiplier and enabled them to accomplish victories against seemingly impossible odds. Zealotry reflects the potency of these dedicated warriors on the field of battle. While expensive, it offers massive payback in the added hardiness of camel and elite units and is crucial when facing a cavalry-based civilization.

Cost:	750 food and 800 gold
Effect(s):	+30 hit points for camels and Mamelukes

Spanish: Supremacy

Spain spent much of the Middle Ages as a battleground. As a result, farmers and peasants had to become soldiers if they were to survive. While Supremacy won't transform villagers into weapons of war, it will give the player another offensive option, as well as an interesting way to surprise an enemy.

Cost:	400 food and 250 gold
Effect(s):	Villagers are better at combat

Teutons: Crenellations

This technology represents the potency of Teutonic castles and the wide area of influence they could have around the surrounding countryside. As a result, castles now become an even better offensive unit. Infantry units (as opposed to just villagers and ranged units) in town centers, castles, and towers can now fire arrows as well, meaning that the defensive ability of your home village is greatly increased.

Cost:	600 food and 400 stone
Effect(s):	+3 range for castles; garrisoned infantry units fire arrows

Turks: Artillery

The Artillery technology reflects the skill of Turkish cannon teams and allows the powerful bombard weapons of the game to strike from a greater range. This lets bombard towers and cannon galleons initiate their attacks from safer distances.

Cost:	450 stone and 500 gold
Effect(s):	+2 range for bombard towers, bombard cannons, and cannon galleons

Vikings: Berserkergang

This expensive technology enhances the Viking unique unit by increasing the self-healing speed of these regenerative warriors. A skilled player can then create multiple battalions of Berserkers and shift them in and out of battle, rotating one group out while another heals.

Cost:	500 food and 850 gold
Effect(s):	Berserkers regenerate faster

New Units

Here you'll learn all of the facts and figures for each new unit in *The Conquerors*, as well as the history of how each fits into the game. You'll also find a few tips and tricks to allow you to make the most of these new military units.

Conquistador and Elite Conquistador

Conquistadors are Spanish warriors sent to the New World to claim the land (and the gold) for Mother Spain. These armored cavalry soldiers packed primitive guns, shocking the Meso-americans they attacked, since guns and mounted soldiers had not been seen before. This unit, while expensive to train, offers a potent attack. It can soften up the enemy with an initial charge and then fall back into a cover/artillery role. The Elite Conquistador is especially hardy.

Available to:	Spanish (unique unit)
Age Available:	Standard: Castle Elite: Imperial
Cost:	60 food and 70 gold
Trained at:	Castle
Hit Points:	Standard: 55 Elite: 70
Attack:	Standard: 16 Elite: 18
Armor:	2
Pierce Armor:	2
Range:	6
Strongest vs.:	Swordsmen, monks, Teutonic Knights, War Elephants
Weakness:	Knights, camels, pikemen

continued

Technology Upgrades:	Hit Points: bloodlines
	Armor: padded, leather archer, ring archer
	Speed: husbandry
	Creation Speed: conscription
	Resistance to Conversion: faith, heresy

Eagle Warrior and Elite Eagle Warrior

Aztec warriors were as much about ritual as combat skill, and the eagle warrior was an integral part of this mythology made real on the battlefield. These fast foot soldiers could deliver a deadly first strike due to their speed.

Since the Aztecs have no mounted units, eagle warriors also serve as scouts. While they don't deliver much of an offensive punch, their hit points make them hold up well in battle. Grouped together, their speed and resiliency make them an exceptional guerilla hit-and-run unit.

Available to:	Aztecs, Mayans
Age Available:	Standard: Castle
	Elite: Imperial
Cost:	20 food and 50 gold
Trained at:	Barracks
Hit Points:	Standard: 60
	Elite: 60
Attack:	Standard: 4
	Elite: 9
Armor:	0
Pierce Armor:	Standard: 2
	Elite: 4
Range:	0
Strongest vs.:	Archers, cavalry, siege weapons
Weakness:	Infantry
Technology Upgrades:	Hit Points: El Dorado
	Attack: forging, iron casting, blast furnace
	Armor: scale mail, chain mail, plate mail
	Sight: tracking
	Speed: squires
	Creation Speed: conscription
	Resistance to Conversion: faith, heresy

Halberdier

The halberd was an evolution of the pike, designed to be a deadlier weapon for frontline troops to use against attacking cavalry. The weapon featured a large axe blade with a spear tip on top and a spear tip at the rear. This allowed the halberd to be used like a pike, but the addition of the axe blade meant that it could be chopped down on a stationary cavalry unit.

Halberd units are a more potent form of pikeman, and are used the same way against mounted units such as knights and War Elephants. Like pikemen, they are best used in strike groups and are a must against a cavalry-based civilization.

Available to:	Byzantines, Chinese, Goths, Huns, Japanese, Koreans, Persians, Spanish, Teutons
Age Available:	Imperial
Cost:	35 food and 25 wood
Trained at:	Barracks
Hit Points:	60
Attack:	6
Armor:	0
Pierce Armor:	0
Range:	0
Strongest vs.:	Stable units, War Elephants
Weakness:	Infantry, archers, scorpions, magonels
Technology Upgrades:	Attack: forging, iron casting, blast furnace Armor: scale mail, chain mail, plate mail Sight: tracking Speed: squires Creation Speed: conscription Resistance to Conversion: faith, heresy

Hussar

The Hussar evolved in Hungary as an elite light cavalry warrior. These riders were skilled in the saddle and were often employed as scouts. The original Hungarian Hussars wore gaudy uniforms to call attention to themselves and their riding skills. Lightly armored, they were not suited for all-out charges, but were deadly against retreating units.

Hussars offer an improvement over the light cavalry unit, and provide speed, resiliency, and a fairly potent attack. They make great late-game scouts or harassment units. They are also effective in small groups when used to draw an enemy unit or two into the open.

Available to:	Byzantines, Celts, Goths, Huns, Koreans, Mongols, Persians, Saracens, Spanish, Turks
Age Available:	Imperial
Cost:	80 food
Trained at:	Stable
Hit Points:	75
Attack:	7
Armor:	0
Pierce Armor:	2
Range:	0
Strongest vs.:	Archers, magonels, cavalry archers, bombard cannons, monks
Weakness:	Knights, camels, pikemen
Technology Upgrades:	Hit Points: bloodlines Attack: forging, iron casting, blast furnace Armor: scale barding, chain barding, plate barding Speed: husbandry Creation Speed: conscription Resistance to Conversion: faith, heresy

Jaguar Warrior and Elite Jaguar Warrior

Like the eagle warrior, these Aztec fighters donned fearsome, ritualistic costumes when they marched into battle. While the eagle warriors were quick and nimble, Jaguar Warriors were armored and slow moving, but far more deadly on the field of battle.

These units form the backbone of the late-game Aztec army. They deliver a powerful attack and their large number of hit points can absorb a great deal of punishment. Used en masse, Jaguar Warriors will provide a deadly frontal attack against an enemy army.

Available to:	Aztecs (unique unit)
Age Available:	Standard: Castle Elite: Imperial
Cost:	60 food and 30 gold
Trained at:	Castle
Hit Points:	Standard: 60 Elite: 75
Attack:	Standard: 10 Elite: 12
Armor:	Standard: 1 Elite: 2
Pierce Armor:	0
Range:	0
Strongest vs.:	Infantry

continued

Weakness:	Archers, magonels
Technology Upgrades:	Attack: forging, iron casting, blast furnace, Garland Wars
	Armor: scale mail, chain mail, plate mail
	Sight: tracking
	Speed: squires
	Creation Speed: conscription
	Resistance to Conversion: faith, heresy

Missionary

The Spanish conquest of the New World brought with it a desire to convert all of the indigenous people to Christianity. To facilitate this, boatloads of missionaries soon ventured into the forests and jungles to deliver their message.

The Missionary unit works just like a monk, but reflects its more adventurous nature by its increased speed (though a lower conversion range). A Missionary's speed allows the unit to keep pace with the Spanish infantry and to quickly move in and convert enemy units.

Available to:	Spanish (unique unit)
Age Available:	Castle
Cost:	100 gold
Trained at:	Monastery (after a Castle is built)
Hit Points:	30
Attack:	0
Armor:	0
Pierce Armor:	0
Range:	7
Strongest vs.:	Teutonic Knights, War Elephants
Weakness:	Archers, knights, light cavalry, Woad Raiders
Technology Upgrades:	Hit Points: sanctity
	Speed: fervor
	Building Conversion: redemption
	Convert Other Monks: atonement
	Range: block printing
	Rejuvenation Time: illumination, theocracy
	Resistance to Conversion: faith, heresy

Note: Missionaries cannot pick up relics.

Petard

With the use of gunpowder on European battlefields, it was soon discovered how this new material could be used as an explosive when packed tightly into casks with other materials. These bombs could do significant damage to buildings and could allow breaching more rapidly than by previous means.

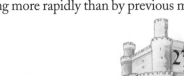

The petard is an armored infantry unit that delivers a cask of explosives to a location. The range of this unit is zero, so it is only useful against buildings. It takes five to destroy a town center.

Available to:	All
Age Available:	Castle
Cost:	80 food and 20 gold
Trained at:	Castle
Hit Points:	50
Attack:	25
Armor:	0
Pierce Armor:	2
Range:	0
Strongest vs.:	Buildings, siege weapons
Weakness:	Archers, scorpions, cavalry archers, mangonels, Cataphracts
Technology Upgrades:	Attack: siege engineers Creation Speed: conscription Resistance to Conversion: faith, heresy

Plumed Archer and Elite Plumed Archer

The Mayans utilized a more primitive bow technology than was seen in Europe, and as a result, their archers couldn't deliver as potent a strike as an English Longbowman. However, their brightly costumed Plumed Archers were strong, fast, and well armored.

These unique units are as powerful as standard archers, but they can move more quickly and can take more punishment. When used in groups, the lesser attack is mitigated and Plumed Archer speed can assert itself in quick strikes and during pursuit.

Available to:	Mayans (unique unit)
Age Available:	Standard: Castle Elite: Imperial
Cost:	46 wood and 46 gold
Trained at:	Castle
Hit Points:	Standard: 50 Elite: 65
Attack:	5
Armor:	0
Pierce Armor:	Standard: 1 Elite: 2

continued

231

Range:	Standard: 4
	Elite: 5
Strongest vs.:	Archers, monks, Teutonic Knights, War Elephants
Weakness:	Cavalry, skirmishers, eagle warriors, Woad Raiders
Technology Upgrades:	Attack: chemistry
	Attack, Ranged: fletching, bodkin arrow, bracer
	Armor: padded archer, leather archer, ring archer
	Targeting: ballistics, thumb ring
	Creation Speed: conscription
	Resistance to Conversion: faith, heresy

Tarkan and Elite Tarkan

The Huns developed the stirrup that allowed their cavalry riders to sit up firmly in the saddle and attack effectively with a lance while charging (the stirrup allowed the Hun rider to remain in the saddle at the moment of impact). When attacking en masse, a horde of Hun riders could instantly demoralize nearly any foe.

The Hun Tarkan unit is resilient, well armored, and can deliver a meaningful attack, making it a very solid unit to comprise the bulk of the late-game Hun cavalry. These units are especially potent against buildings, and so make great harassment raiders in the early Castle Age.

Available to:	Huns (unique unit)
Age Available:	Standard: Castle
	Elite: Imperial
Cost:	60 Food and 60 Gold
Trained at:	Castle
Hit Points:	Standard: 90
	Elite: 150
Attack:	Standard: 7
	Elite: 11
Armor:	1
Pierce armor:	Standard: 2
	Elite: 3
Range:	0
Strongest vs.:	Buildings, archers, magonels, cavalry archers, Bombard Cannons, monks
Weakness:	Knight, camels, pikemen
Technology Upgrades:	Hit Points: bloodlines
	Attack: forging, iron casting, metallurgy
	Armor: scale barding, chain barding, plate barding
	Speed: husbandry
	Creation Speed: conscription
	Resistance to Conversion: faith, heresy

Turtle Ship and Elite Turtle Ship

Late in the sixteenth century, the Korean navy developed the first armored naval vessels. Called Turtle Ships, these oar-powered behemoths lay low in the water and were covered by thick armor plating. The sides sported cannons that could easily dispatch the unarmored ships of Japan.

These unique-looking warships give the Korean player a potent navy, since they allow the use of cannon ships before the cannon galleon becomes available to other players. In a naval game, this gives them a chance to assert early dominance over the seas.

Available to:	Koreans (unique unit)
Age Available:	Standard: Castle Elite: Imperial
Cost:	200 wood and 200 gold
Trained at:	Dock
Hit Points:	Standard: 200 Elite: 300
Attack:	50
Armor:	Standard: 6 Elite: 8
Pierce Armor:	Standard: 5 Elite: 6
Range:	6
Strongest vs.:	Galleys, longboats, demolition ships
Weakness:	Fire ships, bombard cannons, monks
Technology Upgrades:	Armor: careening Speed: dry dock Lower Cost: shipwright Resistance to Conversion: faith, heresy

War Wagon and Elite War Wagon

The Korean kingdom of Koryo was known for its innovative military force and was possibly the first to use rockets in combat. It is believed (based upon limited historical documentation) that the Koreans also developed the first armored land vehicles—War Wagons. These horse-drawn, powerful transports could deliver a deadly attack, thanks to the archers they housed.

Next to the War Elephant, the Korean War Wagon is the closest thing to an armored fighting vehicle in *The Conquerors*. This unit has great resiliency (in both armor and hit points) and can deliver a ranged attack over a significant distance.

Available to:	Koreans (unique unit)
Age Available:	Standard: Castle Elite: Imperial
Cost:	80 wood and 60 gold
Trained at:	Castle
Hit Points:	Standard: 150 Elite: 200
Attack:	9
Armor:	0
Pierce armor:	Standard: 3 Elite: 4
Range:	Standard: 5 Elite: 6
Strongest vs.:	Infantry, archers
Weakness:	Cavalry, skirmishers, pikemen
Technology Upgrades:	Attack: chemistry Attack, Ranged: fletching, bodkin arrow, bracer Armor: padded archer, leather archer, ring archer Targeting: ballistics, thumb ring Creation Speed: conscription Resistance to Conversion: faith, heresy

New Multiplayer Games and Maps

ere you'll learn about the three new game types available in The Conquerors. The chapter also details the new Regular and Real World map types and covers all the strategies required to make the very most of these new experiences.

For updated strategies and tactics relating to this chapter, please visit www.sybexgames.com.

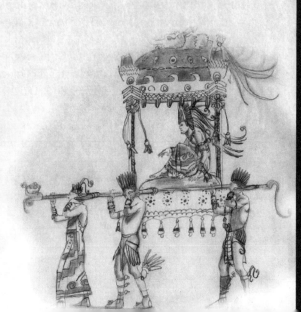

New Game Types

The Conquerors features three new game types—in addition to the original four from *The Age of Kings*—designed primarily for multiplayer gaming.

> **Note** All of the new game types, while designed for multiplayer gaming, are also available for single play via the Standard Game menu. Truth be told, the computer players only offer a reasonable challenge in the Defend the Wonder game, since it best suits their tactical approach.

King of the Hill

🛡 **Victory Condition:** Be the player in possession of the monument in the center of the map at the end of the countdown.

Like the children's game of old, *The Conquerors'* King of the Hill rewards the bully in possession of the prize when the game ends. In the center of the map is a monument (clearly visible to all players at the start of the game and in the possession of a random civilization).

Surrounding the monument is a stone plaza representing the boundary for the "hill." The first unit to move onto the plaza will claim the monument for his civilization and trigger the countdown cycle. If you are in possession of the plaza when the clock reaches zero, you win. The countdown timer is displayed in the upper right corner of the screen with the color indicating the current player in possession of the monument. The years count by at a rate of 20 per minute, meaning that a 550-year countdown takes about 30 minutes.

To claim the monument, you have to move at least one of your units onto the plaza when there are no enemy units present. Of course, during the course of the game, the plaza will rarely be left up for grabs—odds are that you'll have to exert some force to remove the other units from the monument (see Figure 9.1).

Remember that time of possession means nothing in this game; the winner is the player who controls the monument at the moment the countdown timer ticks down to zero.

Since King of the Hill has a limited countdown that begins with the first player to claim the monument, the flow of the game is unpredictable. If a player moves in and claims the "hill" right away, then the game will be short and furious (it's very doubtful that the player will reach Imperial Age). If no one claims the monument at the start, then the civilizations can grow to great power before the battle ensues.

Figure 9.1:
Erect defensive structures to help you hold the monument as soon as you can, but be sure to protect your builders from attack.

Tip For a fast and exciting game, begin in the Imperial Age to allow maximum access to units and technology.

Successful play requires both a strong enough offensive force to take the monument and defensive units with the ability to ward off attackers. Civilizations with good ranged units—such as the British with the Longbowmen—are an excellent choice for this game mode. Given the unpredictable ebb and flow of a battle, waiting until the last minute to take the monument is risky business, since time will clearly be your enemy.

Tip Logistics plays a crucial role in this game variation—keeping a line of supply open between your military structures and the monument is key. Placing gather points near the structure is a good idea.

Wonder Race

🛡 **Victory Condition:** The first player to construct a wonder wins.

In this game, all players are allied at the start of the game and you cannot change your allegiances (players can play cooperatively if they choose the same civilization type). This renders combat unavailable and military buildings functionally useless. In short, this is a game of pure economics. Players race to reach the Imperial Age and accumulate the resource stockpile (1,000 wood, 1,000 stone, and 1,000 gold) needed to build a wonder.

> **Tip** Don't forget the market! You can sell surpluses to buy what you need for the wonder.

Wonder Race is a run to the finish without distractions that rewards both rapid and correct decisions. You should always be moving forward, striving to build a full population of villagers as quickly as possible. Food production is the key early in this game. It's required to grow your population and to have the food needed to advance through the ages. Gold will become vital as you move into the Feudal Age. Early in the game, grow as rapidly as possible (training only villagers) and put two-thirds of your population on food gathering and the other third on gold.

> **Tip** The Huns have an advantage in this game variation since they require no houses. This means that you can start cranking up the maximum villager population from the start. Other civilizations with good economic bonuses (such as the Aztecs, Franks, Koreans, Mayans, or Turks) should also be considered.

When you hit the Feudal Age, begin resource hoarding and move 50 percent of your population to food production (on farms), and spread the other 50 percent on gold, wood, and stone. In the Castle Age, gather the food needed to move to the Imperial Age as quickly as possible. The moment you begin researching Imperial Age, move all villagers to wood, gold, and stone, and begin stockpiling as effectively as possible. As soon as you accumulate the needed resources, begin constructing your wonder. Assign every villager you have to the job.

Defend the Wonder

Victory Condition: The player who starts the game with a wonder wins if it can be held for a 400-year countdown. If the other players destroy the wonder before the timer runs down, they win.

> **Tip** When building walls or other fortifications around your wonder, make sure that you do so beyond the range of a trebuchet or bombard cannon—the last thing you want is an enemy encamped outside of your wall hurling projectiles at your wonder.

In this game, all players begin in the Imperial Age with 10 villagers and a scout unit. Player 1 (the one with the wonder to defend) begins with a stockpile of 900 of each resource type. All other players begin with 600 units of each resource type.

Player 1 plays a purely defensive role and must rapidly build up a defense system to withstand at least 15–20 minutes of constant assault (figure it will take other players at least 10 minutes to launch serious attacks). In order to survive, Player 1 will have to move as quickly as possible, building enough villagers to keep the resources pouring in and constructing defensive (walls and towers—particularly bombard towers, which can offer a deadly shower of defensive artillery) and military structures. Remember to always think defensively when creating a military force. Speed is not as important as potent, effective counter attacks (see Figure 9.2).

Figure 9.2:
A defensive force of rapid-strike fighters and a host of siege engines will allow you to hold on to your wonder until the end.

Defending the Wonder is an exciting struggle in a two-player game, since each can muster roughly equal resources to bring to the conflict. This game variation becomes markedly more difficult when multiple players are all converging on your wonder. In that situation, the defending player must perform flawlessly to succeed.

Attacking the wonder is a tactically straightforward operation—you have one target upon which all of your resources are focused. Remember, though, that a wonder is the toughest structure in *The Conquerors*, and simple infantry or mounted units alone stand no chance of razing it unless the defending player is truly incompetent.

To destroy a wonder, you'll need lots of siege weapons. You'll also need to protect those siege weapons, since they will be the primary targets of any defending forces. In fact, the only use for any non-siege military units should be the protection of your siege weapons. Working together, powerful Imperial Age siege weapons can raze a wonder very quickly—six or more trebuchets or siege onagers can chew through the structure in a few minutes.

The defending player knows you're coming, so all weapons will be focused on destroying your siege equipment before you can take out the wonder. To maximize your chances, attack from two or three fronts at once. Be sure to stagger them slightly, as this will give the defender time to concentrate on one front before you charge in on another. A multipronged assault like this should allow your siege weapons time to do their jobs.

Last Man Standing

♥ **Victory Condition:** remain the last player in the game, turning on your allies once you vanquish your enemies

Last Man Standing isn't so much a unique game type as it is a unique victory condition. In a standard game, one side must defeat the enemy by one of the normal victory triggers: vanquishing foes, building and holding a Wonder, or gathering and holding all relics. Any member of an allied team can achieve the victory condition and the entire team wins. In Last Man Standing, the game continues until all other foes are eliminated, forcing allies to turn on each other in the end-game (which makes for some very exciting conclusions, indeed!).

Last Man Standing requires players to prepare themselves for a very turbulent end-game. Success in a multiplayer game with real-life human allies and foes depends upon diplomacy and allies' cooperation. In this variation, the early game progresses much the same way, with one notable exception: never reveal everything to your allies.

The skilled player will work to achieve a position of power in this game, but will always hold something back, be it resource stockpiles or units, so that when the moment comes when foes are vanquished and allies begin to turn on each other, he will have the upper hand. In general, you can play this variation in one of two ways: aggressive or passive. Aggressive means booming early in the game and striving to a position

of dominance so that you can be in the driver's seat when the end-game approaches. Gather territory rapidly and grow a large army so that you can swoop in and capture defeated player's resources. Played right, you will either be in a fully dominant position at game's end or only have another adversary (rather than two or more) that is your equal.

Passive play is more defensive in nature. Stake out your territory and protect it (though make sure that your piece of the pie holds enough resources to carry you through the game). Work with your allies in the early game, but entrench yourself as fully as possible while you build up a sizable resource "bank" that you can draw upon. Done correctly, you'll be a tough target for any but the strongest of players (who will likely save you for last), as you continue to dig in while the battles are fought outside of your gates. When it is just you and your last adversary, ideally, you'll have far deeper coffers from which to fund your end-game army.

New Maps

The Conquerors splits the maps up into two types: Regular and Real World. Regular maps are generated maps very similar to what you found in the original *Age of Empires* and *The Age of Kings*, while Real World maps are designed to reflect the geography and flavor of actual world locations.

Regular Maps

Regular maps are random maps that are generated based upon the parameters (such as size), set up in the Standard Game screen (for single player) or the Create Game screen (for multiplayer). Each of these new map types possesses a unique personality and play flavor. Feel free to experiment when trying out your tactical acumen on these very divergent environments.

Arena

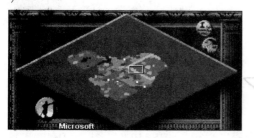

Arena sets the players up in their own little regions of the map, bounded on all sides by endless deciduous trees and fortified walls. Within each player's encampment are just enough forage bushes, gold, and stone to get started. The real wealth of resources lies in the central "arena" area of the map. Players have no choice but to spar for these precious resources if they have any hope of survival.

Ghost Lake

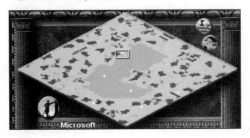

Ghost Lake is a land unit-only game that takes place on the snow-covered territory surrounding a frozen lake. The frozen water acts just like solid ground and the resources are spread about in standard fashion. There is a limited number of trees and no forests on this map, so the terrain offers no real tactical advantages to any player.

Mongolia

The Mongolian map is a flat, arid expanse of sand and hard-packed snow. There is no water, but evenly distributed resources abound. The most notable tactical feature of this map are the myriad cliff faces. These impassible barriers allow for some interesting tactical maneuvering and defensive fortifications.

Nomad

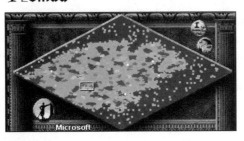

Nomad features a large desert peninsula surrounded by navigable water on three sides. The sandy mainland is packed full of resources and plenty of palm trees. There are many elevation changes but no cliffs. This map offers a traditional game challenge, though the waterways mandate some sort of naval presence as well.

Oasis

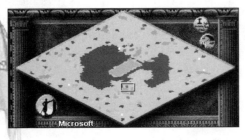

You're forgiven for the assumption, but Oasis isn't a desert map. Rather, it's a winter map of wide-open spaces and snow-capped pine trees. The center of the map boasts a frozen lake surrounded by a thick, defensive forest that features only one opening into this lake area.

The unique layout of the map means that there is one supremely defensible position in an otherwise wide-open map. The first player to lay claim to the lake is clearly in the driver's seat here.

Salt Marsh

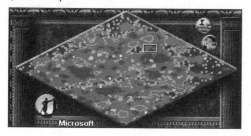

The Salt Marsh is a chaotic and interesting map featuring lush grasslands, groves of palm trees, and many waterways dotted with shallows and marshy areas. This creates an intriguing tactical flow and renders naval forces virtually useless. Exploration is difficult, but key in order to find the best (and sometimes only) paths on the map.

Scandinavia

The Scandinavian map features frozen lakes and snow-packed flatlands surrounded on the east and west by waterways (though there is no water connection between the sides of the map, making these passages useful only for trade and fishing). Resources are plentiful, but the large groves of snow-covered pine trees make navigation and discovery quite challenging. Given the large number of animals to be hunted, civilizations with hunting-related bonuses (Goths, Mongols) are a good choice.

Yucatan

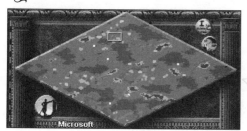

The Yucatan is a large, flat, and lush area. Groves of palm trees dot the landscape and resources are plentiful and evenly distributed. Water comes in the form of small ponds, so navies are useless here. Instead of sheep, your villagers will hunt wild turkeys.

Random Land Map

This choice simply picks one of the standard map types at random and then generates the terrain, so you'll have no idea if your game will be in the frozen tundra or in the arid desert. This is a great option to test out your reaction to unexpected environments.

Real World Maps

Real World maps allow you to play *The Conquerors* in actual geographic areas. These maps represent countries all over the world and offer a great variety of play situations. It should be noted that these maps are not to scale.

When you select Real World from the Map drop-down menu, you will notice that the Size choice disappears—that is because these maps are hand-made and offer no variation in size (though the size will vary from map to map). The paragraphs below detail the specifics of each map and provide the "best fit" as far as the number of players is concerned.

Britain

Britain is a large island surrounded on all sides by water. The large island of Ireland is off the west coast, while Norway and France are off to the east and south, respectively. Four other small islands also surround the main British isle. Terrain is snowy in the north, and the cliffs of Dover line the southern end. Resources are scattered evenly, and the sea is well stocked with fish.

This map plays like a cross between the Coastal and Island map types, except that the sheer size of Britain, in comparison to the other landmasses, mandates that all players must control the main island in order to find sufficient resources to advance fully. This map is best suited for two to three players.

Byzantium

Byzantium encompasses Greece to the west and the more arid Turkish lands to the east. Each region is its own landmass and both support ample resources for civilization growth.

While a sea separates Greece and Turkey, the coastlines are so long and winding that it is extremely difficult to marshal a navy that can gain full control of the waters. Preventing an invading force from coming ashore can be very challenging. This game is clearly about growing and then conquering, and both regions offer very limited natural fortifications or defensive protection. Two players are best for this map.

Central America

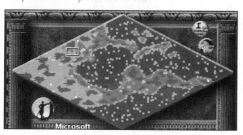

This large-scale map covers the region from Texas to Florida down to Cuba, the Yucatan, and Panama. The terrain ranges from arid to tropical, and resources are scarce except in the Texas and Yucatan regions (though the Gulf of Mexico is packed with fish).

The water is divided into two main areas east and west of Panama. The west is great for fishing but offers no real tactical opportunities for a navy. The east (the Gulf) offers a great opportunity to create a powerful navy that has access to all key regions of the map.

This map is good for between two to eight players, though any more than three will create an interesting "rush for the resources" sub-game.

France

This mid-size map covers all of modern France, as well as the southern tip of Britain to the north and some of Spain to the southwest. The terrain is mostly grassy with deciduous trees.

The mainland possesses very sparse resources, with only six main gold veins (three more can be found in Britain). The land is open and offers no real tactical advantages anywhere (except for the player in southern England, who can fortify himself quite nicely if he doesn't run out of resources). This map is best suited for between two to four players.

245

Iberia

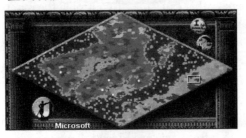

Iberia begins at the southwestern edge of France (covered in occasional snow) and covers all of Spain and the northern coast of Africa. The Straits of Gibraltar separate southern Spain from Africa. The Spanish mainland features a number of gold veins in the north and few stone veins anywhere. The African coast easily holds enough resources for a full civilization.

Water surrounds Spain on three sides and offers a great staging area for naval battles. The Straits are a good place to place deadly defensive structures like bombard towers. Two or three players are recommended.

Italy

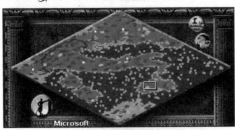

This mid-sized map features all of Italy, as well as the west coast of Greece, the island of Sicily, and a portion of the African continent. The resources are abundant and equally distributed.

Italy is bordered in the north by impassable cliffs, making access to and from the mainland only possible by boat. In fact, the waterways of this map mandate an important naval presence for food, trade, and military strength. This map is ideal for four players (Italy, Sicily, the Greek coast, and Africa).

Middle East

The Conquerors' version of the Middle East is centered on the Arabian peninsula nestled between Iran and the horn of Africa. The area is largely arid, but has plenty of palm trees. The water surrounding the peninsula offers some interesting tactical opportunities for naval warfare.

With the exception of stone, which is very rare indeed, resources are abundant. The eastern coast of Africa, with only a small land bridge to Arabia, is the easiest spot on the map to defend. This map is best suited for two to four players.

Norse Lands

The Norse Lands include modern Norway, Sweden, and Finland, and is entirely covered with snow and ice. The edge of Iceland appears to the far west (though no resources are there). To the south can be seen the northern edge of Eastern Europe (Poland, Latvia, etc.).

Resources are plentiful in all areas of the map and are fairly evenly distributed (with the exception of Iceland). The seas surround the Norse peninsula and offer great fishing, as well as a host of naval options. Two to four players are the best bet for this map.

Sea of Japan (East Sea)

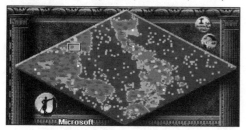

This large map features the island of Japan, along with eastern China and Thailand to the east. The Japanese island is resource-rich (especially in gold) and is surrounded by water on three sides. The island is surprisingly narrow and won't allow too much building if you plan on a lot of troop movement.

China is a large landmass and has sufficient resources spread evenly around, but the Thai peninsula is notably resource-poor (meaning a Thai player will have no choice other than early invasion). This map is best suited for three players.

Texas

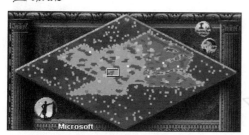

This giant-sized map is a fanciful representation of the state of Texas completely surrounded by water. The panhandle and east are arid, while the western portion of the state is lusher and features more trees.

Resources are plentiful and scattered evenly about, leaving no uniquely defense-worthy position other than the panhandle. Be sure to check out the Ensemble Studios flag, proudly waving over Dallas, Texas. Four to eight players can compete here.